21535

AN INTRODUCTION
to the
NEW TESTAMENT

Volume 3
THE NON-PAULINE EPISTLES
AND REVELATION

AN INTRODUCTION
to the
NEW TESTAMENT

Volume 3
THE NON-PAULINE EPISTLES
AND REVELATION

By
D. EDMOND HIEBERT

MOODY PRESS
CHICAGO

Originally entitled
An Introduction to the Non-Pauline Epistles

Copyright ©, 1962, 1977, by
THE MOODY BIBLE INSTITUTE
OF CHICAGO

Revised and enlarged edition, 1977

All scripture quotations in this book are from the American
Standard Version (1901), except where indicated otherwise.

The use of selected references from various versions of the
Bible in this publication does not necessarily imply publisher
endorsement of the versions in their entirety.

ISBN: 0-8024-4139-4

Printed in the United States of America

CONTENTS

5

Part 2: THE REVELATION

PREFACE TO THE FIRST EDITION

THIS BOOK is intended as an introductory guide to the systematic study of the non-Pauline epistles, that is, Hebrews and the general epistles. It is not a commentary on these epistles, neither is it intended to displace the use of such commentaries. The aim is rather to provide a guide for the concentrated study of these epistles by furnishing the student the *introductory material* needed for their intelligent interpretation and directing him in tracing the thought content of these difficult, much neglected, yet important writings.

The opening section of the book offers an introductory discussion of these eight epistles as a group. The following brief section, setting forth a suggested study procedure, presents the book method of study as the most profitable method for a mastery of these epistles. The method as outlined will require diligent effort, but the results will be highly rewarding. This study guide is not a substitute for the student's own work on these epistles but aims to direct his efforts. A vital grasp of the contents of the Scriptures is not derived from a reading of books about the Bible but from a repeated, attentive personal reading of the Bible itself.

The material concerning each of the eight epistles is divided into three parts: an introduction, an outline, and a book list. The introductions are intended to provide the student with the necessary historical background for intelligent interpretation. The outlines are presented as a guide to aid in the mastery of the contents. And the book lists seek to indicate something of the wealth of resources available for an intensive study of these challenging books.

Since these epistles have been the occasion for much discussion and controversy, it has been thought desirable to deal with the critical problems at some length. An effort has been made to give an ade-

7

quate presentation of the problems, without being exhaustive, and to offer conclusions from a conservative viewpoint. The usual matters of introduction, authorship, readership or destination, occasion, place and date of composition, and purpose are also considered.

The detailed outlines of the epistles were developed in an effort to chart the contents of these writings for the student. Favorable response to their use in the classroom emboldens the writer to present them here. The attempt to develop detailed outlines, especially of these epistles, is not without its serious difficulties. Such outlines invariably reveal one's interpretation of difficult sections while leaving him without any means of justifying the views adopted.

The outlines are not presented with any thought of finality. It is frankly recognized that different outlines are possible and have been made. The independent student will doubtless arrive at different results in many instances. The student is urged to use the outlines critically, testing, altering, and improving them in accordance with the results of his own study. No outline, however correctly developed, can be a satisfactory substitute for a personal study of the epistle itself.

The outlines by themselves will appear quite cold and meaningless. They must be vitalized through a personal study of the book thus outlined. A road map, important as it is to the traveler as a guide, may appear dull and uninteresting until one travels along the route personally and enjoys the scenery. The outlines seek to chart the road for the student as he travels through the epistles himself.

The appended book lists are intended to point out something of the wealth of material available to assist the student in a concentrated study of these epistles. The lists are not exhaustive but present a selection from the vast literature that has been produced. The use of such interpretative volumes is desirable and valuable in opening up the fuller truths presented in the epistles.

It is hoped that the diversity of the books listed will meet the needs of different groups. The brief comments given on the various volumes are not critical reviews but are simply intended to indicate in general the nature of each book. When a volume covers more than one of the non-Pauline epistles, usually a comment has been made on it only when the book is first listed, according to the order of the epistles followed in this volume. A favorable comment does not imply endorsement of all its contents.

PREFACE TO THE ENLARGED EDITION

IT IS A MATTER of deep gratitude that the *Introduction to the Non-Pauline Epistles*, first published in 1962, has been found useful as a study guide for individual study as well as classroom work. In this edition the scope of the volume has been expanded to include the book of Revelation. The new material on the Revelation in Part 2 offers an introduction, an outline, and a book list as a guide for an intensive study of the last book of the New Testament.

The introductions to the various non-Pauline epistles have received a minimum of revision. Circumstances have not permitted, nor has it been deemed necessary, to make extensive revisions of these introductions. The brief revisions that have been made were inserted in the interest of further accuracy and clarity. The book lists, however, have been completely revised, somewhat enlarged, and brought up to date. It is the hope that these annotated book lists will be helpful in calling attention to some of the varied expository volumes available on these epistles. A favorable comment on a volume does not imply endorsement of all its contents.

The material in Part 2 on the Revelation conforms to the three-part format used for the epistolary portion. No separate suggested study procedure has been included for the study of the Revelation. Since the New Testament contains no other book parallel in character and contents to the Revelation, the study procedure suggested in Part 1—the book method of study—is equally appropriate for a concentrated study of the book of Revelation.

May this expanded volume continue to be found useful as a guide in the study of these important but difficult books of the New Testament.

ACKNOWLEDGMENTS

It would be quite impossible to enumerate all the sources from which help has been received, stimulation derived, or materials drawn. Yet the footnotes and the Bibliography will in a large measure reveal the scope of indebtedness to others.

All scriptural quotations, unless otherwise indicated, are made from the American Standard Version (1901), and used through the courtesy of the copyright holders, The National Council of Churches of Christ in the United States of America.

Special acknowledgments are due to the following publishers for the use of some quotations from copyrighted materials:

To William B. Eerdmans Publishing Company (Grand Rapids) for a number of brief quotations from various articles in *The International Standard Bible Encyclopaedia,* two quotations from "The Epistles of James and John" by Alexander Ross in *The New International Commentary on the New Testament,* a brief quotation or two from *The New Testament, An Historical and Analytic Survey* by Merrill C. Tenney, a quotation from the commentary on James by R. V. G. Tasker in the *Tyndale New Testament Commentaries;* to the Lutheran Book Concern (Columbus, Ohio) for a quotation from R. C. H. Lenski's *The Interpretation of the Epistles of St. Peter, St. John, and St. Jude;* to Zondervan Publishing House (Grand Rapids) for a quotation from *A Conservative Introduction to the New Testament* by Samuel A. Cartledge.

To Hodder and Stoughton (London) for two quotations from "The Johannine Epistles" by C. H. Dodd in *The Moffatt New Testament Commentary.*

The outlines were originally developed by the author for his own use in the classroom exposition of these epistles. Various sources have provided suggestions and stimulation in their development, and they can no longer be enumerated. However, in the case of the outline on 1 John, I gladly acknowledge my indebtedness to the work of Raymond E. Gingrich, *An Outline and Analysis of the First Epistle of John.*

A full record of all the literature which has stimulated and molded my understanding of the book of Revelation is no longer possible, since my study of that book reaches back over a period of some forty years. In writing the introduction to Revelation for this volume, a conscientious effort was made to acknowledge in the footnotes all sources directly drawn upon. Indebtedness to various writers for brief quotations is gratefully acknowledged.

Part 1

THE NON-PAULINE EPISTLES

1

A GENERAL INTRODUCTION TO THE NON-PAULINE EPISTLES

OF THE TWENTY-ONE EPISTLES in the New Testament, eight do not bear the name of Paul as the author. The names of these eight epistles, in the order in which they stand in our English Bible, are Hebrews, James, 1 and 2 Peter, 1, 2, and 3 John, and Jude. As to their *expressed* authorship, two of them are anonymous (Hebrews and 1 John), two are ascribed to Peter, two to "the elder," and one each to James and Jude. Although they constitute less than 10 percent of the New Testament, they make a vital contribution to the Christian revelation. Their study has been much neglected by the average Christian. Admittedly they present peculiar difficulties and perplexing problems, yet a diligent mastery of their contents offers rich rewards to the reverent student.

THE DESIGNATION FOR THESE EPISTLES

The thirteen epistles which bear the name of the apostle Paul as their author are naturally designated the *Pauline epistles*. But we have no such comprehensive term for the remaining eight epistles collectively. They are generally described as the general epistles and Hebrews.[1] The division of the New Testament epistles into Pauline and non-Pauline is confused by the fact that there is no unanimity of opinion, past or present, on the question as to which group Hebrews really belongs.

The designation "general epistles" is not a biblical expression. In the King James Version the term does appear in the *title* of five of these epistles, namely, James, 1 and 2 Peter, 1 John, and Jude. But

---

1. Concerning the view that Hebrews is non-Pauline in authorship, see the Introduction to Hebrews under "Authorship."

these titles were not a part of the original documents. They were added later by some unknown hands, before A.D. 300, and are not authoritative. Following the evidence of the oldest manuscripts, the term is rightly omitted in the American Standard Version and other recent translations.

The term *general* or *catholic*[2] has been variously interpreted. It is admitted that the word *catholic* means universal or general, but the precise significance of the adjective in this designation has been differently understood. Some would apply the reference to the *authority* of these writings, while others relate it to the *nature* of these epistles. Under the former view it has been thought to mean either canonical or orthodox. That the basic meaning of the term cannot be *canonical* is evident from the fact that Origen (*Against Celsus* 1. 63) calls the epistle of Barnabas "a Catholic Epistle," and Eusebius, in speaking of the epistles of Dionysius which he wrote to the Lacedaemonians and the Athenians, says, "He was most useful to all in the catholic epistles that he addressed to the churches" (*Ecclesiastical History* 4.23). Nor can the term be held to denote the *orthodoxy* of these epistles, for Eusebius employs the epithet of an epistle which he explicitly affirms to be heretical (*Eccl. Hist* 5. 18).

In applying the connotation of the term to the *nature* of these epistles, the reference may be taken to allude to the general or joint apostolic authorship of this group or to the general scope of the recipients. The view that the term *catholic* or *general* is used to designate the letters of all the other apostles (as distinguished from those of Paul) which formed a common collection designated the "Catholic Epistles," is not in accordance with the usage of the term in ecclesiastical writers. Origen applied the term to the epistle of Barnabas, and Eusebius used it of the epistles of Dionysius and even of the heretical epistle of Themison. The view that the term is used to denote an encyclical or circular writing, general in nature and not addressed to any specific church or individual, is most satisfactory. It is now generally acknowledged that this is the primary meaning of the term. Thus Clement of Alexandria refers to the epistle of the Jerusalem Conference, addressed to the Gentile Christians "in Antioch and Syria and Cilicia" (Ac 15:23), as "the Catholic epistle

2. The term *catholic* (*katholikos*) is of Greek origin, while *general* (*generalis*) is the Latin equivalent. However, in the Vulgate these letters are not called *Generales*, but *Catholicoe*.

of all the apostles" (*The Stromata* 4. 15). In this sense Origen applied the term to the epistle of Barnabas, which is simply addressed to "sons and daughters," that is, Christians generally. The nature of the seven non-Pauline epistles would readily make the terms applicable to them as a group. When these epistles became generally known in the churches as a distinct collection, as distinguished from the Pauline epistles, the feature that seems to have impressed itself most was the fact that they were not addressed to any local church. Hence they came to be known as the "General Epistles." By the time of Eusebius the term had come to denote the group of seven non-Pauline epistles as being descriptive of their nature, for Eusebius speaks of "James, who is said to have written the first of the epistles general" (*Eccl. Hist.* 2. 23). To summarize, the term *catholic*, originally employed to denote epistles which were not addressed to any specific group, with the passing of time became a technical term, used to designate this group of epistles in distinction from the other three groups of writings in the New Testament, namely, the gospels and the Acts, the Pauline epistles, including Hebrews; and the book of Revelation.

The term "General Epistles" is a convenient label for these seven epistles as a group, although the term is not strictly accurate. It obviously must not be pressed to imply that these letters were addressed to Christendom as such. The address of the epistle of James stamps it as decidedly a circular letter. However, the contents of the epistle imply that James had a specific group of readers in mind. But if the epistle was written early, when as yet the Church was composed chiefly of Jewish converts, before the large influx of Gentile converts under Paul's ministry, the epistle is catholic in scope. Second Peter and Jude are obviously encyclical in their address. First Peter is addressed to the believers in five provinces in Asia Minor, hence is encyclical in nature. First John, containing no explicit indication of the circle of its readers, seems originally to have been directed to a circuit of churches in the province of Asia, thus also general in scope. But the two brief letters of John are both definitely local in destination and cannot properly be designated as general. But their brevity and affinity to 1 John as well as the desire to keep the letters of John together, caused them to be included with the longer epistle as a sort of appendix, even helping to interpret the longer epistle.

Since traditional usage does not include the epistle to the Hebrews among the general epistles, to avoid the use of the double designation we will, for convenience, simply designate all eight of these epistles under the term *the non-Pauline epistles*. Admittedly the negative term is not too satisfactory, but due to the diversity of the epistles in the group, only such a vague term seems available for them.

THE CANONICITY OF THESE EPISTLES

From earliest times, and even to the present, the question of the canonicity of most of the non-Pauline epistles has been vigorously debated. All of them, except 1 Peter and 1 John, were listed by Eusebius (*Eccl. Hist.* 3. 25) as among the *Antilegomena*, that is, the disputed books.[3] For one reason or another the canonicity of these epistles was questioned by some section of the Church. The growing tendency, in the time of Eusebius, was toward their universal acceptance. He clearly distinguished them from the rejected writings. The epistles in question were never regarded anywhere in the Church as books that were certainly to be rejected. Barnes asserts, "Those who entertained doubts in regard to them did not argue against their genuineness, but only expressed doubts in respect to their canonical authority."[4]

The ancient Church was not blandly uncritical but applied several specific tests to a book before it was accepted as canonical. At least four tests were applied: (1) *Apostolicity*. Was it written by an apostle or by one closely related to an apostle? (2) *Universality*. Was the book universally received and read in the churches? (3) *Contents*. Were the contents of the book in agreement with the received doctrines of the Church? (4) *Inspiration*. Did the book give evidence of being inspired by the Spirit of God? Each book had to pass the rigid test set by these standards before it was accepted as canonical.

Before the end of the fourth century the doubts concerning all of these epistles were resolved to the general satisfaction of the churches and they were accepted as canonical.[5] It should, however, be remarked that no books were admitted into the canon by the mere vote

3. The books classified by Eusebius as *Antilegomena* were Hebrews, James, 2 Peter, 2 and 3 John, and Jude.
4. Albert Barnes, *Notes on the New Testament, Explanatory and Practical, James, Peter, John, and Jude*, p. 3.
5. For fuller details concerning the canonical questions see the introductions to the various epistles.

of a synod or council. All the books which were admitted were received because there was positive evidence that they were genuine, evidence which satisfied the Church at large. None was received where the evidence was not felt to be clear and positive.

The very fact that the canonicity of six of the non-Pauline epistles was questioned reveals unmistakably that the early Church was not uncritical in its attitude toward the various books that asked for recognition and admission into the New Testament canon. Many spurious books were in circulation and the Church felt constrained to exercise the utmost care in the matter of recognizing a book as authoritative. We are grateful for the critical attitude toward these epistles which prevailed in the early Church. As Miller remarks, "The very fact that these books were thus questioned is an encouragement to us to believe that our New Testament contains 27 well-tested and authenticated books."[6] Having at its disposal information which is no longer available to us, the early Church, we believe, did not err in accepting them as canonical. For centuries now the great majority of Christians have accepted them as a worthy part of sacred Scripture. "They are recommended to our earnest and docile study by the hearts and minds and consciences of devout Christians in all ages. If we accord to them such study, their teaching will assert its authority over us."[7]

THE CANONICAL POSITION OF THESE EPISTLES

The general order of the books in the New Testament in the ancient Greek *manuscripts* is as follows: gospels, Acts, general epistles, Pauline epistles (including Hebrews), Revelation. The several *catalogs* of the sacred books which are found in the writings of the early Christian Church vary in the place they assign to the general epistles, but increasingly they place them after the Pauline epistles.

Modern scholarship is not agreed on the question of the proper place for these epistles in the canon. Influenced by the order generally found in ancient manuscripts, they were placed before the Pauline epistles by Tischendorf, Tregelles, and Westcott and Hort in their editions of the Greek text. But the popular Greek text of Nestle follows the order found in our English canon, which adopts the order

6. H. S. Miller, *General Biblical Introduction. From God to Us,* p. 144.
7. W. H. Bennett, *The General Epistles, James, Peter, John, Jude,* The Century Bible, p. 7.

of Jerome in the Vulgate. This order has strong support from the majority of the catalogs of the canon as well as of some of the Greek manuscripts and the Latin versions. Plummer regrets that the order of the Vulgate has universally prevailed in the Western churches.[8] Credner seeks to justify the order found in the majority of the Greek manuscripts as follows: "First historical notices of Jesus (the Gospels); then such notices of the Apostles; then general (catholic) Epistles of the Apostles; then Epistles to separate congregations and to individuals (the Epistles of Paul)."[9] But this view must be modified considerably by historical relations. It is generally accepted today that Paul's letter to the Ephesians is encyclical in its destination. Then also 2 and 3 John would have to be excluded from the general epistles.

It is our feeling that the general contents of these non-Pauline epistles more logically point to a position after the Pauline epistles. We agree with Bernard when he asserts that "for all internal reasons they are better read in the place which they occupy in our Bibles."[10] He advances four arguments in favor of this order.[11] First is the fact that there is the closest possible relation between the Acts and the Pauline epistles, the latter part of Acts forming the most natural introduction to those epistles. Again, he feels that the unity and mass of the Pauline epistles entitles them to a place of precedence over the fewer, shorter, and less connected group of general epistles. Third, he holds that the internal doctrinal development pleads for this arrangement, since in that order the more thorough and systematic treatment of fundamental subjects found in the Pauline epistles stands before that which is more supplementary. And, lastly, he points out that the reference to the Pauline epistles in 2 Peter 3:15-16 points to the Pauline writings as previously known and implies that the general epistles serve to confirm the Pauline doctrine.

The order of the books within this group is not quite constant in the earliest authorities. Generally James stands first, but a few times Peter is placed before James, doubtless due to the prominence of the apostle. The prevailing order seems to represent the belief that

---

8. Alfred Plummer, "The General Epistles of St. James and St. Jude," in *An Exposition of the Bible*, 6:558b.
9. Quoted by J. P. Lange and J. J. Van Oosterzee, "The Epistle General of James," in Lange's *Commentary on the Holy Scriptures*, pp. 4-5.
10. Thomas Dehany Bernard, *The Progress of Doctrine in the New Testament*, p. 162.
11. Ibid, pp. 223-24.

James is chronologically before Peter. John was naturally placed after them as coming considerably later. Jude was put last because of its brevity and comparative insignificance. The Syrian version, which admitted only James, 1 Peter, and 1 John, gives them in that order. The order in Luther's German translation is unique. Since Luther had some doctrinal objections to Hebrews and James, he took the liberty of putting them after the epistles of Peter and John and making them the last epistles except Jude.

Since Hebrews largely won its place in the canon under the impression that it was Pauline in authorship, or at least Pauline in its ultimate origin, it was not grouped with the general epistles. In the early Greek manuscripts Hebrews was either assigned a place among the Pauline epistles, although the exact position varied, or was placed at the end of the Pauline epistles as a sort of appendix to them.[12] It was this latter position among the Pauline epistles which causes Hebrews to stand before the general epistles in our English canon.

THE IMPORTANCE OF THESE EPISTLES

The importance of these epistles cannot be judged by the amount of space they take in our canon. In comparison to the historical books (gospels and Acts) or the Pauline epistles, the non-Pauline epistles constitute only a comparatively minor part of the New Testament.[13] Yet how enormous would have been our loss if they had been excluded from the canon!

The non-Pauline epistles, written, as we believe, by five different men, are invaluable in the contribution which they make toward the fullness of the New Testament revelation. Without them the New Testament would have been incomplete. From the Acts and the epistles of Paul we would have learned that there were other presentations of Christianity than the Pauline, grounded indeed in the same essential truths which Paul proclaimed, yet placing these truths in a different perspective and regarding them from another point of view. The inclusion of these non-Pauline epistles in the canon completes the picture. "And the boon is all the richer from the Divine diversity

12. For details see Brooke Foss Westcott, *The Epistle to the Hebrews,* pp. xxx-xxxii. The latter position seems to be due to the never quite forgotten objections to the Pauline authorship of Hebrews.
13. These eight epistles account for less than 10% of the pages of the New Testament, while the Pauline epistles constitute nearly 24% of the whole, and the historical books (gospels and Acts) cover a little over 60% of the entire New Testament.

of thought thus preserved for us."[14] These epistles give us an insight into the differing approaches to and presentations of the truth in Christ among the apostolic witnesses. As the four gospels complement each other, so these epistles offer a highly instructive complement to the Pauline epistles. Christianity is so manifold that it required the contribution of each of these writers to set forth its full import. The contribution of Paul stands forth in unmistakable grandeur; but the aspects of truth found in the other apostolic writings were needed to give the full picture. "Each writer, by the strongly distinguished lines of his own individuality, makes still more conspicuous the unity of the common faith."[15] Herein lies one importance of these non-Pauline epistles. As Lange says,

> By this complementing they preserve the Christian consciousness from a one-sided culture of the Pauline expression; by the variety and fulness of their modes of treatment and expression, they guarantee the fulness of Christian cognition and the full vitality and motion of the churchly spirit.[16]

While each of the New Testament writers gives us his own distinctive emphasis and apprehension of the Gospel message, there is yet perfect harmony between them.

These epistles are also important as mirroring the conditions of the Church during the latter part of the apostolic era. Except for James, which appears to be the earliest book in the New Testament, all of the non-Pauline epistles relate to a time within the seventh decade of the Christian era or later. Here we see the growing consciousness of the unity of the true Church in the midst of developing evil. The development of the pernicious weeds of false doctrine in the midst of the pure wheat of the Gospel, already seen in the Pauline epistles, especially the pastorals, here comes into greater prominence. These epistles form a suitable link between the Acts and the Pauline epistles on the one hand and the Revelation on the other.

THE ORIGIN OF THE EPISTLES

The large use of the epistolary form in the New Testament as a means of imparting spiritual teaching is the unique glory of the New

---

14. F. W. Farrar, *The Early Days of Christianity*, p. 48.
15. Bernard, pp. 162-63.
16. J. P. Lange and J. J. Van Oosterzee, p. 5.

Testament. The Old Testament records the fact that the prophet Jeremiah made use of a letter to impart divine revelation to the Jews in the Babylonian captivity (chap. 29), yet no book of the Old Testament is cast into the form of an epistle. Pratt observes, "The Scriptures of other oriental religions—the Vedas, the Zend Avesta, the Tripitaka, the Koran, the writings of Confucius—lack the direct and personal address altogether."[17]

The use of the epistolary form in the New Testament arose directly out of the vital experience of a new fellowship in Christ between the writer and his readers. Letters are the result of fellowship and separation. As soon as the Christian movement spread beyond its Palestinian confines and distance separated the believers, they resorted to the use of letters. "As members of a great household—as fathers or brethren—they spoke to one another words of counsel and warning, and so found a natural utterance for the faith and hope and love which seemed to them the sum of Christian life."[18]

The large use of the epistolary method in the apostolic Church stands in striking contrast to the absence of all mention of written letters in the gospels. There are no epistles that Jesus wrote.[19] This is doubtless due to the fact that during His ministry Jesus restricted Himself to the Jewish people to whom He ministered orally, while His primary task was the training of the twelve through His personal contacts with them. He taught them through His words and deeds, but most important in leading them to firm faith in Him was the impact of His divine-human personality. Their faith was engendered, nurtured, and brought to fruition through their experience with Jesus Christ in personal fellowship. This faith they imparted to others not only through their oral ministry but also through the use of letters to those separated by distance from them.

Like the Pauline epistles, the non-Pauline epistles were the product of the developing life and varied experiences of the early Christian Church. They were called forth by actual life situations and were intended to meet real needs and answer vital questions in the lives of the believers to whom they were addressed.[20]

17. Dwight M. Pratt, "Epistle," in *The International Standard Bible Encyclopaedia,* 2:966a.
18. Brooke Foss Westcott, *A General Survey of the History of the Canon of the New Testament,* p. 20.
19. The letter of Jesus to Abgarus of Edessa, preserved by Eusebius *Ecclesiastical History* 1. 13, is spurious.
20. None of the New Testament epistles was addressed to unbelievers.

The Spirit-filled witness of the followers of Christ resulted in the rapid spread of Christianity. The very success of the apostolic witness as evidenced by the large number of professed believers created a danger that an inadequate apprehension of that faith would lead to improper separation of saving faith from saved conduct. It was the effort to prevent or correct this fallacy in the lives of professed Christians that caused the writing of the epistle of James. Again, the separated lives of believers in the midst of a hostile world evoked persecution of the Church. The experiences of persecution endured by the followers of Christ naturally produced confusion and uncertainty in their hearts. This situation the Spirit used to stir the apostolic leaders to give them words of encouragement and challenge to fidelity and heroic endurance. The first epistle of Peter arose out of such an occasion. The remaining epistles of this group belong to the literature of a controverted faith. The Christian faith soon found itself under attack both from without and from within. The threat of persecution from without and the loss of vital Christian conviction on the part of numerous professed Christians created the danger of apostasy from the faith. The epistle to the Hebrews was written to avert such a danger. The presence of false and licentious members within the professed circles of Christendom threatened to corrupt the moral and doctrinal purity of the Church through their evil lives and pernicious teachings. Second Peter and Jude, as well as the Johannine epistles, were written to combat this danger and to ground believers in the truth.

The apostolic leaders found it possible and desirable to make use of the epistolary method in meeting these situations. The use of letters enabled them to deal with the varied needs of those addressed in a direct and informal manner, to apply Christian truth with such emphases and applications as the occasion demanded, and to adapt their instructions to the particular needs and capacities of the readers. These epistles thus arose out of actual life situations and were intended to meet definite life needs. These occasion-inspired messages, inspired by the Holy Spirit, continue to have relevance and perennial freshness as God's message to men even in our own day. The Holy Spirit made use of this method to bring into existence an important part of the books of the New Testament, therein preserving for all future generations the content of the revelation of God in Christ Jesus and the record of its operation in human lives.

The Groupings Within These Epistles

The eight non-Pauline epistles, written by five different men, form quite a heterogeneous group. Hebrews stands alone among the epistles of this group, both as to contents and traditional canonical treatment. By traditional usage it is not one of the general epistles.

Nor do the general epistles constitute a unified group. Robertson says, "The Catholic Epistles cannot properly be kept together like Paul's Epistles, nor need they be, for there is no special bond of union between them."[21] It is obvious that the Johannine epistles form a distinct group. They show a close affinity of form and content, and traditionally they have been grouped together as being quite late in origin. The two Petrine epistles may be grouped together. The striking similarity in subject matter between Jude and part of 2 Peter draws those two epistles together for consideration. On the other hand, James stands alone, not only because of its early date but also because of its singular style and contents.

The eight epistles of this group may then be arranged in the following order: James, Hebrews, 1 and 2 Peter and Jude, and the Johannine epistles. According to the view herein presented, this order is very nearly chronological, yet seeks to preserve such groupings among these epistles as can be discerned.

---

21. Archibald T. Robertson, *The Student's Chronological New Testament, With Introductory Historical Notes and Outlines,* p. xlix.

2

SUGGESTED STUDY PROCEDURE

THE NON-PAULINE EPISTLES demand and are eminently worthy of serious and prolonged study. Most of them are not among the books of the New Testament whose full significance lies evident upon the surface. They have their full share of passages "wherein are some things hard to be understood" (2 Pe 3:16). Consequently, for the average Christian, they constitute one of the most neglected portions of the New Testament. Yet to those who are willing to give them diligent and concentrated attention they offer rich and lasting treasures. They present a rewarding field for serious, Spirit-taught Bible study.

The logical method for the mastery of these epistles is the book method of study. They were separately produced as independent works and they should be studied as distinct units of Christian thought and teaching. The most rewarding method is to concentrate upon one at a time until its contents are thoroughly mastered.

It is of course desirable that one should have a general view of the contents of the Bible before such a concentrated study of individual books is undertaken. An individual book of the Bible is always of greater significance when seen in its larger relations to the entire biblical revelation. Such a general knowledge is here assumed.[1] It is only preparatory to the book method of study; and such a study in turn will immeasurably broaden one's view of the Scriptures as a whole.

---

1. Along with his intensive study of an individual book of the Bible the Christian student should without fail continue his rapid through reading of the Bible as a whole. It is highly desirable that these two types of Bible reading should be carried on simultaneously. R. A. Torrey testified to his practice of reading "the A.V. through every year, the R.V. through every year, and the N.T. in Greek through every year." *How To Study The Bible For Greatest Profit*, p. 87. This was in addition to his specific biblical studies.

We would suggest the following procedure as the most productive of lasting spiritual results.

1. REPEATED READING

Read the epistle *straight through* at one sitting. It is important to read the whole book at one time to get a clear impression of it as a whole. Disregard chapter and verse divisions; they are very convenient, man-made devices for reference, but they may hinder the apprehension of the author's trend of thought. Read it straight through in an endeavor to follow the writer's general development of his message. Do not stop to puzzle over passages that may appear dim to you. The purpose is not to catch the details but to grasp the central line of thought.

Now read it *again and yet again*. That which at first seemed vague and quite meaningless will with the third or fourth reading begin to assume shape and meaning. There is no substitute for this repeated personal reading of the epistle itself. People often are willing to read numerous books about the Bible but reluctant to read the Bible itself. But the reading of books about the Bible, valuable as that is, will not give one a personal knowledge of the Bible itself. The student of literature does not gain a mastery of the great literary classics by reading books about them; he must read them directly. So also a mastery of these epistles cannot be gained apart from the repeated reading of them.

After two or three readings of the epistle, different versions of the New Testament might be read. The use of a different translation may often serve to shed light on a certain passage not fully understood before. If the student is conversant with other languages, reading the epistle in another language often proves enlightening.

Personal testimony from various sources bears witness to the immeasurable value of such repeated reading of a book of the Bible. That noted Bible expositor, G. Campbell Morgan, "set for his own standard the reading of a book fifty times before putting pen to paper in preparation."[2] It was the secret of his comprehensive grasp of the contents of the Bible.

James M. Gray, noted exponent of synthetic Bible study, relates how he was led to adopt the book method of study through the testi-

2. Jill Morgan, *A Man of the Word, Life of G. Campbell Morgan*, p. 164.

mony of a Christian layman.[3] As a young minister he met a business-
man at a certain Christian convention and was attracted to him by
his serene Christian life. Venturing to ask him how he became possessed of the experience, the answer was, "By reading the Epistle to
the Ephesians." He was surprised, for its reading had not brought
such results to him. Asked for an explanation, the man related his
experience. One Sunday while spending the afternoon out in the
country with his family, he had taken a pocket copy of Ephesians
and, going out into the woods, began to read it, reading it straight
through at a single reading. His interest was aroused, and he read
it again and again. He read it through some twelve or fifteen times.
When he finally arose to return, he was in possession of the epistle
to the Ephesians, or rather it was in possession of him. He had in
an experiential sense come to sit with Christ in heavenly places. It
was the turning point in his spiritual life. Dr. Gray took the lesson
learned from this layman and employed it with transforming results.

In a little tract entitled "How the Bible Became a New Book to
Me,"[4] N. N. Rönning relates how his reading of the experience of
Dr. Gray came to him like a revelation. Early the next morning he
read the entire gospel of Matthew through at one sitting. It too
proved the beginning of a new experience in Bible study for him.

2. HISTORICAL BACKGROUND

Carefully read the epistle again with the aim of discovering in it
all available information concerning the setting and historical background of the epistle. Gather all the material you can find in it concerning the author, the readers, as well as the place, occasion, and
purpose of its composition. To be most profitable, have by your side
different sheets of paper, each sheet labeled "Author," "Readers,"
"Purpose," et cetera, and record the information you find on the
proper sheet with the scriptural references. This is important, for a
letter, especially, cannot be fully understood without acquaintance
with these matters of introduction.

Following your own study of the epistle relative to these matters
of introduction, read the introduction to the epistle. Test, supple-

---

3. James M. Gray, *How to Master the English Bible*, pp. 13-15.
4. Eight-page tract published by the Book Mission of the Evangelical Lutheran
   Church, Minneapolis.

ment, and evaluate your own findings in the light of the materials given on the epistle.

3. GENERAL OUTLINE

Your previous readings will have made you aware of the general divisions of the epistle. Now turn to the outline of the epistle given following the introduction. Notice the main divisions of the epistle and compare this with your own impression concerning the general outline. In some epistles the general divisions are so obvious that there will be little question concerning the main divisions. In other cases different students will reach different conclusions. The outline is important as an aid in setting forth the development of the thought of the epistle. Use the outline given as a guide to the contents of the epistle. Notice first the general divisions and mark them in the margin of your Bible. With these main divisions before you, reread, or perhaps better, seek to rethink the contents of the epistle as best you can with the aid of the outline. Next notice the main subdivisions under each and their relation to the main division.

For example, look at the outline of 1 Peter. Notice that the first twelve verses are designated as introduction, while the last three verses of the epistle form the conclusion. The body of the letter is divided into three main divisions. Each of these is designated as exhortations, in accordance with the author's own characterization of his message in 5:12. Notice the subject and verses included in each division, and then note the subdivisions of each section. With the outline thus before you, read the entire epistle again in the light of the outline.

4. DETAILED STUDY

Having gained a general acquaintance of the contents of the epistle through your repeated reading, plus the suggestions from the outline, you are now in a position to make a detailed study of it. Make an individual study of each verse as you go through the epistle. Seek to determine the precise meaning of each word and phrase in the light of its historical setting and the principles of grammatical interpretation. Keep in mind that each statement must be understood in the light of its context. Study the epistle independently, making an honest endeavor to gain the meaning of its teaching for yourself. Such independent study will be of more lasting benefit to you than simply reading the interpretation which someone has already worked out. For the most lasting benefit, the results of your own study should be preserved in writing for future use.

Following your own study of the text, turn to the writings of others. A list of volumes on the various epistles will be found following the outline. They are intended to present something of the rich variety of tools available for an intensive study of these important writings. Evaluate and supplement your own notes with the materials thus discovered. By reading such interpretative volumes you will share in the blessings which God has given to others who have labored on these epistles. The recording of these findings will not only impress them more firmly on your own mind but will preserve them for future use.

For this detailed study the use of the American Standard Version (1901) is urgently recommended. It is the best substitute for a knowledge of the original Greek available to the English reader. It is our conviction that for purposes of accurate study it is still the best translation available in the English language. The translation is an accurate word-by-word rendering, following the order of the Greek wherever possible. Consequently the resultant reading is not always smooth idiomatic English, but it brings the student as close to the original Greek as consistently possible in a translation. The accurate student must not forget that these epistles were originally written in the Greek.

5. PRAYERFUL MEDITATION

Throughout your reading and study have a prayerful attitude. Trite as that may sound, it is of fundamental importance in true Bible study. For the Christian the study of the Bible is more than merely intellectual. Its greatest values are not gained through intellectual acumen but through spiritual receptivity. The Holy Spirit, who inspired the Bible, is its best Teacher.

Meditate upon and spiritually digest the results of your study. Much Bible study is of little consequence spiritually because of a failure personally to assimilate its results for Christian living. "The ultimate aim of Bible study is not an informed intellect but a transformed personality."

There is no royal shortcut to the mastery of the Bible. The book method of study will demand time and effort. But its values are well worth all that it costs. In thus studying these non-Pauline epistles you will gain not only valued mental discipline and a rich store of precious truths, but you will find that it contributes immeasurably to your spiritual growth and stability. Here are treasures to be gleaned whose values will abide for time and eternity.

3

JAMES

An Introduction to James

THE EPISTLE OF JAMES has been characterized as the Wisdom Literature of the New Testament. That the Old Testament Wisdom Literature had nourished the meditations of the writer is evident. His pithy, pungent sentences, his authoritative tone, and his ethical emphasis declare it. Again, not without reason, James has been styled "the Amos of the New Testament." The epistle has in it the direct thrust of that Old Testament prophet. Like Amos, it draws much of its imagery from nature and offers a stinging rebuke to social injustice. Its remarkable Jewish cast makes it clear that its author had his roots deep in the Old Testament. It is equally clear that the epistle reveals obvious traces of the influence of the teachings of Jesus, especially the Sermon on the Mount.

The Canonicity of James

The epistle of James was not admitted into the canon without considerable hesitation. Eusebius (265-340) bears witness to this in his famous *Ecclesiastical History* by listing it among the *Antilegomena*, that is, the books which were being disputed by some section of the Church (3. 25); yet he himself accepted it as canonical (2. 23). Plummer thus states the reasons for this hesitancy concerning the epistle:

> The doubts were provoked by two facts—(1) the Epistle had remained for some time unknown to a good many Churches; (2) when it became generally known it remained uncertain what the authority of the writer was, especially whether he was an Apostle or not.[1]

---

1. Alfred Plummer, "The General Epistles of St. James and St. Jude," in *An Exposition of the Bible*, 6:560.

These doubts lingered longest in the Western Church where the emphasis was placed upon the apostolic authorship of a book admitted into the canon. During the fourth century the doubts concerning its canonicity subsided and it became universally recognized following the third Council of Carthage in A.D. 397.

1. EXTERNAL EVIDENCE

Although the West was the last to recognize its canonicity, it seems that the epistle of James was early known in Rome and the West. This conclusion is generally drawn from certain rather indefinite allusions to it in Clement (30-100), *The Shepherd*, by Hermas (*c.* 110-140), and Irenaeus (140-203).[2] The view of Mayor that the data from Clement indicated that James was in the mind of that writer is not generally accepted by scholars, but that Hermas was dependent upon James seems clear. Moffatt accepts that the probability of dependence is strong enough in Hermas to establish the terminal date of James.[3]

After these early glimpses of the epistle the traces of it in the West are soon lost in obscurity. It is not mentioned in the Muratorian Canon (*c.* A.D. 170), nor does it receive mention in Tertullian (150-222) and Cyprian (200-258). Gibson concludes that James seems "to have been unknown to the African Churches of the first three centuries."[4] But on the basis of probable allusions in early writers Mayor holds that "our Epistle was more widely known during the first three centuries than has been commonly supposed."[5]

In the East the evidence is fuller. It was not included in the Syriac version (*c.* A.D. 200), but was a part of the Peshitta Syriac (*c.* 425), a revision of the Old Syriac. The first father to quote the epistle as Scripture and ascribe it to James was Origen (185-253). Eusebius classified James among the disputed books, yet he himself quoted James 4:11 as Scripture (*The Psalms*). Although the extant writings of Clement of Alexandria (155-215) contain no reference to James, Eusebius says that Clement made "abridged accounts of all the canonical Scriptures, not even omitting those that are disputed, I mean the book of Jude, and the other general epistles" (*Eccl. Hist.*

---

2. The relevant passages from various early writers are cited in full in Joseph B. Mayor, *The Epistle of St. James*, pp. lii-lxviii.
3. James Moffatt, *An Introduction to the Literature of the New Testament*, p. 467.
4. E. C. S. Gibson, *The General Epistle of James*, The Pulpit Commentary, p. xii.
5. Mayor, p. li.

6. 14). This would of course include James. It was accepted by Athanasius (298-373), Gregory of Nazianzus (330-90), Chrysostom (347-407), and many others. But, as Harmon observes, "even those fathers who accepted it made but little use of it."[6] By the time of Jerome (340-420) and Augustine (354-430) it was all but universally accepted.

The external evidence shows that the epistle came but slowly into general circulation, especially in the West, where its canonicity was long questioned. The evidence for it is predominantly Eastern.

2. INTERNAL EVIDENCE

The evidence drawn from the character of the epistle itself harmonizes with all that we know about the James to whom it is traditionally ascribed. The contents of the epistle, with their lack of emphasis on doctrinal teaching, offer no motive to suspect a forgery. The superiority of its contents to that of the sub-apostolic writings, such as the epistle of Clement, or of Barnabas, or of Ignatius, strongly supports the conclusion that the writer was a man of apostolic rank.

Luther's criticism of James, based on the supposed conflict between James and Paul, is well known. He asserted that James was "a right strawy epistle" (*eine rechte stroherne epistle*), in comparison with John, Romans, Galatians, and 1 Peter and without evangelical character.[7] Luther's prejudice against the epistle was strengthened by the use that the Papists made of it to defend the doctrine of justification by works and the sacrament of extreme unction. But if Luther had only recognized the early date of James and had read it more sympathetically, he would not have passed such an adverse judgment on this epistle. The Lutheran church has not followed him in his evaluation of it. There is no real conflict between the epistle of James and the Pauline epistles.[8] Neither was there any

6. Henry M. Harmon, *Introduction to the Study of the Holy Scriptures*, pp. 711f.
7. Luther's critical position caused him to make a separate group of Hebrews, James, Jude, and Revelation in his German New Testament, placing them at the end of the volume and assigning them no numbers in his table of contents. Since 1603 these books have numbers in the table of contents. This order was followed in English Bibles before the Great Bible in 1539.
8. For a succinct discussion of the harmony between Paul and James see Doremus Almy Hayes, "James, Epistle of," *International Standard Bible Encyclopaedia* 3:1566a-1567a. Also Joseph Agar Beet, *A Commentary on St. Paul's Epistle to the Galatians*, Dissertation 4, "The Epistle of James Compared with That to the Galatians," pp. 203-10.

conflict between James and the true position of Luther. In his famous preface to Romans, Luther uses words that might appropriately have been used instead in an introduction to James:

> O, it is a living, busy, active, mighty thing, this faith; and so it is impossible for it not to do good works incessantly. It does not ask whether there are good works to do; but before the question rises, it has already done them, and is always at the doing of them. He who does not these works is a faithless man.[9]

The bearing of the internal evidence on the question of the canonicity of James is bound up with the problem of the identity of the author. The internal evidence strongly supports the traditional view of the authorship of the epistle.[10] Those who reject the traditional authorship reveal no unanimity among themselves as to their interpretation of the phenomena of the epistle. Critical opinion has variously regarded James as in reality a non-Christian Jewish work with a few Christian interpolations, an Ebionitic anti-Pauline tract written by someone in the name of James the Just after A.D. 70, or a pseudepigraphic writing of the second century.

3. CONCLUSION

The external evidence for James is admittedly not strong. Its slowness in gaining general acceptance in the Syrian church may have been due to the fact that it was addresesd to an indefinite circle of Jewish Christian readers and its author did not claim apostolic authority.[11] With the development of Gentile Christianity, the Jewish Christians to whom the epistle was addressed probably became more and more a self-contained group, thus accounting for the fact that the letter was so little known among the Gentile churches during the first two centuries. The resultant obscurity concerning its earlier history became the fertile soil for subsequent questions concerning its authority.

The internal evidence is thoroughly consistent with the traditional view of the authorship of the epistle. Its strong Jewish cast as well as its unmistakable reflections of the teachings of Jesus confirm this view. If the epistle was a forgery in the name of James the Just

---

9. Martin Luther, *The Works of Martin Luther, With Introductions and Notes,* 6:451-52.
10. See below under "The Author of the Epistle."
11. See R. J. Knowling, *The Epistle of St. James,* Westminster Commentaries, p. li.

there is no adequate explanation for the lack of any emphasis upon the apostle's personality and activities. The view that it was an anti-Pauline tract rests upon the mistaken assumption of a conflict beween the contents of James and the Pauline epistles. The assumption that it was a document Jewish in origin given a Christian flavor by the addition of a few Christian interpolations is highly improbable. Thus Moffatt comments, "A Christian interpolator would scarcely have contented himself with inserting so little, when he could have added references to Christ's life, e.g. at 5:11; and he would probably have left 2:1 clearer."[12] This view overemphasizes the Jewish element in the epistle and neglects the underlying Christian atmosphere in it. Ropes remarks, "There is no sentence which a Jew could have written and a Christian could not; its Jewish ideas are without exception those that a Christian could hold."[13] The theory also assumes that the epistle was not originally written in Greek; but certain features of the style, as for example, his use of similar-sounding Greek words, with the same or varied meaning, as connecting links between his sentences, precludes any view of it being translation Greek.

The fact must not be blurred that historically there was serious question in the early Church concerning the canonicity of the epistle. But the uncertainty arose primarily out of uncertainty regarding its author rather than its authenticity. We unhesitatingly accept the epistle as a worthy member of the Christian canon. We hold that the Church was right in its decision concerning the canonicity of it. We fully concur in the conclusion of Plummer:

> When we examine for ourselves the evidence which is still extant, and which has greatly diminished in the course of fifteen hundred years, we feel that both on external and internal grounds the decision of the fourth century respecting the genuineness of the Epistle of James, as a veritable product of the Apostolic age and as worthy of a place in the canon of the New Testament, is fully justified.[14]

THE AUTHOR OF THE EPISTLE

1. PICTURE IN EPISTLE

The author of this epistle gives his name as James or *Iakōbos* as

---

12. James Moffatt, p. 474.
13. James Hardy Ropes, *A Critical and Exegetical Commentary on the Epistle of St. James*, International Critical Commentary, p. 33.
14. Plummer, p. 562.

the Greek has it. Our English monosyllabic James blurs the fact that the writer bears the name of the great patriarch, Jacob, which had become a commonplace name among the Jews during the day of Jesus.

The author further describes himself as "a servant of God and of the Lord Jesus Christ" (1:1). This identification indicates only his spiritual position. Unlike Jude, who identifies himself as the "brother of James," the author apparently did not feel it necessary to identify himself by an indication of his human relations. Apparently he was a man who would be well known to his readers without any further identification.

Although in the body of the epistle the author makes no further direct reference to himself, there are yet few writings which in the same space reveal more of the individual character of their author. He reveals himself as no dull, commonplace man. He manifests a vigor and alertness that are arresting. His crisp, concise, authoritative tone commands attention. His brief sentences are like piercing arrows which inevitably hit their mark.

He stands before us as a man who is keenly observant of nature, life, and human character. He was an observant student of nature and repeatedly draws his illustrations from that area. He also has deep and penetrating insight into life and human nature. "He knows the fashions of the world, and he notes with unerring clearness and humorous shrewdness the characters of men; he sees their superficial goodness, their indolent selfishness, their vulgarity and the mischief of their untamed thoughtlessness."[15]

He is a man of deep moral and religious convictions. He has a deep sense of right which compels him to speak out against wrong wherever he encounters it. He speaks out with impassioned indignation, yet he is essentially kindly in disposition. He has no use for religious profession unaccompanied by a good life. He has a deep, if reticent, love for Christ, whom he calls "the Lord of glory" (2:1). Although his emphasis is practical, he yet gives expression to the basic Christian convictions. In the words of Manley,

> He regards God as the "eternal changeless One" from whom come all good gifts (1:17), and under whose providence is every detail of life

15. W. Boyd Carpenter, *The Wisdom of James the Just*, p. 12.

(4:15). He holds a strong belief in prayer (5:16), and looks for the coming of Christ (5:7).[16]

Although the author definitely reveals the spirit of the Gospel, it is yet evident that his thinking stems out of a Jewish background. Smith remarks that his "whole mental atmosphere is that of a devout Jew, who has not ceased to be a Jew by becoming a Christian."[17] Christian ideas are still clothed in Jewish forms. The love of the world is condemned in Old Testament terms as adultery against God (4:4). In urging the duty of prayer he enforces it by the Old Testament example of Elijah (5:17-18), and evil speaking is condemned as putting a slight on the Law (4:11). He never uses the word Gospel, yet what apparently takes its place he calls "the law of liberty" or "the royal law" (2:12, 8). The marks of the epistle thus point to an author who was a devout Jewish Christian. Yet there is no trace of the observance of the Jewish rituals and sacrifices.

2. IDENTITY

Some have insisted that the identity of this James, a very common name at the time, cannot be established and that the author was someone otherwise entirely unknown. But on this view it is difficult to account for the authoritative tone and encyclical nature of the epistle. If the traditional identification must be abandoned, then we are forced to the unsatisfactory conclusion that it was indeed written by someone who had no apostolic authority whatever. This contradicts the consensus of the Church concerning it.

The New Testament speaks of four men by the name of James. Scholarly opinion has not been in agreement as to which of these men is the author of this epistle. They may be distinguished as follows: (1) James, the son of Zebedee and brother of John, one of the twelve (Mt 4:21; 10:2; 17:1; Mk 10:35; 13:3; Lk 9:54; Ac 1:13; 12:2). (2) James the son of Alphaeus, one of the twelve (Mt 10:3; 27:56; Mk 3:18; 15:40; Lk 6:15; 24:10; Ac 1:13). (3) James, the Lord's brother (Mt 13:55; Mk 6:3; Gal 1:19). (4) James, the father of Judas "not Iscariot" (Lk 6:16, ASV; Ac 1:13), ASV).[18]

The last of these may at once be eliminated as the possible author.

16. G. T. Manley, *The New Bible Handbook*, p. 396.
17. H. Maynard Smith, *The Epistle of S. James*, p. 4.
18. That we should read *"son"* rather than *"brother,"* as in the King James Version, is evident from the parallel construction about James the son of Alphaeus.

He is entirely unknown except for the fact that he was the father of one of the twelve.

The hypothesis that the author was James the son of Zebedee has had but few advocates.[19] This James was beheaded under Herod Agrippa I not later than the spring of A.D. 44 (Ac 12:2), and it seems highly improbable that an apostle could have written an encyclical letter such as this at that early date. Nor is there any evidence that he had attained a special position of leadership among the Jewish Christians which would justify such an appeal.

We are left with a choice between James the son of Alphaeus and James the Lord's brother. Can we think of the former as the author of this letter? But we are immediately confronted with the preliminary question as to whether or not these two are the same person. The proposal to identify them was stimulated by the views of Jerome in the fourth century.

The view that James the son of Alphaeus and James the Lord's brother are the same is beset with grave difficulties. It assumes that the Clopas in John 19:25 is to be identified with Alphaeus the father of James (Mt 10:3; Mk 3:18; Lk 6:15; Ac 1:13). Linguistically it is possible that the two names are only different forms of the same Aramaic name. Yet it seems unlikely that the same man would have been known by both names in the same company of disciples. Johnstone points out that in the Syriac versions, made by men who doubtless were acquainted with Aramaic names and their renderings, different forms are used for Alphaeus and Clopas.[20]

This view would make John 19:25 refer to only three women, holding that "his mother's sister" is "Mary the wife of Clopas." This view is very common, but it seems highly improbable.[21] Then we would have two living sisters bearing the name of Mary in the same family. A comparison with Matthew 27:56 and Mark 15:40 makes it far more probable that John refers to four women, naming them in pairs, and that the sister of Mary the mother of Jesus is really Salome, the mother of the sons of Zebedee. The Peshitta Syriac ver-

19. Advocated by F. T. Bassett. See rebuttal in E. H. Plumptre, *The General Epistle of St. James,* Cambridge Bible for Schools and Colleges, pp. 6-10.
20. Robert Johnstone, *Lectures Exegetical and Practical on the Epistle of James,* p. 59.
21. See George E. Evans, "The Sister of The Mother of Jesus," *The Review and Expositor,* October 1947, pp. 475-85.

sion inserts a conjunction, thus showing that the translator understood John to speak of four women.

The gospel references to the brothers of Jesus do not harmonize
with the view that one of them was among the twelve. His brothers
are always represented as a different set of men than the apostles
(Jn 2:12; Mt 12:46; Mk 3:31; Lk 8:19; Jn 7:3; Acts 1:14). The fact
that they united with His mother in an attempt to check the intensive
ministry of Jesus reveals their attitude toward Him. The way in
which the people of Nazareth spoke of them does not imply that any
of them were among His disciples (Mt 13:55; Mk 6:3). As late as
the last Feast of Tabernacles, some six months before the crucifixion,
John's gospel informs us that "even his brethren did not believe on
him" (7:5). It is difficult to see how this statement by John can be
harmonized with the view that one of His brothers was among the
disciples of Jesus.

In support of the proposed identification, Jerome argued that in
Galatians 1:19 Paul speaks of James the Lord's brother as an apostle.
But this does not prove that he was one of the twelve. The addition
"except James" may simply mean that he did see another person who
was so important that he felt that he must be mentioned along with
the apostle Peter.[22] But even if we accept as more natural the interpretation that Paul means to call James an apostle, it does not follow
that he was one of the twelve. He may simply be using the term
apostle in a wider sense to include other men of prominence in the
Church. And the fact that the risen Lord appeared to James would
seem to qualify him for that designation. We know that the term
was applied to Barnabas (Ac 14:4, 14), although he certainly was
not one of the original twelve.[23]

The difficulties encountered in attempting to identify James the
son of Alphaeus with James the Lord's brother compel us to reject
the identification. Plumptre categorically asserts, "Except on that
hypothesis, there are absolutely no grounds whatever, external or
internal, to connect the former with the authorship of this Epistle."[24]
Yet, among the Reformers, Calvin thought this view not improbable.
Although he did not identify the two men, he thought that the James

22. See R. C. H. Lenski, *The Interpretation of St. Paul's Epistles to the Galatians, to
the Ephesians, and to the Philippians,* pp. 61-62.
23. Mayor, pp. xvii-xviii.
24. Plumptre, p. 12.

of Galatians 2:9, whom Paul calls a "pillar" of the Church, was indeed the son of Alphaeus.[25] Calvin hesitated to pronounce which of the two was the author. Tasker observes that apparently "Calvin hesitated about assigning the same degree of authority to an apostle other than Paul, if he was outside the number of the original twelve."[26] J. Sidlow Baxter, a modern advocate of this view, insists that to identify the James of Acts 12:17; 15:13-21; 21:18-25 with James the Lord's brother rather than James the son of Alphaeus, an apostle, makes Luke guilty of dropping an apostle without an explanation and putting in his place another leader who was not an apostle.[27] But after the list of the apostles in Acts 1 only three of the twelve are certainly mentioned again. James the son of Alphaeus is known to us only from the mention of his name in the lists of the twelve. A man who made so little impression on the gospel narrative as not to have his name associated with a single gospel event, does not seem to be the forceful personality behind this epistle. That one who was not one of the original twelve should in a short time step into prominence in the early Church need not be surprising when we consider the relation that James the Lord's brother had to Christ as well as his devout personal character.

We are left with the conclusion that the author of this epistle was James the Lord's brother. All that we know about him from Scripture and tradition agrees with this. Three considerations have been advanced in confirmation of this position.

This view is supported by the remarkable coincidences of language between the epistle and the speech of James at the Jerusalem Conference as well as the letter sent by the Conference, which was evidently drawn up by James.[28] The form "to greet" at the beginning of the epistle of James and the Conference letter is an unusual form. James began his speech with the address, "Brethren, hearken unto me"—a form also found in the epistle (2:5). The expression "your souls" in the Conference letter is a Hebraic expression; it is also found in the epistle (1:21). The peculiar use of the word "to visit" is found in both the speech and the epistle. These and other similarities cer-

---

25. John Calvin, *Commentaries on the Catholic Epistles*, p. 277.
26. R. V. G. Tasker, *The General Epistle of James*, The Tyndale New Testament Commentaries, p. 22.
27. J. Sidlow Baxter, *Explore the Book*, 6:292-93.
28. For an elaboration of these coincidences see James Alex. Robertson, *The Hidden Romance of the New Testament*, pp. 222-25.

tainly are remarkable in view of the shortness of the passage in Acts from which they come. They cause us to feel that all the time we are in contact with the same mind.

A second consideration is the fact that in reading the epistle one repeatedly comes across sayings and phrases which recall the teachings of Jesus.[29] Ross asserts, "This Epistle contains more verbal reminiscences of the teachings of Jesus than all the other apostolic writings taken together."[30] But it is not that James is consciously and deliberately quoting from Jesus. He seems rather not to be quoting at all. These thoughts and expressions seem to have become a very part of his thinking as the result of his long association with Jesus. Thus Robertson says, "We can scarcely resist the conclusion that we are listening to the reproduction of thoughts from a mind that had lived and laboured for years alongside the Master-mind which created and gave them perfect utterance."[31]

A third consideration is the fact that the epistle is the work of just that type of mind which all the mentions of James in the New Testament and Christian tradition reveal him to be.[32] The well-known Jewish features of the life of James "the Just" blend harmoniously into the picture of the writer as portrayed in the epistle.

But strenuous objections have been raised to this view as to the author of this epistle. It has been asserted that the reference to persecutions being experienced points to a later date than James. But there is no evidence that the afflictions being suffered by these Jewish Christians were due to governmental persecutions. They were rather the result of the impositions of the rich upon the poor, the injustices of the employers toward their employees. The persecutions were local manifestations of hatred.

It has been claimed that the exhortation to patience suggests that there had already been a considerable delay in the expected return of Christ and so indicates a later date. But the words of James offer no grounds for the assertion that there has been a great delay in the Lord's return. James definitely implies that the coming of the Lord is near, and this attitude is consistent with the time of James.

It is held that the book contains quotations from other New Testa-

29. See the list of parallels under the section, *"The Characteristics of the Epistle."*
30. Alexander Ross, *The Epistles of James and John,* The New International Commentary on the New Testament, p. 16.
31. Robertson, p. 229.
32. For a sketch of the history of James see p. 44.

ment books, especially 1 Peter, hence it must be of later origin. But this argument is inconclusive since it can be turned around and with equal force be used to point to the early date of James.

Much weight has been laid upon the assertion that a Galilean peasant such as James could not have written such excellent Greek as this epistle. Thus Easton thinks that it is impossible "by the wildest stretch of the imagination" to accept that James, the Lord's brother, could have written the Greek of this epistle.[33] But this argument from the language of James is not so formidable as assumed. Carr bluntly replied, "Such an argument implies a preconception of the possibilities of learning available for James which do not rest on evidence."[33a] It must be remembered that "Galilee of the Gentiles" was a bilingual country. Thus Moulton asserts,

> There is not the slightest presumption against the use of Greek in writings purporting to emanate from the circle of the first believers. They would write as men who had used the language from boyhood, not as foreigners painfully expressing themselves in an imperfectly known idiom.[34]

And A. T. Robertson likewise remarks, "The incongruity of such a smooth piece of Greek as this Epistle being written by a Palestinian Jew like James vanishes when we consider the bilingual character of the people of Palestine."[34a]

While admittedly the language of the epistle is good Greek, the assertion concerning the "excellent Greek" must not be overdone. Robertson declares, "The author of Hebrews, Luke and Paul far surpass him in formal rhetoric."[35] Although written in good, vigorous Greek, the form and idiom have a definite Hebrew flavor. While making due allowance for the influence of "international vulgarisms" in Koine Greek, the features of the language point to a Jewish atmosphere of thought and expression. Thus Oesterley says,

> The Greek form of the expression of thought seems to be moulded from a Hebrew pattern, *i.e.*, that the mind of the writer was accus-

---

33. Burton Scott Easton, "The Epistle of James," in *The Interpreter's Bible*, 6:6*b*.
33a. Arthur Carr, *The General Epistle of St. James*, Cambridge Greek Testament, p. xxiii.
34. James Hope Moulton, *A Grammar of New Testament Greek*, 1:8.
34a. A. T. Robertson, *A Grammar of the Greek New Testament in the Light of Historical Research*, p. 123.
35. Ibid, p. 123.

tomed to express itself after the manner of one to whom Hebrew ways of thinking were very familiar, and who in writing Greek, therefore, almost unconsciously reverted to the Hebrew mode.[36]

The contention that James could not have developed such a command of Greek as this epistle shows is not decisive. The general diffusion of Greek in Palestine makes it very probable that James was acquainted with Greek from boyhood. Further, his position of influence in the church at Jerusalem would make it desirable to develop proficiency in its use. From the very beginning there were Hellenists in the Jerusalem church who were completely at home in the Greek language. Aside from the fact that there would have been opportunity for further study of Greek right in Jerusalem, daily contact with these Hellenists, as well as frequent practice in public speaking and debate, might well give James ample opportunity to develop considerable proficiency in the use of the language. Nor should the possibility that James may have had linguistic aptitudes be lightly dismissed. That there were men of high literary proficiency in Greek in Palestine at the time is certain. Mayor points out that a few years earlier the city of Gadara, on the eastern side of the Sea of Galilee, was the home of four highly accomplished literary men. He concludes that "it was no more impossible for a peasant of Galilee to learn to write good Greek, than for one who had been brought up as a Welsh peasant to learn to write good English, or for a Breton to write good French."[37]

3. HISTORY

Apparently James was the oldest of the brothers of Jesus, for his name is always mentioned first (Mt 13:55; Mk 6:3). Following His resurrection, the Lord appeared to him (1 Co 15:7), and that appearance dissolved all his doubts, and he threw in his lot with the followers of Christ. He was with the group in the upper room after the ascension of Jesus (Ac 1:14). When Paul returned to Jerusalem three years after his conversion, he saw Peter and "James the Lord's brother" (Gal 1:18-19). Following his miraculous deliverance from prison, Peter directed that the news should be given to James, apparently now a recognized leader in the Jerusalem church (Ac

36. W. E. Oesterley, "The General Epistle of James," in *The Expositor's Greek Testament*, 6:393.
37. Mayor, p. xlii.

12:17). At the time of the Jerusalem Conference James was recognized as one of the pillars of the Church (Gal 2:9), and he took a leading part in the discussions of the Conference. At the end of Paul's third missionary journey, when he brought the offering for the Judean saints, James was the revered leader of the Jewish Christians in Jerusalem (Ac 21:18-25).

The glimpses which we get of James as the leader of the church of the circumcision in Jerusalem show that he honored and observed the ritual of the Law. At the Jerusalem Conference it was the speech of James that conciliated the Jewish brethren. It was he who suggested the restrictive clauses to the decision of the Conference; he reminded them that "Moses from generations of old hath in every city them that preach him, being read in the synagogues every sabbath" (Ac 15:20-21). He also reminded them that the prophecy concerning Israel's future is relevant for its own time (vv. 15-18). Further, when Paul returned to Jerusalem with the collection for the saints, the suggestion made to Paul by James shows that he had the tenderest sympathies for the "many thousands . . . among the Jews of them that have believed; and they are all zealous for the law" (Ac 21:20). In Galatians 2:12 we read of certain men coming to Antioch who represented themselves as coming "from James." Their refusal to eat with the Gentile believers had a strong effect on affairs at Antioch. It is not asserted that they were sent by James, but it seems clear that their action carried great weight because they could claim the sanction of James for their position. As the leader of the Judaic church, James himself continued to observe the Mosaic Law, not as a means of salvation, but as a way of life. James was not in conflict with Paul. At the Jerusalem Conference James definitely supported the position of Paul that the Gentile believers were not under the Law. He reaffirmed that position when Paul came to Jerusalem with the collection (Ac 21:25). But the Jerusalem Conference said nothing about Jewish Christians and their keeping of the Law. From his suggestion to Paul it is clear that James was in full sympathy with those Jewish believers who continued to do so (Ac 21:20-25). In Galatians 2:9 James is among those who agree to continue their ministries "unto the circumcision."

Nonbiblical references to James place special emphasis upon his Jewish character. The account of Hegesippus, preserved by Eusebius

(*Eccl. Hist.* 2. 23), says that he lived the life of a Nazarite and spent so much time in prayer on his knees in the Temple that his knees became hard as a camel's. Because of his life of piety and strict uprightness he was given the title "James the Just," a title which implies not only his integrity but his faithful adherence to the requirements of the Law. His rigid observance of the Law secured for him the veneration even of the unbelieving Jews. The account of Hegesippus contains some fanciful features, and there is some disagreement in his account of the death of James and that given by Josephus.[38] But it is plain that he died a violent death at the hands of the Jewish leaders because of his great influence in leading people to accept Jesus as the Messiah. His violent death was openly condemned by the masses of the Jews, and there was a widespread conviction that the afflictions which shortly thereafter befell the city of Jerusalem were in punishment for the crime of his death. It is easy to see how a man so Jewish and so insistent upon practical morality could have written this epistle.

4. RELATION TO JESUS

The conclusion that James the Lord's brother is the author of this epistle at once raises the difficult question as to the exact significance of that designation. It is a thorny problem on which the scholars have badly torn their exegetical robes. It must be treated with due respect for the sincere convictions of those who differ on the answer. Three main views have been advocated.[39]

The *Helvidian* theory, so named from an obscure writer who advocated it in the latter part of the fourth century, holds that these brothers of Jesus were the sons of Joseph and Mary, hence they were all younger than Jesus.[40] A reading of the various New Testament references to these brethren by one unprejudiced by historical or doctrinal considerations would naturally lead to the conclusion that they were the sons of Joseph and Mary. In the scriptural accounts they are always called brothers, and not cousins; their relationship is always defined with reference to Christ, not to Joseph and Mary; they

---

38. Flavius Josephus *The Antiquities of the Jews* 20. 9. 1.
39. For the history of these views see Ropes, pp. 54-59.
40. This is the view of perhaps the majority of modern Protestant scholars. See the defense in Mayor, *The Epistle of James,* chap. 1; John Eadie, *Commentary on the Epistle of Paul to the Galatians,* pp. 57-100; H. E. Jacobs, "Brethren of the Lord," *International Standard Bible Encyclopedia,* 1:518b-20b.

always appear in connection with Mary (except in Jn 7:3) as if her children, members of her household. The impression that they were the real sons of Mary is deepened by the statement in Matthew 1:25 that following the birth of Jesus, Joseph and Mary lived as husband and wife. The statement in Luke 2:7 about Jesus as Mary's "firstborn son," although a technical term indicating certain privileges, may fairly well, in the light of the gospel record, be construed to imply the existence of children born subsequently. If Luke had meant to teach that Mary had no other children, the word *monogenēs* (used in Lk 7:12; 8:42 of an "only" child) would have been available.

Tertullian (150-222) is the first known writer who expressly asserted that the "brethren" were the uterine brothers of Jesus. Mayor points out that in the statement of Tertullian, written about the end of the second century, there is no trace of a contrary tradition which Tertullian is seeking to controvert.[41] Ropes holds that this was the view of most persons in the Christian Church during the second century and finds confirmation of that in a statement of Origen to the effect that the opposite opinion was held by "some," in apparent distinction from the majority.[42]

Objection is raised to this view on the ground that the majority of the ancient writers who discuss the question hold to the position that Mary had no other children. But it is clear that by the time the subject came into full discussion the theory of the perpetual virginity of Mary, though unsupported by scriptural teaching, had already begun to project itself into the theology of the Church. The objections to the Helvidian theory were prompted by the desire to preserve the virginity of Mary. Ascetic feeling which placed a higher sanctity upon celibacy than marriage caused men to shrink from the thought that the virgin womb of Mary, in which the eternal Word was made flesh, should also have been the habitation of other babes.

Objections to this view are also raised on biblical grounds. It is asserted that the way in which the brothers of Jesus attempted to interfere with His ministry is, according to Jewish custom, inconsistent with the view that they were younger. But it has well been replied that "those who pursue an unjustifiable course are not models of consistency."[43]

41. Mayor, p. x.
42. Ropes, p. 54.
43. Jacobs, 1:520a.

Again, it is held that the fact that Jesus on the cross committed His mother to John's care implies that she did not have other children. But this does not necessarily follow from the historical facts. In that tragic hour none of her other sons understood Jesus and hence could not sympathize with Mary as could John the beloved disciple. As the son of her sister Salome there was a closer bond between him and Mary than between her nearer blood relation.

The *Epiphanian* theory, so called from its most vigorous defendant in the fourth century, holds that these brothers were the sons of Joseph by a former marriage, hence they were all older than Jesus.[44] By the fourth century this had become the prevailing view in the Church. It received the support of Origen (185-253), Eusebius (265-340), and Gregory of Nyssa (332-98). This view had its origin in the second century and finds its earliest expression in the apocryphal gospels; there the assertion is made that Joseph was an old man and had children when he married Mary (*The Protevangelion* 8. 13). But these legends need not be taken seriously; Jerome, the author of a third theory, denounced them as "apocryphal nonsense."

This view had great appeal in the early Church because it safeguarded the virginity of Mary. The view appeals to the sacred feelings of many modern Christians without implying any support for certain doctrinal implications. However, it does not seem to do full justice to the statement that Jesus was the "firstborn son." Again, if the brothers were older than Jesus it is difficult to explain their continued presence with His mother; we would have expected them to be married, having homes of their own, but the impression left by Scripture is that they constituted one household. Later when Paul wrote 1 Corinthians (9:5) they were widely known as Christian workers who were married. This view is also open to the objection that if the brothers are His seniors Jesus could not have been the heir to David's throne, as His elder brothers would have ranked before Him.

The *Hieronymian* theory, originated by Jerome to refute the position of Helvidius, holds that the "brethren" of Jesus were really His cousins, the children of Clopas and Mary the sister of the mother of

---

44. This is the view of the Orthodox churches. It has some strong defenders among modern Protestant scholars. See J. B. Lightfoot, *Saint Paul's Epistle to the Galatians*, Dissertation 2, "The Brethren of the Lord," pp. 252-91; Smith, pp. 33-37.

Jesus.[45] Although it became widely accepted, this view rests upon several questionable suppositions, namely, that Alphaeus and Clopas are the same man, that Mary the wife of Clopas was the sister of the virgin Mary, and that the word "brother" is used in a lax sense to mean cousin. These assumptions are open to serious question. If they were the sons of Mary the wife of Clopas, it is inexplicable that, their mother being alive, they should always be spoken of as the "brothers of the Lord" and be associated with Mary the mother of Jesus rather than with their own mother. If they were cousins of Jesus the Greek had the word *anepsios* to express that relationship. Jerome could produce no earlier ecclesiastical tradition to support the view.

The problem is admittedly a complex one and probably will never be settled to the satisfaction of everyone. We concur in the following conclusion of Mombert:

> The view that Jesus had actual brothers and sisters is as old as any of the other theories and we believe, with Neander, Winer, Meyer, Stier, Alford and Farrar, that it accords best with the evangelical record, and barring dogmatical prejudices or feeling, is at once the simplest, most natural and logical solution of this otherwise hopelessly confused question.[46]

THE READERS OF JAMES

1. JEWISH CHRISTIANS

James indicates the circle of his readers with the words "to the twelve tribes which are of the Dispersion" (1:1). Those who reject the authorship of James and place the epistle late hold that these words must be taken figuratively as denoting "Christendom in general conceived under the oecumenical symbol of ancient Israel."[47] Others have taken the words literally as addressed to the Jews of the Dispersion whether Christians or not. The common, and doubtless the correct, view is that it was addressed to Jewish Christians outside Palestine.

That the recipients of the epistle were Christians is evident from its contents. James repeatedly addresses them as "brethren," and he

---

45. This is the established view of the Roman Catholic church.
46. Addition by J. Isidor Mombert in J. P. Lange and J. J. Van Oosterzee, "The Epistle General of James," Lange's *Commentary on the Holy Scriptures*, p. 22.
47. Moffatt, p. 464.

bases his authority upon the fact that he is a "'servant of God and of the Lord Jesus Christ" (1:1). He views his readers as having been born again by the Word of God (1:19), as persons holding "the faith of our Lord Jesus Christ" (2:1); he reminds them of "the honorable name by which ye are called" (2:7). The exhortation to them to "be patient until the coming of the Lord" (5:7) presupposes that the readers were Christians.

That the readers were Jewish Christians is evident from the salutation as well as the contents of the epistle. The designation of their place of meeting as the "synagogue" (2:2), the prominence given to monotheism (2:19), the enumeration of Jewish formulae of oaths (5:12), as well as the characteristic Jewish features of the ethical errors which are censured, all point to that conclusion.

2. LOCALITY

The epistle gives no further indication where the readers were located beyond the fact that they are "of the Dispersion" (1:1), hence living outside of Palestine. Some, like Jones, think that "the readers are Jewish Christians probably belonging to the Eastern Dispersion," as distinguished from the churches of the Western Dispersion to whom Peter later addressed his epistle.[48] But since the epistle is written in Greek, it seems much more probable that they belonged to the Greek-speaking Jews who had accepted Jesus as Messiah. Since we have no evidence that Christianity gained a footing in Mesopotamia before A.D. 60, we seem to be limited to the Jewish Christians of the Greek Dispersion. From Acts 9:2; 11:19; and 13:1 it is clear that Christianity early spread beyond Palestine into Greek-speaking territory. Gloag holds that the epistle is addressed "to the Greek Jews or Hellenists, who had embraced Christianity, and who in all probability were chiefly congregated in the countries in closest proximity to Judea, namely Phoenicia, Syria, Cilicia, and Proconsular Asia."[49] Dana, feeling that the locality of the readers was even more restricted, concluded that "the Epistle was written to Jewish Christian congregations in Syria."[50] This seems to us to be the most probable and to be supported by Acts 11:19.

48. Maurice Jones, *The New Testament in the Twentieth Century*, p. 319.
49. Paton J. Gloag, *Introduction to The Catholic Epistles*, p. 48.
50. H. E. Dana, *Jewish Christianity*, p. 107.

3. RELATION TO JAMES

As Jews the readers had been accustomed to look to Jerusalem for religious leadership. This background conditioned them to look for and accept guidance and doctrinal instruction from James, the recognized leader of the Jewish Christians at Jerusalem. As the leader of the Jerusalem church, the care of these Jewish Christian congregations would in a special way fall to the province of James. He would come into contact with various representatives of these congregations as different members came to Jerusalem for business or to attend the Jewish national feasts. His discovery of conditions among them led him to use the epistolary method to meet their needs, a method also proposed by him at the Jerusalem Conference.

THE OCCASION FOR JAMES

It was his discovery of the unsatisfactory conditions among these Jewish Christian congregations that prompted James to write this epistle. The circumstances are discernible from the epistle. They were being beset by manifold trials (1:2). Yet they were not in a proper attitude to profit thereby. They were failing to appropriate the available resources through prayer (1:5).

Being of the poorer classes, many of them were suffering social injustices. While there were some wealthy members among them (1:10), the majority seem to have been of the laboring classes (1:9; 5:1-8). Employed by the rich Jews, the poor suffered at the hands of their wealthy employers who dragged them before the judgment seat (2:6-7) or wrongfully withheld their wages (5:4). But the complaints of these sufferers reveal that they were not bearing their trials with that patience and humility befitting them as Christians. Their perturbed spirits and worldly attitude found expression in complaints against one another (4:11-12; 5:9-10) and even led to strife and dissensions (4:1-3).

They were prone to yield to a materialistic, independent attitude which failed to submit itself to the providence of God (4:13-17). They were in danger of neglecting their self-preservation from the world (4:4-10), and they seemed to imagine that their Christian faith would suffice to save them without a holy life (2:14-26). It was evident that they needed seriously to test themselves to see if their faith was genuine.

THE PLACE AND DATE OF COMPOSITION

1. PLACE

The view that James the Lord's brother is the author carries with it the conclusion that the place of composition was Jerusalem, the fixed place of his residence. The physical allusions in the epistle lend confirmation to this conclusion. The reference to "the early and latter rain" (5:7), the effect of the hot winds on vegetation (1:11), the existence of salt and bitter springs (3:11), the cultivation of figs and olives (3:12), and the familiar imagery of the sea as near by (1:6; 3:4) all are reminiscent of conditions in Palestine.

2. DATE

Among those who reject the authorship of James the dates assigned to the epistle vary greatly. Even among those who accept that authorship there is considerable divergence of opinion. Some would date it shortly before the martyrdom of James, while others place it early, even before the Jerusalem Conference. The contents of the epistle seem to point to an early date.

One phase of the evidence for an early date is the "very slight line which appears to exist between Judaism and Christianity."[51] There is likewise an absence of developed Christian phraseology and a lack of elaborated Christian doctrine. The Christian distinctives mentioned in the epistle—the lordship of Christ and the hope of His early return (1:1; 2:1; 5:8)—were characteristic of Christianity from its very inception.

The fact that there is no mention of circumcision points to a time before this burning question arose in the Church. Before the admission of Gentiles into the Church the obligation of the ceremonial Law upon believers was taken for granted by Jewish Christians, hence needed no discussion. But with the Jerusalem Conference this became a critical problem, and it seems unlikely that James in writing to Jewish Christians would have nothing to say about it if the problem had already arisen.

The total absence of any reference to Gentiles and their relation to Christianity is strange indeed if Gentile Christians are already a prominent element in the Church. The epistle gives no hint of the existence of Gentile churches. Neither does it contain any directions

51. E. C. S. Gibson, *The General Epistle of James,* The Pulpit Commentary, p. ix.

concerning the social relations between Jewish and Gentile believers, a problem which was acute after the Jerusalem Conference (cf. Gal 2:11, ff.).

The Church order reflected in the epistle is most elementary. Neither "bishops" nor "deacons" are mentioned. The reference to "the elders of the church" (5:14) is consistent with the view that these were Jewish Christian congregations organized largely after the pattern of the Jewish synagogue. The warning against many being teachers (3:1) seems to point to an early free type of organization.

It is highly improbable that the epistle was written after the outbreak of the controversy concerning faith versus works. If James wrote in reaction to Paul's teaching of salvation by faith, surely he would have more explicitly expressed himself on the relation between himself and Paul. It is very likely that later in the controversy the antagonists of Paul used the words of James, taken out of their context, as a weapon against Paul's teaching. The epistle belongs to a period before the finer distinctions which arose out of that question were developed. Thus Smith says,

> There was, when the letter was written, no need to distinguish between *works*, *good works*, and *works of the Law*, but these distinctions became vital for subsequent controversialists. The word *justification* had evidently not acquired a technical sense, and the author shows no acquaintance with the doctrine of Paul.[52]

We conclude that the evidence points to a date before the Jerusalem Conference. The date may thus be suggested as about A.D. 46, at least before A.D. 49. This view makes James the earliest book in the New Testament.

THE PURPOSE OF THE EPISTLE

Since the epistle contains no formal statement of purpose, the author's purpose must be gathered from the general contents of the letter. Obviously the purpose was not theological exposition. James seems not to have felt it necessary to expound the contents of the faith which his readers must hold. His purpose is practical. Information concerning the condition of the readers had led him to realize that their faith was not vitally operative in their lives. He accordingly presents to them a series of practical tests whereby they may test the

52. Smith, p. 34. Italics in original.

genuineness of their Christian faith. It is sometimes said that the purpose of James was to emphasize the importance of works. This is a failure to apprehend the larger purpose of James. Rather, as Lenski remarks, "This entire epistle deals with Christian faith, and shows how this faith should be genuine, true, active, living, fruit-ful."[53] The epistle develops the theme of tests for the Christian faith. The central truth of the epistle is the blessedness of enduring trials (1:12).

Following the brief salutation (1:1), James at once plunges into his subject—the tests of faith. From different angles the subject of tests is discussed in the next seventeen verses (1:2-18). Then he proceeds to set forth a series of six tests whereby his readers are to test their own faith. In the remainder of chapter one (1:19-27) he points out that faith must be tested by its attitude toward the Word of God. Chapter two presents two further tests: Faith tested by its reaction to social distinctions (2:1-13) and by its production of works as the evidence of its vitality (2:14-26). Chapter three points out that faith must be tested by its production of inner self-control (3:1-18). The fact that his readers manifested a spirit of worldliness leads him to devote a long section to the matter of faith's reaction to the world and the various ways whereby worldliness manifests itself in the believer (4:1—5:12). The concluding test of faith which James presents is its resort to prayer under all circumstances of life (5:13-20). James concludes abruptly with an appeal to restore those that have strayed.

The Characteristics of the Epistle

1. style

The language of James is clear, uninvolved, and straight to the point. There is generally no reason for a failure to understand what he wishes to say. His sentences are brief and free from those long involved grammatical constructions which characterize the writings of Paul.

The epistle is characterized by the vividness of its presentation. James must have been an arresting preacher. He makes frequent use of rhetorical questions, vivid similes, and pointed illustrations. Abstract ideas are presented in concrete form (2:2-4; 5:1-6) or per-

53. R. C. H. Lenski, *The Interpretation of the Epistle to the Hebrews and of the Epistle of James*, p. 538.

sonalized (1:15; 3:6). "His utterance glows with the fervor of his spirit; it is rapid, exclamatory, graphic, abrupt, sometimes poetical in form, and moving with a rhythmical cadence."[54]

He assumes the position of an official teacher, sure of his ground, with no questions about his authority. In the 108 verses of the epistle, he uses 54 imperatives.

A singular feature of his style is the use of *duadiplosis*, that is, the linking together of clauses and sentences by the repetition of the leading word or some of its cognates. As an illustration, note 1:2-6: patience (3), patience (4); nothing lacking (4), if any of you lack (5); let him ask (5), but let him ask (6); nothing doubting (6), he that doubteth (6). The same practice is observed in other parts, as in 1:12-15; 1:21-25; 3:2-8. The use of such a method by an ordinary writer would be fatally monotonous, but the vividness of his imagery and the force of his thoughts save him from this danger.

2. OMISSIONS

The epistle of James is distinctive among the books of the New Testament for its omissions. Cadoux remarks,

> The Epistle of St. James is theologically notorious for having no mention of incarnation, atonement or future life, doctrines of which the other Epistles of the New Testament are full. It has no mention of the sufferings, death and resurrection of Jesus, tidings of which other Epistles are full.[55]

Although Christ is mentioned once as the object of faith and He is called "the Lord of glory" (2:1), no further development as to His person and work is found. Although the Jewish atmosphere of the epistle is obvious, there is no mention of Jewish rituals or ceremonies.

But these omissions do not mean that the writer was devoid of doctrinal convictions. The practical purpose of James did not call for an exposition of his doctrinal views, but there is a good deal of what has been called "compressed theology" in the epistle. Expressions like "Of his own will he brought us forth" (1:8), "the implanted word" (1:21), "the perfect law of liberty" (1:25), "heirs of the kingdom" (2:5), or "the Spirit which he made to dwell in us" (4:5), are rich in doctrinal implications.

54. Marvin R. Vincent, *Word Studies in the New Testament*, 1:619.
55. Arthur Temple Cadoux, *The Thought of St. James*, p. 5.

The epistle lacks entirely those autobiographical touches which characterize the letters of Paul. Beyond the statement of his name and his spiritual position, he offers no further information about himself. He gives no indication of his relation to his readers, no thanksgiving for them nor praise of them. It has no formal benediction in conclusion.

3. CONTENTS

It is not infrequently asserted that the epistle lacks unity, that James rambles from thought to thought without any unifying theme.[56] The book gives that impression on the surface, but looks deceive. We firmly hold that he does have a unifying theme, namely, the tests of faith. As though preaching a sermon, James generally states his point and then proceeds to a fuller elaboration of it. Studied in the light of its unifying theme, the epistle is seen to have order and coherence.

The epistle is characterized by the Jewish coloring of its contents. Hayes asserts that James "is the most Jewish writing in the New Testament."[57] The very opening address is Jewish in origin (1:1); he speaks of Abraham as "our father" (2:21); he draws his illustrations from the Old Testament—Abraham (2:21), Rahab (2:25), Job (5:11), Elijah (5:17-18). He is the only New Testament writer who employs the Old Testament designation "the Lord of Sabaoth" in speaking of God.[58]

The author's abundant use of illustrations from nature is characteristic of the epistle. For example, he makes mention of "the surge of the sea driven by the wind and tossed" (1:6), "the flower of the grass" (1:10), "the sun ariseth with the scorching wind" (1:11), "a vapor that appeareth for a little time and then vanisheth away" (4:14), and others. Howson remarks, "There is more imagery from mere natural phenomena in the one short Epistle of St. James than in all St. Paul's Epistles put together."[59]

---

56. "The Epistle has been called 'an ethical scrapbook'; and truly, it is so disconnected, as it stands, that it is the despair of the analyst." A. M. Hunter, *Introducing the New Testament*, p. 96.
57. Hayes, p. 1562a.
58. The name occurs in the New Testament elsewhere only in a quotation from the Old Testament in Romans 9:29.
59. John S. Howson, *The Character of St. Paul*, p. 8, note.

The similarities between the teaching of this epistle and the Sermon on the Mount are striking. Compare the following:

James	Matthew	James	Matthew
1:2	5:10-12	3:17-18	5:9
1:4	5:48	4:4	6:24
1:5; 5:15	7:7-12	4:10	5:3-4
1:9	5:3	4:11	7:1-2
1:20	5:22	5:2	6:19
2:13	5:7; 6:14-15	5:10	5:12
2:14-16	7:21-23	5:12	5:33-37

The epistle offers a larger number of similarities to the Sermon on the Mount than any other book in the New Testament. If the apostle Paul developed the significance of the death of Jesus, it may be said that James developed the teaching of Jesus. Scott asserts, "There is scarcely a thought in the Epistle which cannot be traced to Christ's personal teaching. If John has lain on the Saviour's bosom, James has sat at His feet."[60]

4. RELATION TO CHRISTIANITY

The epistle of James occupies a distinctive place in the growing stream of historic Christianity. It finds its place in the early days of that history when as yet the distinction between Judaism and Christianity had not been fully brought to view. It offers us a glimpse of the Christian faith as held by Jewish believers during the early chapters of the Acts. The picture which it presents is that of Judaic Christianity before the thirteenth chapter of Luke's history of the Church.

The conception of Christianity underlying the epistle is that it is the consummation of the hopes of Judaism. It is thought of not in antithesis to Judaism but rather as its true consummation. Judaism was the flower, while Christianity was the fruit. The Christian faith is viewed as the final manifestation of what was latent in the Jewish revelations. Viewed in this light the distinctive characteristics of James become significant and instructive. The epistle thus makes its

60. Robert Scott, "The General Epistle of James," in *The Speakers' Commentary, New Testament,* 4:109a.

own distinctive contribution to the canon of the New Testament, a
contribution which we could ill afford to lose.

5. TIMELINESS

There is a tendency within certain circles to depreciate the epistle
of James by asserting that it was written to the "Jewish Church,"
hence is no longer of abiding significance for the Church today. Admittedly it was addressed to Jewish Christians, who without having
all the additional light of the Pauline epistles were yet members of
the Body of Christ, and in Christ there is neither Jew nor Gentile.
His stern insistence upon Christian practice consistent with profession, his open contempt for all sham, and his stinging rebukes of
worldliness are notes that are urgently needed today. We are again
living in an era when the message of James has striking relevance for
the Christian Church.

An Outline of James

I. The Introduction, 1:1-18
    A. The salutation, v. 1
    B. The theme: tests of Christian faith, vv. 2-18
        1. The Christian attitude toward tests or trials, vv. 2-12
            a) The proper attitude toward trials, vv. 2-4
                (1) The attitude commanded, v. 2
                (2) The reason indicated, v. 3
                (3) The outcome to be realized, v. 4
            b) The use of prayer in trials, vv. 5-8
                (1) The need for wisdom realized, v. 5*a*
                (2) The request for wisdom to be made, v. 5*b*
                (3) The assurance of answered prayer, v. 5*c*
                (4) The condition for answered prayer, vv. 6-8
            c) The correct estimate of life by the tried, vv. 9-11
                (1) The attitude of the lowly brother, v. 9
                (2) The attitude of the rich, vv. 10-11
            d) The result of enduring trials, v. 12
        2. The true nature of temptation, vv. 13-16
            a) The origin of temptation, vv. 13-14
                (1) Negative—not from God, v. 13
                (2) Positive from our own lusts, v. 14

  b) The result of yielding to temptation, vv. 15-16
   (1) The picture of the result, v. 15
   (2) The warning against deception, v. 16
 3. The beneficent activity of God, vv. 17-18
  a) The Giver of all good gifts, v. 17
  b) The Regenerator through His Word, v. 18

II. Faith Tested by Its Attitude Toward the Word of God, 1:19-27

 A. The reaction to the Word, vv. 19-20
  1. The knowledge possessed, v. 19*a*
  2. The reaction commanded, v. 19*b*
  3. The reason stated, v. 20
 B. The reception of the Word, v. 21
 C. The obedience to the Word, vv. 22-27
  1. The nature of obedience, vv. 22-25
   a) Negative—not being hearers only, vv. 22-24
   b) Positive—being a doer also, v. 25
  2. The kinds of obedience, vv. 26-27
   a) The false—form without inner control, v. 26
   b) The true—activity with inner control, v. 27

III. Faith Tested by Its Reaction to Social Distinctions, 2:1-13

 A. The rebuke for partiality, vv. 1-4
  1. The prohibition against partiality, v. 1
  2. The illustration of partiality, vv. 2-3
  3. The question of condemnation, v. 4
 B. The results of partiality, vv. 5-11
  1. The consequent inconsistency in conduct, vv. 5-7
   a) The contrast to God's dealing with the poor, vv. 5-6*a*
   b) The contrasted actions of the rich, vv. 6*b*-7
  2. The consequent breach of the law of love, vv. 8-11
   a) The importance of the law of love, vv. 8-9
    (1) The commendation upon its fulfillment, v. 8
    (2) The consequences of its violation, v. 9
   b) The seriousness of the breach of the Law, vv. 10-11
    (1) The statement of the principle, v. 10
    (2) The illustration of the principle, v. 11

C. The appeal to live according to the law of liberty, vv. 12-13
1. The statement of the appeal, v. 12
2. The reason for the appeal, v. 13

IV. Faith Tested by Its Production of Works, 2:14-26

A. The signs of useless faith, vv. 14-20
1. The uselessness of inoperative faith, vv. 14-17
   a) The questions concerning inoperative faith, v. 14
   b) The illustration of inoperative faith, vv. 15-16
   c) The application to inoperative faith, v. 17.
2. The barrenness of orthodox faith without works, vv. 18-20
   a) The assertion of the objector, v. 18*a*
   b) The challenge to the objector, vv. 18*b*-19
      (1) The demonstration of faith by works, v. 18*b*
      (2) The character of faith without works, v. 19
   c) The application to the objector, v. 20
B. The manifestation of saving faith through works, vv. 21-25
1. The faith of Abraham had works, vv. 21-24
   a) The evidence of Abraham's faith, v. 21
   b) The results of Abraham's working faith, vv. 22-23
      (1) The perfection of his faith, v. 22
      (2) The fulfillment of Scripture, v. 23*a*
      (3) The friendship with God, v. 23*b*
   c) The conclusion from Abraham's example, v. 24
2. The faith of Rahab had works, v. 25
C. The union of faith and works, v. 26

V. Faith Tested by Its Production of Self-Control, 3:1-18

A. The significance of a controlled tongue, vv. 1-2
1. The application to the teacher, v. 1
2. The evidence of the perfect man, v. 2
B. The importance of control over the tongue, vv. 3-6
1. The effects of a controlled tongue, vv. 3-5*a*
   a) The illustrations of control, vv. 3-4
      (1) The control over the horse by the bridle, v. 3
      (2) The control over the ships by the rudder, v. 4
   b) The nature of the tongue needing control, v. 5*a*
2. The damage of an uncontrolled tongue, vv. 5*b*-6

C. The natural inability to control the tongue, vv. 7-8

D. The inconsistency of an uncontrolled tongue, vv. 9-12
  1. The inconsistency indicated, vv. 9-10*a*
  2. The inconsistency rebuked, v. 10*b*
  3. The inconsistency illustrated, vv. 11-12

E. The wisdom controlling the use of the tongue, vv. 13-18
  1. The marks of the wise man, v. 13
  2. The evidence of false wisdom in control, vv. 14-16
    a) The manifestations of this wisdom, v. 14
    b) The character of this wisdom, v. 15
    c) The outcome of this wisdom, v. 16
  3. The evidence of the true wisdom in control, vv. 17-18
    a) The character of this wisdom, v. 17
    b) The fruit of this wisdom, v. 18

VI. Faith Tested by Its Reactions to the World, 4:1—5:12

A. The manifestation of worldliness through strife and faction, 4:1-12
  1. The condition manifesting worldliness, vv. 1-6
    a) The description of the condition, vv. 1-3
      (1) The questions revealing the condition, v. 1
      (2) The outcome of the condition, v. 2*a*
      (3) The reasons for the condition, vv. 2*b*-3
    b) The rebuke for the condition, vv. 4-6
      (1) The adulterous character of the condition, v. 4
      (2) The attitude revealed by the condition, vv. 5-6
  2. The exhortations to the worldly, vv. 7-12
    a) The appeal to resume a right relation to God, vv. 7-10
      (1) The basic attitude required, v. 7
      (2) The elements in the attitude Godward, vv. 8-10
        (*a*) The return to God, v. 8*a*
        (*b*) The personal cleansing, v. 8*b*
        (*c*) The repentance for sin, v. 9
        (*d*) The attitude of humility, v. 10
    b) The appeal to cease censoriousness of others, vv. 11-12
      (1) The prohibition against censoriousness, v. 11*a*
      (2) The reasons for the prohibition of censoriousness, vv. 11*b*-12

(*a*) The assumption of an unwarranted authority, v. 11*b*

(*b*) The usurpation of the divine prerogative, v. 12

B. The manifestation of worldliness through business planning, 4:13-17

1. The rebuke for the wrong attitude, vv. 13-14
2. The indication of the proper attitude, v. 15
3. The sinfulness of the present attitude, vv. 16-17

C. The manifestation of worldliness through wrong reactions to suffering, 5:1-11

1. The impending judgment upon the oppressive rich, vv. 1-6
   a) The announcement of judgment, v. 1
   b) The description of the judgments, vv. 2-3
   c) The charges in the judgment, vv. 4-6
2. The Christian reaction under suffering, vv. 7-11
   a) The exhortation to patience, vv. 7-8
   b) The warning against a wrong reaction, v. 9
   c) The examples of suffering and endurance, vv. 10-11
      (1) The example of the prophets, v. 10
      (2) The example of Job, v. 11

D. The manifestation of worldliness through swearing, 5:12

VII. Faith Tested by Its Resort to Prayer, 5:13-20

A. The resort to prayer in emotional reactions, v. 13
B. The resort to prayer in sickness, vv. 14-16*a*
C. The power of prayer, vv. 16*b*-18
   1. The statement of the power of prayer, v. 16*b*
   2. The illustration of the power of prayer, vv. 17-18
D. The message to the one restoring the erring one, vv. 19-20
   1. The supposition of an erring one, v. 19
   2. The assurance to the one restoring the erring one, v. 20

A BOOK LIST ON JAMES

Barclay, William. *The Letters of James and Peter.* The Daily Study Bible. Philadelphia: Westminster, 1958.

Barclay holds that our book of James is the substance of a sermon preached by James, the Lord's brother, taken down by someone else and translated into Greek with a few additions. Barclay's own translation is printed at the beginning of each of the paragraphs into which the epistle is divided. Most valuable for its word studies and background material.

Carr, Arthur. *The General Epistle of James.* Cambridge Greek Testament. Reprint. Cambridge: U. Press, 1930.

Greek text. A scholarly interpretation of the original text by a conservative British scholar. Good introductory material. Adapted to the Greek student.

Easton, Burton Scott; and Poteat, Gordon. "The Epistle of James." In *The Interpreter's Bible,* vol. 12. New York: Abingdon, 1957.

The work of two noted liberal scholars, supporting the view that the epistle is most likely an adaptation of the work of a Jewish author by a later Christian editor, not the Lord's brother. Introduction and exegesis by Easton, exposition by Poteat.

Gaebelein, Frank E. *The Practical Epistle of James. Studies in Applied Christianity.* Great Neck, N.Y.: Doniger & Raughley, 1955.

The substance of a series of popular lectures on James; neither exhaustive nor technical. The author's aim is to apply the incisive ethical and spiritual teaching of James to our own times.

Gwinn, Ralph A. *The Epistle of James. A Study Manual.* Shield Bible Study Series. Grand Rapids: Baker, 1967.

A concise interpretation of James based on the original Greek but adapted to the English reader. A brief introduction simply indicates the critical problems. A conservative guide for individual or group study of James.

Johnstone, Robert. *Lectures Exegetical and Practical on the Epistle of James.* 1871. Reprint. Grand Rapids: Baker, 1954.

A new translation of the epistle with notes on the Greek text. The lectures give an interesting, full, and rewarding practical exposition.

King, Guy H. *A Belief That Behaves. An Expositional Study of the Epistle of James.* London: Marshall, Morgan & Scott, 1945.

Devotional and expository studies of James. Abundant homiletical suggestions and practical applications.

Knowling, R. J. *The Epistle of St. James.* Westminster Commentaries. London: Methuen, 1904.

A valuable commentary by a conservative British scholar of the past century. Emphasizes the linguistic parallels to the epistle. Important introduction.

Lange, J. P.; and Van Oosterzee, J. J. "The Epistle General of James."

In Lange's *Commentary on the Holy Scriptures*. Trans. from the German by J. Isidor Mombert. Reprint. Grand Rapids: Zondervan, n.d.

> A careful exegetical study of the epistle. Contains in addition a mass of homiletical material, much of which is of little value today.

Lenski, R. C. H. *The Interpretation of the Epistle to the Hebrews and of the Epistle of James*. Columbus, Ohio: Lutheran Book Concern, 1938.

> A full and penetrating interpretation by an accomplished conservative Lutheran scholar. Enables the English reader to get at the meaning of the Greek text. Important for exegetical study.

Mayor, Joseph B. *The Epistle of James*. Reprint of 3d ed. Grand Rapids: Zondervan, 1954.

> Greek text. The standard commentary for linguistic study of the Greek text. The long introduction (260 pp.) is a treasury of information about the epistle. Invaluable for the advanced student.

Mitton, C. Leslie. *The Epistle of James*. Grand Rapids: Eerdmans, 1966.

> A thorough, scholarly work by a British Methodist with a twofold aim: to expound the teaching of the epistle and to show that its teaching is an integral part of the total message of the New Testament. Critical problems are carefully dealt with and the Greek occasionally quoted in transliteration. Introductory problems are considered in an appendix.

Moffatt, James. *The General Epistles—James, Peter, and Judas*. The Moffatt New Testament Commentary. Reprint. London: Hodder & Stoughton, 1947.

> Prints the Moffatt translation. The work of a noted liberal British scholar. The comments are rather slight.

Moyter, J. A. *The Tests of Faith*. London: Inter-Varsity, 1970.

> A straightforward explanation of James by an Anglican evangelical scholar; stresses the practical value of James for Christians today. Holds that the address is symbolic of the Church as a whole in the world.

Neibor, J. *Practical Exposition of James*. Erie, Pa.: Our Daily Walk Publishers, 1950.

> An intensely practical and reverent verse-by-verse treatment. Abounds in keen observations and numerous illustrations. Does not deal with critical problems; devotional in approach.

Oesterley, W. E. "The General Epistle of James." In *The Expositor's Greek Testament*. Reprint. Grand Rapids: Eerdmans, n.d.

> Greek text. A scholarly introduction sets forth the critical problems; author holds that the name of James is rightly attached to this document, but that in its present form it contains various additions and adaptations. The comments on the Greek text are of most value to the advanced student.

Plummer, Alfred. "The General Epistles of St. James and St. Jude." In *The Expositor's Bible*. Reprint. Grand Rapids: Eerdmans, 1943.

> An important exposition of these two epistles by a noted British author of the past generation. Valuable for expository and homiletical purposes.

Plumptre, E. H. *The General Epistle of St. James*. Cambridge Bible for Schools and Colleges. Reprint. Cambridge: University Press, 1915.

> A concise, conservative commentary intended for the layman. Good discussion of introductory problems.

Reicke, Bo. *The Epistles of James, Peter, and Jude*. The Anchor Bible. Garden City, N.Y.: Doubleday, 1964.

> A liberal interpretation by the New Testament professor at the University of Basel. Prints author's own translation. Reicke rejects the traditional authorship and dates James around A.D. 90, during the reign of Domitian. The comments, reflecting the author's views concerning the occasion and purpose of James, are disappointingly brief.

Robertson, A. T. *Studies in the Epistle of James*. Rev. ed. Nashville: Broadman, 1959.

> A practical study of James by a master of the Greek; originally published in 1915 under the title *Practical and Social Aspects of Christianity*. This revision by Heber F. Peacock has eliminated some of the more technical and dated material but retains the flavor and challenge of the original work.

Ropes, James Hardy. *A Critical and Exegetical Commentary on the Epistle of St. James*. International Critical Commentary. New York: Scribner's, 1916.

> Greek text. Much valuable introductory material. Important commentary by an accomplished liberal scholar. Does not accept the traditional authorship.

Ross, Alexander. *The Epistles of James and John.* The New International Commentary on the New Testament. Grand Rapids: Eerdmans, 1954.

    A helpful, practical exposition by a noted, conservative, Scottish scholar. Follows in the Reformed tradition, including eschatology.

Simmons, Billy. *A Functioning Faith. Expositions on the Epistle of James.* Waco, Tex.: Word, 1967.

    A devotional and sermonic treatment of James, essentially producing the essence of the author's pulpit ministry in his Texas Baptist church. Technical matters are not dealt with. Vivid applications of the message of James to our own day.

Smith, H. Maynard. *The Epistle of S. James. Lectures.* Oxford: Blackwell, 1914.

    A series of expository lectures on the epistle by a Church of England minister.

Stevenson, Herbert H. *James Speaks for Today.* Westwood, N.J.: Revell, 1966.

    A lucid, popular-level sermonic study of the epistle of James with emphasis upon the relevance of the letter to our day. The author, an evangelical minister, brings the teaching of James into logical balance with the rest of the New Testament.

Strauss, Lehman. *James Your Brother.* New York: Loizeaux, 1956.

    A well-outlined, practical interpretation of the epistle with pointed illustrations and sermonic appeal by a conservative minister.

Tasker, R. V. G. *The General Epistle of James.* Tyndale New Testament Commentaries. Grand Rapids: Eerdmans, 1957.

    A concise, readable, verse-by-verse commentary by a noted British scholar. Better than the author's other volumes in this series.

Vaughan, Curtis. *James, A Study Guide.* Grand Rapids: Zondervan, 1969.

    A well-outlined expositional and devotional commentary by a distinguished Southern Baptist seminary professor. Vaughan frequently quotes various modern translations as an aid in presenting the precise force of the original for the lay reader. Has a three-page bibliography of commentaries and translations.

Winkler, Edwin T. "Commentary on the Epistle of James. In *An American Commentary on the New Testament.* 1888. Reprint. Philadelphia: Amer. Bapt. Pub. Soc., n.d.

A concise and rewarding exposition by a conservative Baptist of the last century.

Zodhiates, Spiro. *The Behavior of Belief.* Formerly published as three volumes, *The Work of Faith, The Labor of Love,* and *The Patience of Hope.* Grand Rapids: Eerdmans, 1959, 1960, 1970.

A series of expository and devotional studies, at least one to a verse, setting forth in a practical and heartwarming manner the teaching of the epistle. Working from an intimate knowledge of his native Greek, the General Secretary of the American Mission to Greeks gives a clear explanation of the original for the non-Greek reader. Contains a full bibliography of the expository and sermonic literature on the epistle. Has indexes of subjects, scripture references, and English words with Greek equivalents.

4

HEBREWS

THE IMPRESSIVE GRANDEUR of the epistle to the Hebrews has left an indelible mark on the literature and theology of the Christian Church. It is unexcelled in its literary excellence and makes a unique theological contribution to the New Testament revelation. No other book of the New Testament breathes more deeply the Spirit of God nor more clearly authenticates its own inspiration than Hebrews, yet no other book leaves us with so many puzzling and enigmatical problems as does this book. Nearly all of the usual points of introduction have been the occasion of much controversy. And most of these matters are still keenly debated and the majority of them seem quite incapable of a decisive solution.

THE LITERARY CHARACTER OF HEBREWS

The literary structure of Hebrews is distinctive. That it is rightly among the epistles is evident from its epistolary conclusion (13:18-25). But like 1 John[1], it lacks entirely the customary opening salutation. The stately sentence with which it begins does not create the impression of opening an epistle but rather resembles the carefully worded introduction to an eloquent oration. Yet one does not read far in it before he is made keenly aware of the didactic and hortatory purpose of the author. The practical intention of the author is prominent throughout the book. Rees rightly remarks, "Hebrews begins like an essay, proceeds like a sermon, and ends like a letter."[2]

The singular structure of Hebrews has given rise to considerable

---

1. First John 1:1-4 does not offer an exact parallel since verse 4 definitely expresses an epistolary purpose.
2. T. Rees, "Hebrews, Epistle to The," in *The International Standard Bible Encyclopaedia,* 2:1355b.

discussion as to its true literary character. By common consent it has been classified as an epistle. This has been the historic view concerning it. Westcott remarks, "Whenever the nature of the book is defined by early writers it is called an 'Epistle'."[3] Deissman, however, evaluates it differently. He boldly asserts,

> The so-called "Epistle to the Hebrews" is not an epistle but a religious tract. . . . It is, on account of its polished form and scholarly contents, the first example of what we can consider Christian art-literature.[4]

But the assertion that Hebrews is "art-literature" is not as sure as Deissmann would have us think. Although Hebrews by its cultivated and philosophical language and cast of thought does make excellent literature, it is by no means certain that it is merely the artistic literary effort of an individual theologian intended for public consumption. Like a true letter, in its present form it appears definitely to have been occasion inspired. It is grounded in the truths which were a part of the common Christian confession and arose out of the author's earnest desire to meet the specific needs of the people to whom it was first sent.

The contents of Hebrews, however, suggest that it is a homily cast into an epistolary form. The reading of Hebrews reminds one of an animated sermon, and at times it rises to magnificent eloquence. The author himself lays stress upon the homiletical aspect of his work when he calls it a "word of exhortation" (13:22). It is very probable that the main argument of Hebrews is an elaboration of a sermon or several sermons cast into epistolary form to meet the particular needs of the group to whom it was sent. The epistolary notes at the end would agree with this view. Doubtless the argument of the book had been previously developed by the writer, but the actual composition of the book was inspired by the realization of a definite need that must be met. This view would account for its dual features of a speech and a letter.

The phenomenon of an epistle without an opening address has given rise to speculation. It has been thought that the salutation was accidentally lost. But if the original did contain such a salutation, surely some trace of it would have survived. The supposition that

3. Brooke Foss Westcott, *The Epistle to the Hebrews*, p. xxix.
4. Adolf Deissmann, *The New Testament in the Light of Modern Research*, p. 51.

the original salutation was deliberately suppressed is untenable. An "editor" who would remove the salutation would certainly not leave chapter 13 as it stands. There is no evidence, either textual or historical, that Hebrews ever had a formal salutation. Doubtless the author did not feel it necessary to begin with the salutation, since the bearer, who would read it to the recipients, would orally impart the name of the writer to them. Ancient explanations of the omission are not very convincing to the modern student.[5]

THE CANONICITY OF HEBREWS

The history of the New Testament canon reveals that the full admission of Hebrews as canonical was beset with considerable uncertainty. Eusebius of Caesarea (265-340) in his *Ecclesiastical History* (3. 3) acknowledged that Hebrews was disputed,[6] although he himself regarded it as one of the "fourteen epistles" of Paul. The dispute was regarding its Pauline authorship.

Hebrews was not questioned on the point of its inspiration. Its invincible strength lay in the very nature of its contents; it gave undeniable proof of its inspiration. The uncertainty concerning its canonicity was caused by the question of its authorship. On this there were different views.

It is certain that Hebrews was known and held in highest honor in Rome before the end of the first century. Clement of Rome (30-100) in his epistle to the Corinthians (*1 Clement*), written about A.D. 96, quotes from it as authoritative. His quotations are made "in such a way as to show that he had the text before him; but the adaptations of words and thoughts are made silently, without any mark of quotation or any indication of the author from whom they are borrowed."[7] After this early yet unmistakable appearance of the epistle in the West, it passed into a period of obscurity, apparently largely due to the fact that it was caught in the vortex of the Novatian controversy and so fell into disfavor.

From very early times the epistle was received as canonical in the

5. Pantaenus of Alexandria thought that Paul, out of modesty, had refrained from putting his name to a letter addressed to Hebrews, because the Lord Himself had been their Apostle. Clement accounted for the omission by supporting that the apostle Paul had prudently omitted his name in order not to offend the Hebrews. Eusebius *Ecclesiastical History* 4. 14.
6. The books which Eusebius classified as *Antilegomena*, or disputed, were Hebrews, James, 2 Peter, 2 and 3 John, and Jude.
7. Westcott, p. lxii.

churches of the East. Justin the Martyr (100-165) in his first *Apology* (chap. 63) speaks of Christ as "apostle," thus apparently showing his acquaintance with Hebrews (cf. 3:1). Toward the close of the second century Clement of Alexandria (155-215) frequently quoted it as of apostolic authority. Origen (185-253) did likewise. In the West, however, it was not until the fourth century that its canonical authority was recognized. With the beginning of the fifth century it was firmly established in the canon of the Western Church, largely through the influence of Jerome (340-420) and Augustine (354-430). The reason for the difference in attitude is thus summarized by Miller: "The East considered apostolic authority sufficient; the West stressed apostolic authorship."[8]

Once accepted as Pauline, the question of the canonicity of Hebrews remained undisturbed for the next eleven hundred years. With the coming of the Reformation the question was raised anew and freely discussed by both Roman and Reformed scholars. Luther had doubts about its canonicity and placed Hebrews, followed by James, Jude, and Revelation, after 3 John. Calvin accepted it as canonical apart from the question of its authorship. Most of the Reformation scholars who rejected the Pauline authorship yet steadily upheld the canonicity. Experience had shown that the acknowledgment of its canonical authority was independent of its Pauline authorship.

The Authorship of Hebrews

The question of the authorship of Hebrews presents one of several apparently insoluble problems in connection with this epistle. The ancient Church was not united in its answer to the question and the modern Church presents even a greater diversity of answers.

1. HINTS IN EPISTLE

In the King James Version the title of this book reads, "The Epistle of Paul the Apostle to the Hebrews." This title rests on late manuscripts and is unauthoritative. The title in the oldest manuscripts is simply "To Hebrews." This title was not part of the original document, "but it must have been given to the book at a very early date, when it first passed into public use as part of a collection of Apostolic letters."[9]

8. H. S. Miller, *General Biblical Introduction*, p. 143.
9. Westcott, p. xxvii.

The epistle is anonymous. No statement in it serves to disclose the writer's precise identity. Yet it is clear that the original readers well knew from whom it came (13:18-24). Only in the last chapter does the author refer to himself in the first person and then his statements are of such a nature as to afford no ground for a positive identification.

The contents of Hebrews, however, cannot be said to be impersonal. It is not as though the author were addressing an ideal audience in a literary treatise intended for Christendom as a whole. While the author never names his audience directly, it is yet clear that he was intimately acquainted with their local situation (cf. 5:11–6:12; 10:32-39; 12:4-5; 13:1-9). The writer knew the needs of the people whom he was counseling. It appears that the unnamed writer was a friend and teacher of the readers and was closely acquainted with their circumstances and spiritual condition.

2. EXTERNAL EVIDENCE

The traditions respecting the authorship of Hebrews fall into three divisions, according to geography.

In Alexandria, Egypt the epistle was associated with the name of Paul and more or less directly attributed to him. Eusebius quotes Clement of Alexandria (155-215) to the effect that Hebrews "was written by Paul, to the Hebrews, in the Hebrew tongue; but that it was carefully translated by Luke, and published among the Greeks. Whence, also, one finds the same character of style and phraseology in the epistle, as in the Acts" (*Eccl. Hist.* 6. 14). The scholarly Origen (185-253) was well aware of the language difficulty in the Pauline tradition, yet he definitely accepted the Pauline connection with Hebrews, and when using popular language ascribed it to Paul. Eusebius quotes the words of Origen at some length on this point:

> That this epistle is more pure Greek [than Paul's] in the composition of its phrases, every one will confess who is able to discern the difference of style. Again, it will be obvious that the ideas of the epistle are admirable, and not inferior to any of the books acknowledged to be apostolic. . . . But I would say, that the thoughts are the apostle's, but the diction and phraseology belong to some one who has recorded what the apostle said, and as one who noted down at his leisure what his master dictated. If, then, any church considers this

epistle as coming from Paul, let it be commended for this, for neither did those ancient men deliver it as such without cause. But who it was that really wrote the epistle, God only knows. The account, however, that has been current before us is, according to some, that Clement, who was bishop of Rome, wrote the epistle; according to others, that it was written by Luke, who wrote the gospel and the Acts (*Eccl. Hist.* 6. 25).

From this it will be seen that Clement and Origen, both familiar with the traditions of those before them, agree in regarding the Greek epistle as Paul's only in a secondary sense. Yet in their writings both used the epistle as being Paul's without any qualification. Impressed with the spiritual insight of the epistle, they were concerned with preserving its canonicity. Eusebius (*c.* 265-340) himself popularly classified Hebrews among the "fourteen" epistles of Paul (*Eccl. Hist.* 3. 3), yet when dealing with the question of exact authorship he adopts the mediating position of Clement (3. 38). Beginning with Athanasius (298-373), the ecclesiastical writers of Egypt and Palestine uniformly ascribed it to Paul.

In North Africa there is evidence of another tradition, namely, that Barnabas was the author. Tertullian of Carthage (150-222) introduces a quotation from Hebrews 4:1, 4-6 with the words, "There is also an Epistle to the Hebrews under the name of Barnabas" (*On Modesty*, chap. 20). Zahn points out that Tertullian is reproducing a current tradition (apparently circulating in the Montanist churches) and not merely giving his own opinion.[10] Zahn adds, "Since, however, Montanism was introduced into the West from the province of Asia, there is the greatest probability that the tradition concerning Barnabas as the author of Hebrews originated there."[11] But this tradition gave way to the Alexandrian view in the course of the fourth century. Thus the third Council of Cathage, A.D. 397, in its canon of New Testament books made mention of "thirteen Epistles of the Apostle Paul, one Epistle of the same [writer] to the Hebrews." But in the canons of the Council of Hippo, A.D. 419, this circumlocution is dropped and mention is made of "fourteen epistles of Paul."[12] Thus there is apparent the advance of the Pauline tradition.

10. Theodor Zahn, *Introduction to the New Testament*, 2:302.
11. Ibid., p. 303.
12. Brooke Foss Westcott, *A General Survey of the History of the Canon of The New Testament*, pp. 408-9.

In Italy and in Western Europe the Pauline tradition was not accepted. No tradition of authorship was espoused there before the fourth century. It appears that Hippolytus (*c.* 160-235) and Irenaeus (*c.* 140-203), bishop of Lyons, did not accept the Pauline tradition. Hebrews is not found in the Muratorian Canon (*c.* A.D. 170), and "by this catalogue it is distinctly excluded from the Epistles of St. Paul (*septem scribit ecclesiis*)."[13] Eusebius, in speaking about the view of a certain Caius at Rome who excluded Hebrews from the Pauline epistles, remarks, "There are even to this day, some of the Romans who do not consider it to be the work of the apostle" (*Eccl. Hist.* 6. 20). Thus it is clear that in the West the Pauline tradition concerning the authorship of Hebrews was not accepted. But Jerome (340-420) and Augustine (354-430) adopted the view of the East and through their influence the authority and Pauline authorship of Hebrews became established in the West. By the middle of the fourth century we find Latin writers like Hilary, Victorinus of Rome, and Ambrose using it unhesitatingly as of Paul. When the West, with its insistence upon apostolic authorship, thought that point confirmed, Hebrews was accepted without further question.

Papyrus 46, dating back to about A.D. 200, placed Hebrews between Romans and 1 Corinthians. It represents the early view in Egypt. This position for Hebrews is unique among the early manuscripts, but it does occur in some later manuscripts. The majority of the early Greek copies place it after 2 Thessalonians, the position assigned to it in the Westcott and Hort Greek text. This latter position seems to imply scribal acceptance of Pauline authorship in a secondary sense.

This brief review of the external evidence makes it clear that there was no uniform tradition in the early Church concerning the authorship of Hebrews. The names of Paul, Barnabas, Luke, and Clement were connected with it, or it was regarded as an anonymous work. Only gradually did the view that it was Pauline come into general favor.

3. SUBSEQUENT HISTORY

The tradition upholding the Pauline authorship prevailed undisturbed from the fifth to the sixteenth century. During the time of the Reformation the question of authorship was reopened. On linguistic

13. Westcott, *The Epistle To The Hebrews*, p. lxiii.

grounds Erasmus rejected the Pauline authorship. Luther rejected the Pauline authorship and conjectured that Apollos was the author. Calvin forthrightly rejected the Pauline authorship of Hebrews yet maintained its full apostolic authority. Beza held that it was written by a disciple of Paul. The Council of Trent reaffirmed the old traditional position, thus in effect closing the question for the Roman Catholic. Callan, a Roman Catholic scholar, remarks, "For Catholics the question is a closed one, inasmuch as we must hold that Hebrews is not only divinely inspired, but that it is Pauline in origin."[14] Yet he accepts the view that "the thoughts and ideas of Hebrews are those of St. Paul, but that the language and style were supplied by someone else."[15] The Pauline authorship still has its advocates among some Protestant scholars,[16] yet the general consensus of opinion rejects it.[17]

Subsequent history has brought the clear realization that the question of the authorship of Hebrews is independent of the question of its authority. It is seen that a rejection of the Pauline tradition is not inconsistent with an unquestioned acceptance of the inspiration of Hebrews.

4. INTERNAL EVIDENCE

A study of the internal evidence in the light of the Pauline tradition as to its authorship has likewise produced conflicting answers. Hebrews unquestionably contains many things that seem to point to Paul as the author. Among these may be noted the reference to Timothy (13:23), the centrality of the person and work of Christ, the characteristically Pauline form of the closing benediction, and certain affinities in language and thought between Hebrews and the acknowledged epistles of Paul.[18]

The reference to Timothy's release seems to fit in with the idea that he came to Rome at Paul's request (2 Ti 4:9, 21), and was imprisoned because of his relations to the apostle, but, being an inconspicuous leader, was later released. Yet the uncertainty concerning

14. Charles J. Callan, *The Epistles of St. Paul with Introductions and Commentary for Priests and Students*, 2:343.
15. Ibid., p. 352.
16. As recent advocates see E. Schuyler English, *Studies in the Epistle to the Hebrews*, pp. 15-26; J. Sidlow Baxter, *Explore the Book*, 6:274-80.
17. "If there is one point on which modern scholars agree, it is that Hebrews is *not* Paul's work." A. M. Hunter, *Introducing the New Testament*, p. 90.
18. For a strong pro-Pauline presentation of the internal evidence see William Kay, "Hebrews," in *The Speaker's Commentary, The New Testament*, 4:7-16.

the place of composition of Hebrews, as well as our lack of all information concerning Timothy's later movements, shrouds the precise significance of the statement. All that the reference does conclusively prove is that the author did move in the circle of Paul's friends.

The remarkable affinities of language and thought, as well as the characteristically Pauline features of the conclusion of the epistle (13:22-25), are confidently pointed to by advocates of this view as confirming Pauline authorship. But the opponents reply that these Pauline features do not prove his authorship. They do prove that "the writer had adopted much of the Apostle's teaching and had been deeply influenced by his companionship."[19]

While admitting these similarities, opponents of the Pauline tradition assert that they only serve to set into sharper contrast the positive dissimilarities. Thus it is held that the theology of Hebrews is different from Paul's. Rees asserts, "Paul's Christology turns around the death, resurrection and living presence of Christ in the church, that of Hebrews around His high-priestly function in Heaven."[20] But Paul is not absolutely silent with regard to Christ's present work in heaven (Ro 5:9-10; 8:34), nor is Hebrews silent in regard to the death and resurrection of Christ (2:9; 9:24-28; 10:12-14; 13:20-21). Paul was a man of many parts, and he may well have decided to devote one epistle to the development of a theme not elaborated elsewhere. Neither can a valid argument against the Pauline authorship be drawn from the absence of a discussion of justification by faith in Hebrews. The writer does recognize the importance of faith in salvation (10:38-39) and lays great stress on the importance of faith as the condition of acceptance with God (chap. 11). Similar instances of the lack of emphasis on a characteristic teaching of Paul can be found in his recognized epistles. As to the theological content of Hebrews, it must be affirmed that there is no disagreement between it and the Pauline epistles. Yet taken as a whole it seems clear that the writer of Hebrews and Paul arrive at their conclusions by different routes.

The absence of a salutation in Hebrews has been urged in favor of a non-Pauline authorship, for all the recognized epistles of Paul begin with his name. The explanation of Clement of Alexandria that

19. F. W. Farrar, *The Early Days of Christianity*, p. 163.
20. Rees, p. 1357.

Paul prudently omitted his name in order not to offend his Jewish readers does not seem to be satisfactory. It was very unlike Paul to hide his identity because there was a known antagonistic feeling toward him. Paul was well aware of the strained attitude toward him on the part of many in the Jerusalem church, yet when there on his third missionary journey he did not seek to conceal his identity from them. That certainly was not his method in dealing with the Judaizing influences in Galatia. It seems rather that his burning love for his kinsmen according to the flesh, as revealed in Romans 9-11, would most naturally have expressed itself in his usual salutation, if he were the author.

Of more weight as an argument against the Pauline authorship is the observation that the author of Hebrews uses the Septuagint throughout, even where it differs from the Hebrew text. Paul, however, uses both the Hebrew and the Septuagint in his epistles. It seems probable that the writer of Hebrews did not know the Hebrew. The use of the Septuagint in Hebrews seems to point to an author lacking the formal Hebrew training of Paul.

Of significance is the observation that the titles applied to the incarnate Son in Hebrews are unlike Paul's practice. The author of Hebrews generally uses only a single term such as *Jesus, Christ,* or *Lord,* while Paul is fond of compound titles. While Paul does at times use the single name in his epistles, the frequency of this practice in Hebrews is not like Paul.

The writer's description of his religious position in Hebrews 2:3 seems to imply that he, like his readers, was among those who had received their knowledge of the Gospel from the disciples of Jesus. It seems improbable that Paul would thus describe himself. Vaughan says, "This reference to the testimony of the original hearers of Christ is exactly that of Luke 1:2. But it is most unlike St. Paul, who everywhere claims to be himself an original witness (I Cor. 9:1; 11:23; 15:8; Gal. 1:1, 12; Eph. 3:3)."[21] With this interpretation of the expression most scholars agree.[22]

The style and vocabulary of Hebrews are relied upon to tell heavily against the Pauline authorship. Admittedly, the argument from style

21. C. J. Vaughan, *The Epistle to the Hebrews,* p. 29.
22. Baxter, p. 278, objects and holds that it does suit Paul in that the historical facts concerning Christ were "confirmed" to him "by them that heard."

is always a precarious thing; yet here the case seems quite marked. From earliest times the fact of the non-Pauline style has been recognized and commented on. Thus Clement of Alexandria thought that the Hebrew original by Paul was translated by Luke into Greek. But Hebrews shows no trace of being translation Greek. Origen bypassed the suggestion of a translation and thought it was written by a disciple of Paul. The stylistic differences between Paul and Hebrews can only be fully appreciated by the student of the Greek New Testament. It is quite impossible to seek to explain them merely on the basis of difference of subject matter. Farrar eloquently states his argument against the Pauline authorship as follows on this point:

> The difference between the Epistle to the Hebrews and the Epistles of St. Paul are differences which go down to the roots of the being. That the same pen should have been engaged on both is a psychological impossibility. The Greek is far better than the Greek of St. Paul. St. Paul is often stately and often rhetorical, and sometimes writes more in the style of a treatise than of a letter; but the stateliness and rhetoric and systematic treatment of the Epistle to the Hebrews in no way resemble his. The form and rhythm of its sentences are wholly different. Paul is often impassioned and often argumentative, and so is the author of the Epistle to the Hebrews; but the passion and the dialectics of the latter furnish the most striking contrast to those of the former. The writer cites differently from St. Paul, he writes differently; he constructs and connects his sentences differently; he builds up his paragraphs on a wholly different model. St. Paul is constantly mingling two constructions, leaving sentences unfinished, breaking into personal allusions, substituting the syllogism of passion for the syllogism of logic. This writer is never ungrammatical; he is never irregular; he is never personal; he never struggles for expression; he never loses himself in a parenthesis; he is never hurried into an anacoluthon.[23]

5. CONCLUSION AS NON-PAULINE

The external evidence for the Pauline authorship allows us to connect the epistle with his name only in a secondary sense, while the association of other names with it or the assertions of its anonymity tell heavily against the Pauline authorship. The internal evidence bears definite traces of Pauline influences, yet the dissimilarities are

23. Farrar, pp. 163-64.

quite strongly against the direct Pauline authorship. We are thus left with the conclusion that Hebrews is not the work of the apostle Paul, but that it arose within the Pauline circle of influence. We hold that the decision against the Pauline authorship in no way impairs the value and authority of this remarkable epistle. Its canonicity is not dependent upon its Pauline authorship.[24] In foregoing the Pauline authorship of Hebrews we are not spiritually impoverished. We are rather enriched by the discovery that we have another remarkable writer among the authors of the New Testament. In the words of Thiersch:

> We may compare it to a painting of perfect beauty, which had been regarded as a work of Raphael. If it should be proved that it was not painted by Raphael, we have thereby not lost a classical piece of art, but gained another master of first rank.[25]

6. SUGGESTED AUTHORS

Not content with such a negative conclusion, the scholars have expended great ingenuity in the effort to discover the real author of Hebrews. Various names have been nominated for the honor—Luke, Barnabas, Clement of Rome, Silas, Philip the deacon, Ariston, Mark, Apollos, and Priscilla and Aquila. Of these some of the more probable may be briefly considered.

The combination of *Paul and Luke,* first suggested by Clement of Alexandria, has attracted a number of scholars.[26] Color is added to this suggestion by the undoubted affinities of language and style between Hebrews and the Lucan writings. But Hebrews shows no traces of being translation Greek, as Clement's suggestion held. The fatal objection to this view is the fact that the writer of Hebrews was undoubtedly a Jew, while Luke was a Gentile (cf. Col 4:11-14).

Origen mentioned the fact that *Clement of Rome* was thought by some to be the author. A comparison with *1 Clement* does show many resemblances to Hebrews. The fatal difficulty is that "the weak, diffuse style of Clement's epistle is quite unworthy of the

---

24. The rejection of the Pauline authorship of Hebrews stands in a different category than the rejection of the Pauline authorship, for example, of Ephesians or the Pastorals. If the claim to Pauline authorship of those epistles can be refuted, then they must be dropped as spurious. No such necessity follows in the case of Hebrews, since it does not make any such claim to Pauline authorship.
25. Quoted in Adolph Saphir, *The Epistle To The Hebrews,* 1:14.
26. Such as Calvin, Hug, Ebrard, Delitzsch, Field, Zill, Cowles.

author of Hebrews, from a literary point of view the most able writer in the New Testament."[27] The view probably arose from the fact that his epistle contains several indubitable allusions to Hebrews.

The name of *Barnabas,* mentioned by Tertullian, has been advocated by a number of scholars.[28] This view has the advantage of having ancient tradition in support of it. Barnabas was a cultured Jew, familiar with the teachings of Paul and in thorough sympathy with his world view of Christianity. He was a Levite from Cyprus, and the nature of the epistle would agree with his title "son of exhortation" (Ac 4:36; 11:22-25). But the relation of Barnabas to the original apostles probably was closer than that implied in Hebrews 2:3. If Barnabas was the author it seems difficult to understand how the name of Paul instead became connected with it. Clogg feels that "the reference to Timothy suggests that the author was a junior, not a senior, member of the Pauline circle."[29]

Silas had been advocated by certain scholars as the author.[30] He was a member of the Pauline circle and acquainted with Timothy. Certain striking coincidences between 1 Peter and Hebrews lend some color to the view. But the evidence is entirely too weak to support the weight of the theory.

Harnack made the ingenious suggestion that *Priscilla,* aided by her husband, was the author.[31] Certainly she was a woman of great force of character and insight. She was closely associated with the work of Paul and was capable of further instructing Apollos. Harnack's suggestion that her authorship of Hebrews would account for the early loss of the name of the author is clever but unconvincing. The supposed signs of femininity in Hebrews are extremely doubtful. If she had written the epistle we would have expected a mention of Deborah instead of Barak in chapter eleven. Hunter remarks, "At the end of the argument, we are hardly convinced, and may even have a sneaking sympathy with Hausrath's sarcastic remark that there is no evidence that Aquila was plagued with a learned wife!"[32]

27. W. H. Bennett and Walter F. Adeney, *A Biblical Introduction,* p. 425.
28. Such as Schmidt, Ullman, Wiessler, Thiersch, Ritschl, Renan, Salmon, B. Weiss, Bartlet, Wickham, Riggenbach, Gregory, Heinrici, Badcock, Endemann, and others.
29. Frank Bertram Clogg, *An Introduction to the New Testament,* p. 135.
30. Mynster, Boehme, Riehm, Godet, Wohlenberg, Kallenback, Hewitt.
31. So also Rendel Harris, Peake, J. A. Robertson.
32. Hunter, p. 115.

The original suggestion by Luther that *Apollos* was the author has received warm support from a number of scholars.[33] Much can be said in favor of this suggestion. Apollos was closely connected with Paul and his work (1 Co 16:12; Titus 3:13). He was "an eloquent man" (Ac 18:24), and Hebrews is characterized by rhetorical skill. He was "mighty in the scriptures" (Ac 18:24), and Hebrews shows that the author was a man who had a masterly grasp of the Old Testament. Apollos was an Alexandrian Jew of high culture, and much in the epistle seems to point to just such a man as its author. We have no extant writings of Apollos to offer a basis of comparison. The difficulty with the suggestion is that no one ever thought of it until the time of Luther. As Purdy remarks, "The most that can be said for him is that there is nothing decisive against the hypothesis that Apollos could have been the author."[34]

We must conclude that none of the conjectures concerning the author can be demonstrated beyond the point of probability. However well the arguments may seem to fit the situation, we must confess that in truth we do not know. We feel that the dictum of Origen of old still stands, "Who it was that really wrote the Epistle, God only knows."

The more we contemplate this enigma concerning the authorship of this marvelous revelation of the supremacy of our Lord Jesus Christ, the more we feel that our ignorance is divinely intended to direct our attention rather to the message of the book. In this Spirit-breathed book the attention is centered upon Christ. He must ever remain preeminent. Throughout the epistle the unnamed author refrains from any mention of men, except to set them aside if they come at all, in the minds of the readers, in competition with Christ.

The Readers of Hebrews

1. NATIONALITY

Although not a part of the original document, in our oldest manuscripts the title is uniformly given as "To Hebrews." The title represents an inference from the general contents of the epistle rather than being based on any specific assertion in it. Manifestly the epistle is written to professed Christians. The designation "To Hebrews"

33. Bleek, deWette, Lunemann, Tholuck, Alford, Moulton, Plumptre, Farrar, T. W. Manson, Selwyn, A. T. Robertson, Howard, Lenski, Spicq, and others.
34. Alexander C. Purdy and J. Harry Cotton, "The Epistle to the Hebrews," in *The Interpreter's Bible*, 11:590b.

might be regarded as a language designation (cf. Ac 6:1) and thus indicate that the readers were Christian Jews who spoke the Aramaic. But the fact that the epistle was written in elegant Greek points to the readers as being Hellenistic Jews. The term thus has reference to race and makes no reference to language.

The traditional view has been that the readers were Christians of Jewish extraction. The general contents and tone of the epistle support this conclusion. The author's argument assumes an exclusively Jewish point of view. "The entire message of the epistle, the dominant claims of Christ and the Christian faith, rests upon the supposition that the readers held Moses, Aaron, the Jewish priesthood, the Old Covenant and the Levitical ritual, in the highest esteem."[35] The fathers of the Hebrews are naturally regarded as their fathers (1:1; 3:9; 2:16). Zahn points out that the epistle nowhere "so much as intimates that the readers *became* members of God's people who descended from Abraham. . . . They were the people of God through birth and training."[36]

Within comparatively recent times the view has been advanced that the epistle was addressed to Gentile Christians.[37] These advocates would detach the epistle from its Jewish-Christian moorings and float it into the midstream of Gentile Christianity. They point to the entire absence in the epistle of any reference to the distinction between Jew and Gentile in the Church, the omission of all allusion to such matters as circumcision, the authority of the Law in relation to the Christian, or the antithesis between faith and works. These matters, it is held, point to a later time when the Jewish-Christian distinctions had receded into the background. It may be replied that all of these omissions would also be natural if the epistle is written to a group of Christians of unmixed Jewish extraction who formed a self-contained society within the larger Church.

It is urged that the faults which the writer warns the readers against were characteristic of a Gentile rather than a Jewish Christian community. This argument, Peake retorts, "depends for its force on a too optimistic view of converts from Judaism."[38] Certainly such warnings would not be amiss for Jewish Christians.

35. Rees, p. 1359b.
36. Zahn, 2:323.
37. So Harnack, McGiffert, Moffatt, E. F. Scott, Strachan, Norborough, Kümmel, Käsemann, G. Vos, and some others.
38. Arthur S. Peake, *A Critical Introduction to the New Testament*, pp. 74-75.

It is claimed that the writer's extensive use of the Old Testament does not favor a Jewish Christian community any more than a Gentile community, since the Septuagint was the Bible of the Church as a whole, not only the Jewish Christians. It is granted that the use of the Septuagint does not prove that the readers were Jewish Christians. But if the readers were Gentiles who were in danger of a lapse into paganism or Gnosticism, as this view would have us believe, then we would have expected quite a different form of argument than that which he follows. The very fact of the author's use of the Old Testament in his argument proves the Jewish-Christian character of his readers. For Jews, whether Christians or not, the Old Testament was accepted as authoritative. But to a Gentile Christian the Old Testament had no authority apart from his Christianity. If there was danger of his apostasy from Christianity, of what value would be the author's arguments from a book which was losing its authority for him? "The author's argument has force only if his readers accepted the Old Testament independently of the acceptance of the Gospel, and this suits Jewish Christians but not Gentiles."[39]

It is asserted that the reference to "the first principles of Christ" (6:1-2) could not be properly addressed to Jewish-Christians, since they were already familiar to the average Jew, but would form an important part of the training of the ordinary Gentile convert. But the true significance of these points would have to be expounded to a Jew as well on becoming a Christian.

We adhere to the traditional view that the readers were Jewish Christians.

2. CIRCUMSTANCES

A general picture of the circumstances of the readers may be gathered from the epistle. It is obvious that it was directed to a specific group of Christians rather than an indefinite public. Hebrews is *not* a general epistle. Its recipients are members of a church at a definite place which the writer hopes soon to visit (13:19, 23). They seem to be a fairly small group and are quite homogeneous in feeling and condition.

They had received the Gospel from "them that heard" (2:3), that is, from personal disciples of the Lord. They had witnessed "signs and wonders" by the Spirit in their midst (2:4). They have been

39. Ibid., p. 76.

Christians for some time already (5:12). They had been fruitful in good works, ministering to the saints, and were still doing so (6:10). They had endured "a great conflict of suffering" and had helped those who had been imprisoned for the sake of the Gospel (10:32-34). They had taken "joyfully the spoiling of their possessions" (10:34) as Christians. Their former teachers have passed away (13:7) and they are called upon to obey their present leaders (13:17).

The persecutions they had formerly endured had died down. But with the favorable change in circumstances had come a dangerous change in them. They have experienced spiritual degeneration, having "become dull of hearing" (5:11), and need again to be cared for as spiritual babes (5:12-14). There is danger of their drifting away from the things they had heard (2:1). They need to be warned against "an evil heart of unbelief, in falling away from the living God" (3:12). They have become worldly minded (13:5) and there is a tendency among them to forsake their assembling together (10: 25).

In their moral dullness and spiritual lethargy the renewed persecution now coming upon them renders the danger of their falling away all the more acute. Although the persecution has not yet been unto martyrdom, it has shaken them and left them bewildered (12: 4-6). Such is the condition of the readers to whom this epistle was addressed.

3. LOCALITY

The question of the location of the readers is wrapped in obscurity. The only place reference in the epistle is found in the words, "They of Italy salute you" (13:24). The meaning is ambiguous. The statement may mean that the writer was in Italy when he wrote, or that he was writing to Italy and that friends with him from there were sending greetings.

Numerous places have been suggested as the place of residence—Jerusalem, Alexandria, Rome, Antioch, Caesarea, Colossae, Berea, Corinth, Thessalonica, Cyprus, Ephesus, Galatia, Lycaonia, and even Spain. The traditional view has been that the epistle was addressed to Jewish Christians resident in Jerusalem, or at least in Palestine. The majority of modern scholars seem inclined to place the readers in Rome.

Jerusalem has been advocated on the ground that the epistle implies that the readers lived under the very shadow of the Temple service. But the author really makes no mention in the Temple at all; his entire discussion centers around the tabernacle, and all Christians, regardless of residence, would be familiar with the details as found in their Septuagint. Again, it is held that the reference to the past persecutions fits the Jerusalem Christians. But persecutions of Christians were common enough in different places so that the statement might apply equally well elsewhere. But the statement that they have "not yet resisted unto blood" (12:4) does not fit the Jerusalem church, for it was there that the blood of the martyrs first flowed. The statement that they were ministering to the saints (6:10) does not quite fit Jerusalem; the Jerusalem believers were rather the recipients of such ministry. It is further argued that in no place was the danger of apostasy for Christians so great as in Jerusalem. It is held that as patriotic Jews they would be strongly inclined to throw in their lot with their countrymen during the crisis of A.D. 65-70 to preserve from destruction that which was sacred to them. But it seems quite impossible that Christians in Jerusalem who were witnessing the disintegration of the Jewish nation should think of throwing in their lot wtih Judaism. The Temple had become the site of revolting scenes; fanatical parties were seeking to exterminate each other. When the fate of Jerusalem became evident, the Christians, on the contrary, forsook the city and fled to Pella. Furthermore, it is improbable that the author would address a group in Jerusalem in the terms of 2:3.

The more probable location is Rome. Thus the salutation, "They from Italy," receives its most satisfactory explanation; those sending greetings were Italians with the author outside of Italy. It is more natural to think of the writer as being with a small group of Italians who were away from home than to think that the author is in Italy and designates the little group around him by the vague term "they of Italy." The preposition *apo*, translated "from, away from," supports this view.

Advocates of the Roman destination have frequently associated the readers with the original Christian church in Rome. But the readers addressed seem too homogeneous in feeling and position to represent the entire church there. Of late the tendency has been to equate them with one of the household groups found in the church of Rome (cf. Ro 16:5, 10-11, 14-15). Lenski, on the other hand, sharply distinguishes the readers from the members of the original Roman congregation. He identifies the readers as the Jewish Christians in Rome who were converted under the ministry of Paul in Rome, as recorded in Acts 28:17-28, and had formed themselves into independent Jewish-Christian synagogues distinct from the original church.[40]

While the evidence is too slender to form a dogmatic conclusion concerning the exact location of the readers, we hold that the Roman destination is the most probable.

THE OCCASION FOR HEBREWS

After a peaceful time the readers were again being subjected to renewed persecution, and it looked as though more serious things were ahead. In view of their spiritual laxness they were in danger of falling away from their Christian faith. It was the recognition of this danger that furnished the occasion for the writing of Hebrews.

But the scholars are not in agreement as to the exact nature of the danger which threatened. The traditional position has been that the Hebrews were in danger of forsaking their Christianity and going back into Judaism. The distinctly Jewish tone of the entire epistle, the form of the argument employed by the writer, as well as the fact that the readers were Jewish in their background, all point to this conclusion.

More recently the position has been advanced that the danger has no relation at all to any apostasy into Judaism. It is pointed out that the epistle does not actually speak of apostasy to Judaism but rather speaks of "falling away from the living God" (3:12). This does mean a desertion of the truths of Christianity but need not imply a return to Judaism. The apostasy, it is held, may be to a form of paganism. This view is related to the contention that the readers were Gentile Christians. Thus Narborough, who conceives of the readers as Gentile Christians around Ephesus, thinks that the danger is that of being led astray by some form of Gnosticism such as prevailed at Colossae.[41]

40. R. C. H. Lenski, *The Interpretation of the Epistles to the Hebrews and of the Epistle of James*, pp. 15-21.
41. F. D. V. Narborough, *The Epistle to the Hebrews*, in The Clarendon Bible, pp. 20-27.

But if the danger was an apostasy to Gnosticism of a kind, surely the author would not have built his whole argument upon a Jewish background which would have no special appeal or authority for them. Paul, when refuting the "Colossian Heresy," never made any appeal to the Old Testament to buttress his position.

It is urged that the warning against "falling away from the living God" (3:12) would be very appropriate if directed to Gentile readers about to relapse into heathenism but would be inappropriate if the readers were Jewish Christians in danger of going back into Judaism, since the living God is common to both Jews and Christians. But this entirely overlooks the author's argument that Christianity has superseded the old, and to forsake this new revelation would certainly be a falling away from the living God who has now fully revealed Himself in His Son. "To go back to the old economy of types and shadows, the economy of partial access to God, would be literally to depart from the living God."[42]

But even among those who hold that the epistle was addressed to Jewish Christians in Rome there is a difference of opinion as to the exact nature of the danger that threatened. All agree that the readers were in danger of deserting the cause of Christ. But is this due to a relapse into Judaism or is it a falling into unbelief and infidelity?

Those who hold to the latter view point out that Hebrews never speaks of an actual apostasy to Judaism. They recall that the danger is described as falling away from God through unbelief (3:12-13; 10:26), as an abandoning of their "confidence" (10:35), as a drifting away from the things heard (2:1). The view that their danger is a return to Judaism does not find its support so much in isolated passages as in the form of the argument of the epistle as a whole. The author throughout proves that the Christian faith is infinitely superior to Judaism and supersedes it. To allow the pressure of adverse circumstances to drift them back into the obsolete forms of Judaism would indeed be a forsaking of their true confidence and a falling away from the living God.

If we may think of the readers as members of the Jewish-Christian synagogues in Rome, the situation may be conceived as follows. With the outbreak of the Neronian persecution Christianity became

42. Marvin R. Vincent, *Word Studies in the New Testament*, 4:370.

an illegal religion. The fury of the persecution at first fell directly on the old, established Roman congregation consisting chiefly of Gentile Christians. These Jewish Christians, still meeting in their synagogues, were as yet officially regarded as Jews by the government. But their sympathy with their suffering brethren had expressed itself in definite efforts to help these unfortunate victims. This had aroused popular resentment against them also. They too were beginning to feel the weight of the persecution. Although martyrdom had not yet been extended to them, there was danger that it might. Because of this prospect their temptation was to minimize as much as possible their Christian distinctives and to emphasize their Jewish background and beliefs. Their danger lay in the temptation to hide their Christian faith under the protective coloring of Judaism. Perhaps, as Manson thinks, they had no intention of actually giving up their Christian profession to return to open Judaism, but they were hanging back and not accepting the full consequences of their Christian profession.[43] Thus they were not pressing on unto perfection and were in danger of falling short of the rest of God through unbelief (4:1-9). Such a compromising position resulted in spiritual dullness and foreshadowed a casting away of their confidence (10:35). They are therefore urged to "go forth unto him without the camp, bearing his reproach" (13:13).

THE PLACE AND DATE OF HEBREWS

1. PLACE

Tradition is silent concerning the place from which Hebrews was written. The expression "They of Italy" (13:24) leaves the matter undecided. It may denote Italians with the author as he writes from Italy or natives from Italy sending greetings to the readers in Italy. We can only agree with Westcott, "The place of writing must be left in complete uncertainty. Plausible conjectures unsupported by evidence cannot remove our ignorance even if they satisfy our curiosity."[44]

2. DATE

The latest possible date for Hebrews is about A.D. 95 since it is

43. William Manson, *The Epistle to the Hebrews*, pp. 15-16, 163-67.
44. Westcott, *The Epistle To The Hebrews*, p. xliv.

definite that Clement of Rome in A.D. 96 made use of it in his epistle to the Corinthians. It seems further that the time is before the destruction of Jerusalem in A.D. 70. There is no reference to that event in the epistle. If the Jewish sacrificial system had already been destroyed it seems improbable that the author would have failed to mention it in confirmation of his position. The statements in 8:4 and 13 seem to imply that Jewish sacrifices in accordance with the Old Covenant were still being carried on, yet this inference is not positive. A generation of Christian leaders had already passed away (13:7), yet the majority of the members were still first converts (2:3; 10:32). The prospect of hard times ahead, perhaps even leading to martyrdom (12:4), suggests the critical time when the Neronian persecution had just begun to run its fearful course in Rome. Accordingly we would suggest as a date the latter part of the year A.D. 64.

THE PURPOSE OF HEBREWS

1. WARNING AND ENCOURAGEMENT

The dangerous and depressing circumstances in which the readers were clearly called for serious warning and rousing encouragement. The author's purpose is to keep them from "drifting away" from the things heard (2:1), to guard them from "an evil heart of unbelief, in falling away from the living God" (3:12), to arouse them out of their dullness of hearing (5:11), and to encourage them to retain their "boldness" and "patience" unto the end (10:35-36). To achieve this end the writer repeatedly shakes up the readers with increasingly sharp warnings of the danger of apostasy (6:4-8; 10:26-31; 12:14-29).

2. INSTRUCTION

The writer further realized the need for instruction concerning the nature of Christianity on the part of his readers. He declares in unmistakable terms the finality of Christianity as it centers in the person of the incarnate Son of God. He begins by showing the supremacy of the incarnate Son, next sets forth the sufferings and triumph of Christ as our Redeemer, and then expounds the nature and work of Christ as our High Priest after the order of Melchizedek. The instructional sections are interspersed with words of warning and encouragement, and the latter part of the epistle seeks to apply the truths laid down to the needs of the readers.

THE CHARACTERISTICS OF HEBREWS

1. UNSOLVED PROBLEMS

Hebrews is remarkable in that the problems concerning its author-ship, place of composition, occasion, and destination seem to be with-out a final solution. These problems have aroused much controversy but are of a different nature than those usually encountered. Salmon aptly points out that usually we have "the deniers of the supernatural ranged on one side, and those who acknowledge a Divine revelation on the other. There is no such division of parties in the controversies concerning the Epistle to the Hebrews, which may be described as being more important from a literary than from an evidential point of view."[45]

2. LANGUAGE AND STYLE

The epistle to the Hebrews is written in some of the most elegant Greek in the New Testament. "The language of the Epistle," says Westcott, "is both in vocabulary and style purer and more vigorous than that of any other book of the New Testament."[46] The vocabu-lary is remarkably copious, having no fewer than 157 words which are peculiar to it. "The vocabulary, like the style," Robertson points out, "is less like the vernacular *koinē* than any book in the N.T."[47] The language of Hebrews is that of a practiced scholar. It shows everywhere the traces of care and effort. The imagery of the epistle is drawn from many sources and is singularly vivid and expressive (cf. 4:12; 6:7-8; 6:19; 12:1; 12:8-10).

3. CONTENTS

The contents of Hebrews point to a man who was a competent Old Testament scholar. The epistle reveals a full and remarkable use of the Old Testament. Scroggie asserts that "there are no fewer than eighty-six direct references to the Old Testament in Hebrews, and these are traceable to at least one hundred Old Testament pas-sages."[48] All the quotations are from the Septuagint Version. Ap-

---

45. George Salmon, *An Historical Introduction to the Study of the Books of the New Testament,* p. 414.
46. Westcott, *The Epistle To The Hebrews,* p. xliv.
47. A. T. Robertson, *A Grammar of the Greek New Testament in the Light of His-torical Research,* p. 132.
48. W. Graham Scroggie, *Know Your Bible. A Brief Introduction to the Scriputres,* Vol. 2, *The New Testament,* p. 282.

parently the author knew no Hebrew and read the Old Testament only in the Septuagint. He has a distinctive way of introducing his quotations; he does not give the human author of the quotation but always lays stress upon the fact that the Holy Spirit is speaking, thus bringing the reader face to face with God in what is said.

Hebrews makes its unique contribution to the teaching of the New Testament in its exposition of the present ministry and priesthood of Christ. There are numerous references to the ascension and exaltation of Christ at the right hand of the Father in other parts of the New Testament, but with the exception of Romans 8:34, only Hebrews explains His present heavenly ministry. Here as nowhere else in Scripture do we get an unfolding of the significance of that ministry. Nowhere are the main doctrines of our faith more purely and majestically set forth. In no other book of the New Testament do we find the Old Testament used and urged with greater authority and cogency.

The epistle is marked by some outstanding passages. The stately opening sentence of the epistle is worthy to stand beside the most exalted passages of Scripture. Of it Scroggie remarks,

> In its superb introduction many of the characteristics of the Epistle are discernible, its originality, its stateliness, its artistic balance of the language, its rhythm, its play upon words, its sweep of thought, and its profoundness.[49]

Doubtless the best known and most read portion of Hebrews is the marvelous eleventh chapter, the "Faith Chapter." It enshrines in lasting glory the mighty heroes of faith of the Old Testament and, with 12:1-2, presents a ringing challenge to a life of faith today.

The epistle bristles with exhortations in the midst of the great argument. No less than five different times does the author suspend the course of his argument to issue a solemn warning to his readers (2:1-4; 3:7—4:13; 5:11—6:20; 10:26-39; 12:25-29). Although in form Hebrews is a theological argument, yet in its intended effect it is a stirring practical appeal. "All through the Epistle, the doctrinal interest goes hand in hand with the practical, and towards the close is merged in it entirely."[50] These "stern passages," as they have been called, especially those in chapters six and ten, have been the oc-

49. Ibid., pp. 269-70.
50. Ernest Findlay Scott, *The Literature of the New Testament*, p. 202.

casion of much heartsearching and perplexity for the common reader and the occasion for definite disagreement among the theologians.

The epistle to the Hebrews is one of the great but much neglected treasures of the New Testament. "For all time this Epistle must have supreme value because it so richly reveals Jesus Christ."[51] In it Christ Jesus is exalted as supreme and unique. He cannot be rejected without eternal loss. In these days when there is a marked tendency in many areas of Christendom to be content with a ritualistic religion without personal spiritual experience, when there is a hesitancy to pay the price of an out and out identification with a rejected Christ, when there is a subtle or boldly open movement to ignore or even belittle the eternal Son of God, the epistle to the Hebrews cries out its stern warnings while it offers rousing encouragement and sweet comfort to the Lord's misunderstood and often oppressed saints.

An Outline of Hebrews

Part 1—Doctrinal, 1:1—10:18

I. Christ the Incarnate Son of God—His Supremacy, 1:1—2:4

  A. His essential glories, 1:1-3

    1. The contrast between the old and new revelation, vv. 1-2*a*

    2. The nature and work of the Son, vv. 2*b*-3

      a) His relationship to the Father, v. 2*b*

      b) His divine personality, v. 3*a*

      c) His incarnate work, v. 3*b*

  B. His superiority over angels, 1:4-14

    1. His supremacy indicated, v. 4

    2. His supremacy confirmed from Scripture, vv. 5-14

      a) The essential dignity of the incarnate Son, vv. 5-6

      b) The supremacy of the Son as anointed King, vv. 7-9

      c) The superiority of the Son as Creator, vv. 10-12

      d) The superiority of the Son as enthroned, vv. 13-14

  C. *Warning:* The danger of neglect, 2:1-4

    1. The nature of the peril warned against, v. 1

    2. The peril in view of punishment under the old revelation, vv. 2-3*a*

    3. The superior authority of this salvation, vv. 3*b*-4

---

51. Henry Cowles, *The Epistle To The Hebrews*, p. 25.

II. Christ the Son of Man—His Suffering and Death, 2:5–4:13
  A. The fulfillment of man's promised sovereignty in Jesus, 2:5-9
    1. The sovereignty over the coming world, v. 5-8*a*
    2. The delay in the fulfillment, v. 8*b*
    3. The fulfillment in the glorified Jesus, v. 9
  B. The fulfillment grounded in the incarnate work of Jesus, 2:10-18
    1. The relationship between the Son and the sons, vv. 10-13
      a) The fitness of the sufferings of the Son, v. 10
      b) The oneness of the saved with the Son, vv. 11-13
    2. The object of the incarnation of the Son, vv. 14-15
    3. The necessity of the Son's incarnation, vv. 16-18
  C. The glory of the Son over the house of God, 3:1-6
    1. The call to consider Jesus, vv. 1-2
    2. The superiority of Jesus over Moses, vv. 3-6
  D. *Warning:* The danger of failing of God's rest through unbelief, 3:7–4:13
    1. The exclusion from God's rest through unbelief, 3:7-19
      a) The example of unbelief in the wilderness, vv. 7-11
      b) The application of the wilderness example, vv. 12-15
      c) The interpretation of the lesson from the psalm, vv. 16-19
    2. The abiding reality of the promised rest, 4:1-13
      a) The application of the promise to believers in Christ, vv. 1-2
      b) The nature of this rest, vv. 3-10
        (1) The Christian experience of rest, v. 3*a*
        (2) The identity of the rest of Christians, vv. 3*b*-10
          (*a*) Neg.—what this rest is not, vv. 3*b*-8
            (i) Not the rest of creation, vv. 3*b*-5
            (ii) Not the rest of Canaan, vv. 6-8
          (*b*) Pos.—what this rest is, vv. 9-10
      c) The exhortation to those having this promise of rest, vv. 11-13

III. Christ the Great High Priest—His Superior Priesthood, 4:14–10:18

A. His Person: The Melchizedek priesthood of Christ, 4:14–7:28
   1. The appropriation of Christ as our High Priest, 4:14-16
   2. The characteristics of Christ as High Priest, 5:1-10
     a) The necessary qualifications for priesthood, vv. 1-4
       (1) The purpose of the office of priest, v. 1
       (2) The qualifications for the office of priest, vv. 2-4
         (*a*) The necessary relation to men, vv. 2-3
         (*b*) The call of God to priesthood, v. 4
     b) The qualifications of Christ as High Priest, vv. 5-10
       (1) His divine appointment to the priesthood, vv. 5-6
       (2) His qualification for priesthood through discipline, vv. 7-10
   3. *Warning:* The danger of failure through sloth and apostasy, 5:11–6:20
     a) The rebuke for spiritual degeneration, 5:11-14
     b) The exhortation to go on to spiritual maturity, 6:1-3.
     c) The warning against falling away, 6:4-8
       (1) The description of the apostates, vv. 4-6
       (2) The illustration of apostasy from nature, vv. 7-8
     d) The encouragement to press on in their spiritual life, 6:9-20
       (1) The expression of apostolic encouragement, vv. 9-12
       (2) The certainty of the divine promises, vv. 13-20
         (*a*) The encouragement from the example of Abraham, vv. 13-15
         (*b*) The double certainty of the promise to us, vv. 16-18
         (*c*) The nature of the hope set before us, vv. 19-20
   4. The supersedure of the Aaronic priesthood by the Melchizedek priesthood, 7:1-28
     a) The person of Melchizedek, vv. 1-3
     b) The relation of Melchizedek to the Levitical priesthood, vv. 4-10
       (1) The call to consider the greatness of Melchizedek, v. 4
       (2) The evidence of the superiority of Melchizedek, vv. 5-10
         (*a*) His superiority to Abraham, vv. 5-7

(*b*) His superiority to the Levitical priesthood, vv. 8-10

c) The contrast between the two priesthoods, vv. 11-25

    (1) The imperfections of the Levitical priesthood, vv. 11-19

        (*a*) Its transitional and nonpermanent nature, vv. 11-14

        (*b*) Its temporal and noneternal nature, vv. 15-19

    (2) The superiority of Christ's priesthood, vv. 20-25

        (*a*) The immutability of its foundation, vv. 20-22

        (*b*) The permanence in its unchanging Person, vv. 23-25

  d) The suitableness of Christ as our High Priest, vv. 26-28

B. His work: The perfection of Christ's atoning work, 8:1—10:18

  1. The ascended Christ as High Priest in the new sanctuary, 8:1-6

    a) His status as our High Priest, vv. 1-2

      (1) His enthronement in the heavens, v. 1

      (2) His ministry as Priest in the new sanctuary, v. 2

    b) His work as our High Priest, vv. 3-6

      (1) His offering as High Priest, v. 3

      (2) His present ministry as High Priest in heaven, vv. 4-6

  2. The supersedure of the old covenant by the new, 8:7-13

    a) The need for the new covenant, vv. 7-8*a*

    b) The prophetic announcement of the new covenant, vv. 8*b*-12

      (1) The source of the new covenant, v. 8*b*

      (2) The recipients of the new covenant, v. 8*c*

      (3) The nature of the new covenant, vv. 9-12

    c) The passing of the old covenant, v. 13

  3. The better sacrifice of Christ, 9:1—10:18

    a) The atonement under the old covenant, 9:1-10

      (1) The description of the tabernacle, vv. 1-5

        (*a*) The tabernacle associated with the old covenant, v. 1

        (*b*) The parts and contents of the tabernacle, vv. 2-5

(i) The holy place and its furniture, v. 2
(ii) The Holy of Holies and its furniture, vv. 3-5
(2) The priestly service in the tabernacle, vv. 6-7
(3) The lessons from the tabernacle services, vv. 8-10
b) The perfect atonement of Christ, 9:11-28
   (1) The summary description of His priestly work, vv. 11-12
   (2) The significance of the shedding of the blood of Christ, vv. 13-22
      (a) The superior efficiency of His blood, vv. 13-14
      (b) The ratification of the new covenant in Christ's blood, vv. 15-22
         (i) The validation of the covenant through death, vv. 15-17
            a. The effects of the death of Christ, v. 15
            b. The necessity of death for a valid covenant, vv. 16-17
         (ii) The blood conveying the thought of atonement, vv. 18-22
            a. The recognition of the principle under the old covenant, vv. 18-21
            b. The necessity of shedding of blood for atonement, v. 22
   (3) The significance of Christ's entry into the presence of God, vv. 23-28
      (a) The necessary cleansing of the heavenly things, v. 23
      (b) The entry in fulfillment of His atoning work, vv. 24-26
      (c) The anticipated return of the High Priest, vv. 27-28
c) The abiding efficacy of His sacrifice, 10:1-18
   (1) The ineffectiveness of the old sacrifices, vv. 1-4
      (a) The evidence from their repetition, vv. 1-2
      (b) The evidence from their nature, vv. 3-4
   (2) The nature of the self-sacrifice of Christ, vv. 5-10
      (a) The source in the will of God, vv. 5-7

(*b*) The character of it as obedience to God's will, vv. 8-9

(*c*) The effect of the sacrifice, v. 10

(3) The evidence of the efficacy of His sacrifice, vv. 11-18

(*a*) The evidence from the exaltation of Christ, vv. 11-14

(*b*) The witness of the Holy Spirit, vv, 15-17

(*c*) The conclusion from the evidence, v. 18

PART 2—PRACTICAL, 10:19—13:25

I. The Privileges and Peril of Believers, 10:19-39

A. The present privileges possessed by believers, vv. 19-25

1. The possession of glorious privileges by believers, vv. 19-21

a) The privilege of entry into the presence of God, vv. 19-20

b) The possession of a great High Priest, v. 21

2. The exhortation to use these privileges, vv. 22-25

a) The exhortation to approach as worshipers, v. 22

b) The exhortation to maintain a public profession of hope, v. 23

c) The exhortation to mutual stimulation, vv. 24-25

B. *Warning:* The peril in the willful rejection of Christ, vv. 26-39

1. The warning against apostasy from Christ, vv. 26-31

a) The description of the apostasy warned against, vv. 26-27

b) The confirmation of the fate of apostates, vv. 28-29

(1) The fate under the Mosaic Law, v. 28

(2) The fate under the present revelation, v. 29

c) The certainty of the punishment of apostates, vv. 30-31

2. The encouragement to perseverance, vv. 32-39

a) The reminder of their past courageous faith, vv. 32-34

b) The admonition to retain their confidence to the end, vv. 35-39

II. The Triumphs of Faith, 11:1-40

A. The meaning of faith, vv. 1-2

B. The illustrations of faith. vv. 3-38
  1. The function of faith in relation to creation, v. 3
  2. The faith of the antediluvians, vv. 4-7
    a) The faith of Abel, v. 4
    b) The faith of Enoch, vv. 5-6
    c) The faith of Noah, v. 7
  3. The faith of the patriarchs, vv. 8-22
    a) The faith of obedience and patience, vv. 8-16
      (1) The faith of patient obedience seen in Abraham, vv. 8-12
      (2) The characteristics of the faith of obedience, vv. 13-16
        (*a*) The perseverance of faith, supported by trust in the invisible, v. 13
        (*b*) The satisfaction in heavenly things, vv. 14-16*a*
          (i) The meaning of their pilgrim testimony, v. 14
          (ii) The heavenly nature of their quest, vv. 15-16*a*
        (*c*) The divine response to their faith, v. 16*b*
    b) The overruling of natural judgments by faith, vv. 17-22
      (1) The triumph of Abraham's faith under trial, vv. 17-19
      (2) The operation of faith in the patriarchal blessings, vv. 20-21
      (3) The faith-prompted command of Joseph, v. 22
  4. The faith of conquest in the beginning of national Israel, vv. 23-31
    a) The faith of Moses the leader of Israel, vv. 23-28
      (1) The faith of Moses in its personal workings, vv. 23-26
        (*a*) The faith of the parents of Moses, v. 23
        (*b*) The faith of Moses shown in his personal choice, vv. 24-26
      (2) The faith of Moses in its public workings, vv. 27-28
    b) The faith of the people of Israel, vv. 29-31
      (1) The victory by faith over difficulties of nature, v. 29
      (2) The victory by faith over Jericho, v. 30
      (3) The eliciting of saving faith in Rahab, v. 31

5. The operation of faith in Israel's national life, vv. 32-38
   a) The victorious successes of faith, vv. 32-35a
   (1) The enumeration of representative heroes of faith, v. 32
   (2) The characteristic achievements of faith, vv. 33-35a
   (a) The public victories through faith, v. 33ɪ
   (b) The personal deliverances through faith, vv. 33b-34a
   (c) The personal gifts attained through faith, v. 34b
   (d) The victory over death through faith, v. 35a
   b) The victorious sufferings of faith, vv. 35b-38
   (1) The refusal by faith to yield in suffering, vv. 35b-36
   (2) The varied forms of the sufferings of faith, vv. 37-38
C. The conclusion concerning these heroes of faith, vv. 39-40

III. The Application of These Examples to the Present Trials, 12:1-29

A. The significance of suffering as Christians, vv. 1-11
   1. The motives for enduring suffering, vv. 1-4
      a) The recognition of the Christian life as a race, vv. 1-2
      (1) The position of the believer in the arena, v. 1a
      (2) The preparation of the believer for the race, v. 1b
      (3) The effort of the believer in the race, v. 1c
      (4) The goal of the believer in the race, v. 2
      b) The consideration of the sufferings of Christ, v. 3
      c) The comparative slightness of their sufferings, v. 4
   2. The interpretation of suffering as discipline, vv. 5-10
      a) The scriptural exhortation regarding suffering, vv. 5-6
      b) The view of suffering as divine chastening, vv. 7-8
      c) The comparison between human and divine chastening, vv. 9-10
   3. The result of enduring the divine chastening, v. 11
B. The consequent exhortations to Christian duty, vv. 12-17
   1. The exhortation to personal duty, vv. 12-13
   2. The exhortation to social duties, vv. 14-17
      a) The duty toward men generally, v. 14
      b) The duty toward fellow church members, vv. 15-17
C. *Warning:* The danger in rejecting Christ, vv. 18-29

1. The nature of the believer's privileges, vv. 18-24
   a) The awesome approach to God at Mount Sinai, vv. 18-21
      (1) The physical terrors of Mount Sinai, vv. 18-20
      (2) The confession of the lawgiver himself, v. 21
   b) The privileged approach of believers under grace, vv. 22-24
2. The warning not to reject the One speaking from heaven, vv. 25-27
3. The exhortation to go on having grace, vv. 28-29

IV. The Concluding Admonitions About Practical Duties, 13:1-17

A. The moral duties of believers, vv. 1-6
   1. The general duty of continued brother-love, v. 1
   2. The social duties of believers, vv. 2-4
      a) The duty of hospitality, v. 2
      b) The duty of aiding the suffering, v. 3
      c) The duty of chastity, v. 4
   3. The duties as to personal attitudes, vv. 5-6
      a) The duty to avoid covetousness, v. 5a
      b) The duty of contentment, vv. 5b-6
B. The religious duties of believers, vv. 7-17
   1. The duty to remember their past leaders, v. 7
   2. The duty of complete devotion to Jesus Christ, vv. 8-16
      a) The centering of our life in Christ, vv. 8-9
      b) The continuous support for life from Christ, vv. 10-12
      c) The duty of union with Christ in suffering and service, vv. 13-16
         (1) The union with Christ in reproach, vv. 13-14
         (2) The union with Christ in sacrifice, vv. 15-16
   3. The duty to obey their present leaders, v. 17

V. The Personal Matters in Conclusion, 13:18-25

A. The request of the writer for their prayers, vv. 18-19
B. The prayer of the writer for the readers, vv. 20-21
C. The concluding comments of the writer, vv. 22-23
D. The concluding salutations, v. 24
E. The closing benediction, v. 25

A Book List on Hebrews

Archer, Gleason L., Jr. *The Epistles to the Hebrews. A Study Manual.* Shield Bible Study Series. Grand Rapids: Baker, 1957.
>A concise, thorough, conservative study of the epistle suitable for group study. Much valuable material in outlined form.

Barclay, William. *The Letter to the Hebrews.* The Daily Study Bible. 2d ed. Edinburgh: The Saint Andrew Press, 1957.
>Valuable for its word studies and quotations from varied writers, sacred and secular.

Bruce, F. F. *The Epistle to the Hebrews.* New International Commentary on the New Testament. Grand Rapids: Eerdmans, 1964.
>A monumental tome of reverent scholarship, the work of an internationally known evangelical British teacher and author. The numerous footnotes give evidence of the author's vast learning.

Davidson, A. B. *The Epistle to the Hebrews.* Reprint. Handbooks for Bible Classes and Private Students. Edinburgh: T. & T. Clark, 1950.
>This compact volume, the work of a noted Hebrew scholar, contains much valuable material. A number of extended notes on the Son, the two covenants, the Day of Atonement, et cetera, are most helpful.

Delitzsch, Franz. *Commentary on the Epistle to the Hebrews.* 2 vols. Edinburgh: T. & T. Clark, 1868-1870.
>Greek text. An exhaustive treatment, dealing with many of the critical problems in Hebrews. Draws heavily upon the literature of his day.

English, E. Schuyler. *Studies in the Epistle to the Hebrews.* Travelers Rest, S.C.: Southern Bible House, 1955.
>A thorough exposition by a well-known evangelical, premillennial Bible teacher. Holds to the authorship of Paul.

Erdman, Charles R. *The Epistle to the Hebrews. An Exposition.* Philadelphia: Westminster, 1934.
>A concise, conservative, practical exposition by a noted Presbyterian teacher and author. Well adapted to the average lay student.

Fudge, Edward. *Our Man in Heaven. An Exposition of the Epistle to the Hebrews.* Athens, Ala.: C. E. I., 1973.
>A scholarly yet simple commentary on Hebrews which stresses the present heavenly priesthood of Christ; the work of a conservative minister working with the Church of Christ.

Hewitt, Thomas. *The Epistle to the Hebrews.* Tyndale New Testament Commentaries. Grand Rapids: Eerdmans, 1960.

> A compact, scholarly interpretation of the teaching of Hebrews by a conservative Church of England scholar and leader. Silas is viewed as the most likely author of the epistle.

Kendrick, A. C. "Commentary on the Epistle to the Hebrews." In *An American Commentary on the New Testament.* 1889. Reprint. Philadelphia: Amer. Bapt. Pubn. Soc., n.d.

> Brief discussion of introductory problems. A thorough exposition of the epistle, with a new translation of Hebrews by the author.

Kent, Homer A., Jr. *The Epistle to the Hebrews. A Commentary.* Grand Rapids: Baker, 1972.

> Prints the author's own, quite literal translation. A thorough, conservative exposition built upon careful exegesis of the text. The author ably elucidates the theological import of the epistle. Varied views on problem passages are fairly presented and evaluated.

Lang, G. H. *The Epistle to the Hebrews. A Practical Treatise for Plain and Serious Readers.* London: Paternoster, 1951.

> A fresh, provocative interpretation by a noted British evangelical scholar. Lang does not always follow the beaten path but often breaks new ground in his views. Valuable for the serious student.

Lenski, R. C. H. *The Interpretation of the Epistle to the Hebrews and of the Epistle of James.* Columbus, Ohio: Lutheran Book Concern, 1938.

> A scholarly, exegetical study from a conservative Lutheran standpoint.

MacDonald, William. *The Epistle to the Hebrews. From Ritual to Reality.* Neptune, N.J.: Loizeaux, 1971.

> A well-outlined, devotional exposition by a well-known Plymouth Brethren writer.

Moffatt, James. *A Critical and Exegetical Commentary on the Epistle to the Hebrews.* International Critical Commentary. New York: Scribner's, 1924.

> Greek text. A work of massive scholarship by a famous liberal scholar which espouses a non-Jewish background for the recipients of this letter. Valuable introduction and interpretative notes for the advanced student. Has a helpful section on the rhythmic cadences of the epistle.

Montefiore, Hugh. *A Commentary on the Epistle to the Hebrews.* Harper's New Testament Commentaries. New York: Harper & Row, 1964.

Prints the author's own translation. A critical, perceptive, exegetical study of Hebrews based on the original text but suited to the English reader. The introduction presents a strong case for accepting Apollos as the author of Hebrews.

Murray, Andrew. *The Holiest of All. An Exposition of the Epistle to the Hebrews.* Reprint. New York: Revell, 1965.

A series of 130 expository meditations covering the entire epistle in order. A rich treasure of devotional material from a Calvinistic standpoint with a practical application to daily life.

Newell, William R. *Hebrews Verse by Verse.* 1947. Reprint. Chicago: Moody, n.d.

An independent, popular, heartwarming, verse-by-verse exposition by a competent, conservative Bible teacher. Contains a clear premillennial emphasis. A variety of rich summaries and comments in the footnotes.

Owen, John. *Hebrews: The Epistle of Warning. Verse by Verse Exposition.* Grand Rapids: Kregel, 1953.

A condensation of the eight-volume work on Hebrews on which Owens spent sixteen years of his life. A valuable guide for the study of Hebrews under this noted Puritan theologian and preacher.

Pfeiffer, Charles F. *The Epistle to the Hebrews.* Everyman's Bible Commentary. Chicago: Moody, 1962.

A brief exposition by a conservative Bible scholar. Well suited for a beginner's study of Hebrews.

Pink, Arthur W. *An Exposition of Hebrews.* 3 vols. Grand Rapids: Baker, 1954.

An exhaustive exposition by a noted Calvinistic writer with a ready pen. A reprint of a series of expositions published over a number of years in the late author's magazine, *Studies in the Scriptures.*

Ridout, S. *Lectures on the Epistle to the Hebrews.* 6th ed. New York: Loizeaux, 1943.

A series of expository messages covering the entire epistle by a Plymouth Brethren scholar of the past generation. Prints the translation of F. W. Grant. Warmly devotional, with a clear premillennial emphasis.

Saphir, Adolph. *The Epistle to the Hebrews. An Exposition.* 7th American ed. 2 vols. New York: Loizeaux, n.d.

Warm, expository studies by an accomplished Jewish Christian Bible teacher. Originally published in 1874-76.

Schneider, Johannes. *The Letter to the Hebrews.* Grand Rapids: Eerdmans, 1957.

A straightforward, paragraph-by-paragraph interpretation by a German Baptist professor. Generally conservative in its presentation. Translated into readable English by William A. Mueller.

Thomas, W. H. Griffith. *Hebrews: A Devotional Commentary.* Reprint. Grand Rapids: Eerdmans, 1962.

Forty-one devotional messages unfolding the teaching of Hebrews by a noted Bible teacher of the past generation. Stresses the necessity and conditions of spiritual growth.

Vine, W. E. *The Epistle to the Hebrews. Christ All Excelling.* London: Oliphants, 1952.

A warm, rich exposition by a noted Plymouth Brethren scholar of the past generation. Contains a clear analysis of the epistle. Opens up the meaning of the Greek for the English student.

Westcott, Brooke Foss. *The Epistle to the Hebrews:* Reprint. *The Greek Text with Notes and Essays.* London: Macmillan, 1909.

Greek text. The standard, older commentary on this epistle, still valued for its wise comments. The additional notes offer much helpful material to the serious Bible student.

Wiley, H. Orton. *The Epistle to the Hebrews.* Kansas City, Mo.: Beacon Hill, 1959.

A thorough study of Hebrews by a Wesleyan theologian. Gives a warmhearted development of the person of Christ and His priesthood as central pillars of the Christian faith.

Wuest, Kenneth S. *Hebrews in the Greek New Testament for the English Reader.* Grand Rapids: Eerdmans, 1947.

A commentary on Hebrews, largely in the form of Greek word studies and an expanded translation. Designed to put the English reader into possession of the riches of the Greek text.

5

FIRST PETER

AN INTRODUCTION TO 1 PETER

THE FIRST EPISTLE of Peter has appropriately been called "the epistle of the living hope." It sets forth the hope of the believer in the midst of a hostile world. Addressed to those who stood as strangers in the midst of an antagonistic and oppressive world, it is a ringing appeal to steadfast endurance and unswerving loyalty to Christ. The epistle is finding renewed significance and relevance in these days when again, in many areas, to be known as a Christian may be fraught with dire consequences.

THE AUTHENTICITY OF 1 PETER

1. TRADITIONAL ACCEPTANCE

The early Church had no doubts concerning the authenticity of 1 Peter. The evidence for the epistle is early and clear, and it is as strong as for any other book in the New Testament. It was universally received as an acknowledged part of the Christian Scriptures.[1] Lumby observes, "Heretics, no less than the faithful, regarded it as a portion of authoritative Christian literature."[2] The testimony to the epistle comes from all sections of the Church.[3] This unquestioned acceptance of the epistle is reflected in the fact that Eusebius in his *Ecclesiastical History* (3. 25) placed it among the *homologoumena*, that is, the books acknowledged by the Church. The traditional view of the Church seems abundantly confirmed by the internal evidence. Only

---

1. The omission of it in the Muratorian Canon (*c.* 170) is evidently due to its imperfect condition, perhaps due to the carelessness of the scribe. Marcion rejected it simply because it *was* Peter's work.
2. J. Rawson Lumby, "The Epistles of St. Peter," in *An Exposition of the Bible,* 6:671.
3. For the external evidence see Charles Bigg, *A Critical and Exegetical Commentary on the Epistles of St. Peter and St. Jude,* International Critical Commentary, pp. 7-15.

105

since the nineteenth century have radical critics sought to discredit the epistle.

2. CRITICAL ATTACKS

Although the epistle is so abundantly attested by the ancient Church, negative critics have not hesitated to assail its genuineness. Their attacks have proceeded solely on internal considerations.

Attempts are made to sever the Petrine salutation from the body of the epistle. It is advocated that the epistle was originally an anonymous homily, perhaps a baptismal sermon, and that the salutation and conclusion, linking it with the apostle Peter, were later erroneously added to it. It is held that the style of the opening sentence is different from that of the rest of the epistle, thus revealing that the salutation is a later addition. As confirmation of this it is pointed out that while Polycarp (*c*. 69-155) and Clement of Rome (*c*. 30-100) quoted from the epistle they did not mention Peter's name. Irenaeus (140-203) is the first to mention Peter as the author. We can reply that any attempt to build an argument upon a difference of style in the body of the letter and the few common words of the salutation is "an excessive bit of doubting criticism."[4] The difference in style is not as apparent as is claimed. Bigg asserts,

> In style, the address and subscription are indistinguishable from the body of the Epistle. The language of the address paves the way with great propriety for the admonitions which follow, and contains a sort of abstract or premonition of all that was in the writer's mind.[5]

Those who theorize that the salutation with its claim of Petrine authorship is an erroneous addition have no explanation for the origin of such an addition. Thus Scott admits, "The attribution to Peter must have been due to some misunderstanding, but how it arose we cannot now discover."[6] If Peter was not the author, it would have been more probable, due to the apparent Pauline influence in the epistle, to have ascribed it to Paul. And if the epilogue was not originally written by Peter, it is difficult to conceive how it became attached to the epistle. A forger would not have introduced the unnecessary difficulty of making Mark and Silvanus the special com-

4. Homer Kingsley Ebright, *The Petrine Epistles, A Critical Study of Authorship*, p. 42.
5. Bigg, p. 79.
6. Ernest Findlay Scott, *The Literature of the New Testament*, p. 221.

panions of Peter rather than of Paul with whom they are elsewhere associated.

That Polycarp and Clement of Rome do not name Peter in making their quotations is quite in accord with the practice of their time. Clement quoted or alluded to some twenty-two books of the New Testament without naming his authority. Although he quoted Paul without naming him, he well knew that Paul was the author of the epistles thus quoted. It may be confidently concluded that he had the same knowledge when quoting Peter.

We conclude that the attempt to decapitate the epistle and to make it an anonymous homily is unwarranted.

Objection is raised to the Petrine authorship on the ground of an alleged lack of personal reminiscences of Jesus in it. The conservative student at once recalls that 2 Peter is cast out because it does contain marks or claims of the writer's personal acquaintance with Jesus (1:14-18), while here the critics would deny the genuineness of 1 Peter because it lacks such marks. The critics cannot have it both ways.

The asserted absence of such personal reminiscences in 1 Peter is a matter of personal impression. Ebright cites thirty-two passages in 1 Peter which find equivalents in the teachings of Jesus and concludes that they definitely prove the writer's acquaintance with Jesus.[7] And Farrar, in proof of the Petrine authorship, points out the natural way in which we may trace in the epistle the influence of the prominent events which occurred during Peter's associations with Jesus.[8] Thus, the allusions to Christ's passion and resurrection, events which made a deep impression upon Peter, are clearly evident. He has been "a witness of the sufferings of Christ" (5:1). He speaks as an eyewitness of the Lord's death in the flesh (3:18; 4:1) and His quickening in the Spirit. His words of exhortation, "Let them also that suffer according to the will of God commit their souls in well-doing unto a faithful Creator" (4:19), are reminiscent of the Saviour's word on the cross, "Father, into thy hands I commend my spirit" (Luke 23:46). He appeals to the readers to "gird yourselves with humility" (5:5) and the figure arose out of his memory of the scene in the upper room. That the resurrection of Christ had a transform-

7. Ebright, pp. 50-55.
8. F. W. Farrar, *The Early Days of Christianity*, pp. 69-70.

ing effect on the writer is evident from his word that God "begat us again unto a living hope by the resurrection of Jesus Christ" (1:3).

The general contents and tone of the epistle are consistent with the Petrine authorship. The writer's description of himself as a "fellow-elder" (5:1) is certainly not inappropriate of Peter. He had been thrice commissioned to tend and feed Christ's flock (John 21:15-17) and the pastoral image is prominent in his mind (2:25; 5:2); the very purpose of this letter is a fulfillment of that commission. The tone of the epistle is what we would expect of an apostle. In the words of Farrar,

> It is characterized by the fire and energy which we should expect to find in his forms of expression; but that energy is tempered by the tone of Apostolic dignity, and by the fatherly mildness of one who was now aged, and was near the close of a life of labour.[9]

The Petrine authorship has also been denied on the ground that the references to the persecution in 1 Peter cannot be fitted into the time of Peter. The persecution mentioned in the epistle, it is urged, could not be earlier than the time of Trajan, described in Pliny's correspondence with that emperor, when the acknowledgment of being a Christian was a crime punishable by law. But that is reading too much into the suffering mentioned in the epistle. Suffering "for the Name" was known to Christians even before the time of the Neronian persecutions. But if it is held that the persecutions in Asia Minor mentioned in the epistle arose out of a definite governmental policy against Christians, it is very likely that the governors in those provinces, inspired by the prevailing hatred against Christians, would readily follow the example of Nero at Rome in taking action against them. But it is not even certain that the persecutions seen in the epistle arose from such a cause. They may be explained as the result of the spasmodic outbursts of pagan fanaticism against the Christians (4:4). At any rate, it is now generally admitted that there is nothing in the epistle which *compels* us to date it later than the Neronian persecutions.

It is argued that the obvious traces of Pauline influence in the epistle militate against the Petrine authorship. Is it likely, it is asked, that such a leading spirit as Peter would be so dependent upon

9. Ibid., p. 68.

another apostle? Many scholars readily admit that 1 Peter shows undeniable traces of acquaintance with the Pauline epistles, especially Romans and Ephesians.[10] But the admission does not disprove Peter's authorship of the epistle. Peter, it must be remembered, had an impressionable nature (cf. Gal 2:12), and it is but natural that he would reveal the results of his associations with Paul and especially the impression of these epistles upon him. Romans was the longest and most important of Paul's epistles and there is no reason to hold that he was not acquainted with it, since it was addressed to the saints in the very city where perhaps Peter was when he wrote his epistle. And Ephesians, apparently a circular letter addressed to some of the very churches to whom Peter was writing, would readily be available to him. It is but natural to suppose that Peter had recently read these letters, which would result in the use of similar thoughts and expressions in his letter. But the matter of his dependence upon the Pauline epistles must not be overdrawn. Bigg, upon examining the parallels, concludes, "In the case of Romans as in that of Ephesians the resemblances to 1 Peter are quite superficial, attaching only to current commonplaces."[11] Many scholars are not convinced that there is any real evidence of direct dependence upon the Pauline epistles in 1 Peter. The supposed examples of dependence may well be due to the fact that these ideas were common to all the preaching of the early Church.[12]

On the other hand, the epistle shows marked originality. The author of 1 Peter was no mere copyist. Accepting the fact of affinities to Paul in the epistle, however they may be accounted for, "more decisive than the resemblances are the differences between the two writers."[13] He is not merely an imitator, for the favorite Pauline expressions are missing from the epistle. The contents of the epistle reveal a strong personality, a man able to present his thoughts in his own way.

It is also asserted that the excellent Greek of 1 Peter is such that we cannot think of Peter as the author. It is asserted that Peter, for

10. For lists of parallels see Farrar, p. 72; E. H. Plumptre, *The General Epistles of St. Peter and St. Jude*, Cambridge Bible for Schools and Colleges, pp. 68-70; Bigg, pp. 16-20.
11. Bigg, p. 20.
12. The most recent explanation points to the influence of the catechetical forms in common use in the apostolic Church. See Edward Gordon Selwyn, *The First Epistle of St. Peter*, Essay II.
13. Ebright, p. 60.

whom Greek was a foreign tongue, and who according to Papias needed an interpreter at Rome to translate his Aramaic, could not have written the Greek of this letter. To this Zahn replies,

> The idea that Mark performed the office of an interpreter, translating Peter's Aramaic discourses into Greek, or what is still more impossible, his Greek sermons into Latin, cannot be held by anyone having any knowledge at all of language conditions in the apostolic age.[14]

That Peter did know Greek need no longer be doubted. Galilee was a bilingual country. The other New Testament writers who came from Galilee could speak Greek. James, who as far as we know never left Palestine, could write good Greek. Matthew had a good command of Greek. If Mark, whose home was in Jerusalem, the stronghold of the Aramaic, could speak and write Greek, why should not Peter be able to do so? Moffatt admits that "as a native of Galilee, he cannot have been wholly unfamiliar with colloquial Greek."[15] If Peter knew Greek in his old home in Galilee, why should it be thought impossible that thirty years later, after much travel and practice in the use of the Greek language, he should be unable to compose an epistle in that language?

The statement in Acts 4:13 that Peter and John were "unlearned and ignorant men" simply means that they were laymen and unschooled in the theological institutions of the day. Admittedly Peter was not a polished scholar, and the Greek of the epistle is consistent with that fact. As Ebright says,

> The Greek of the First Epistle of Peter is not so very remarkable. . . . The constructions are very simple. The sentences are of average length, the fifty-three sentences averaging thirty-four words. The thirty-one quotations from the LXX contribute considerably to the color of the epistle. There are no marks of familiarity with the literature of Greece. . . . There is a beauty in the epistle, but it is the charm of the soul rather than the charm of sound; it is the grace of the spirit rather than the grace of the letter.[16]

Ebright reminds us of the parallel case of John Bunyan, the author of *Pilgrim's Progress*. Bunyan was not a scholar, and if we did not know

14. Theodor Zahn, *Introduction to the New Testament*, 2:443.
15. James Moffatt, *An Introduction to the Literature of the New Testament*, p. 332.
16. Ebright, p. 81.

the facts, an irresistible argument could be developed that he was not the author of that masterpiece.[17] It is clear that the Greek of the epistle cannot be used to overthrow the evidence for the Petrine authorship.

The consensus of modern scholarship, however, holds that the phenomena of the epistle can best be accounted for by the view that Silvanus was more than a mere amanuensis and had a share in the formulation of the language as we have it in the epistle. This view is not improbable, especially in view of the Greek of 2 Peter, and is quite consistent with the tradition claim of its Petrine authorship.

3. CONCLUSION

The external evidence is very strong for the Petrine authorship of the epistle. Nor is the internal evidence inconsistent with that position. We cannot believe that the universal acceptance of the Petrine authorship in the early Church must be discredited by the supposedly superior insights of the modern critics. We agree with Adeney,

> It must be felt by the thoughtful reader of this epistle that its author was a man of rare spiritual gifts, who stood very near to the fountains of inspiration. This is one of the very choicest gems in the New Testament, worthy of the great apostle whose name it bears.[18]

THE LATER YEARS IN THE LIFE OF PETER

1. BIBLICAL REFERENCES

The name of Peter is one of the most familiar to the reader of the New Testament, occurring no less than 160 times. Our space permits only a brief consideration of the closing years of his life.[19]

For convenience the life of Peter may be divided into four parts as follows: (1) from the beginning of his life to his meeting with Jesus; (2) from his meeting with Jesus until Pentecost; (3) from Pentecost to the Jerusalem Conference; (4) from the Jerusalem Conference to his death. Of the first part comparatively little is known; the gospels give us a vivid picture of the second part, while the third part is covered quite fully in the Acts. Our information about the last part again is quite meager.

---

17. Ibid.
18. W. H. Bennett and Walter F. Adeney, *A Biblical Introduction*, p. 441.
19. For a full study of Peter see A. T. Robertson, *Epochs in the Life of Simon Peter;* E. Schuyler English, *The Life and Letters of Saint Peter.*

Following the Jerusalem Conference the name of Peter disappears from the book of Acts; the references to him in the rest of the New Testament are scanty indeed. From Galatians 2:11-21 we know that Peter made a visit to Syrian Antioch where, because of his inconsistent conduct, he was publicly rebuked by Paul. From 1 Corinthians 9:5 it is plain that Peter traveled a lot, taking his wife with him. The name of Peter (Cephas) was used as a rallying point for one of the factions in the Corinthian church (1 Co 1:12). This does not, however, prove that Peter had already been at Corinth, although this inference was early drawn.

We hear nothing more of Peter until we come to the two epistles which bear his name. In the first letter Peter is writing to the Christians in five provinces of Asia Minor. It is not stated or even implied that Peter had personally visited these provinces, but that inference has often been drawn.[20] The second letter bearing Peter's name was apparently written to the same groups shortly after. A final reference in the New Testament to the closing years of Peter's life is found in John 21:18-19. John's record of the prediction of Jesus and his own interpretative comment on it make it clear that the reference is to Peter's violent death. Beyond this the New Testament is silent concerning the closing years of Peter's life. That Peter went east to preach the Gospel in Babylon is in itself probable, but the only scriptural basis for the assertion is the disputed expression "in Babylon" found in 1 Peter 5:12.

2. RELATION TO ROME

Tradition uniformly asserts that Peter did go to Rome, that he labored there, and that he was martyred there. The elaborately developed "Legend of St. Peter,"[21] setting forth his relations to Rome and long received in the Roman Catholic church, may be safely set aside as unreliable. Scripture is silent concerning Peter's residence and martyrdom at Rome, and the question is still debated, but the uniform tradition of the Church, when stripped of its embellishments, is strong enough to make it reasonably certain.[22] That Peter was the bishop of Rome for twenty-five years may confidently be rejected as

20. The inference is accepted by Paton J. Gloag, *Introduction to the Catholic Epistles,* pp. 130-31, but rejected by Zahn, 2:145, 154-55.
21. For the traditional account and its evaluation see Plumptre, pp. 53-59.
22. See Gloag, pp. 144-60. For the history of the debate see Oscar Cullman, *Peter, Disciple—Apostle—Martyr,* translated by Floyd V. Filson, pp. 71-77.

"unquestionably a colossal chronological mistake,"[23] and the claim is abandoned by some modern Catholic scholars.[24]

Apparently Peter came to Rome shortly after Paul's release from his first imprisonment there. If Peter was in Rome when Paul wrote the prison epistles, it is incredible that he should not have mentioned his name among those sending greetings in those letters. Upon his release Paul doubtless revisited his churches in the east and spent the winter in Nicopolis (Titus 3:12). Presumably the following spring he left for Spain, doubtless touching at Rome on the way there. It may even be that Paul and Peter now met in Rome. Mark and Silas apparently remained with Peter while Paul went on to Spain, where he remained perhaps two years. In the absence of Paul, Peter would feel a special responsibility toward the churches in Asia Minor. It is probable that Peter remained in Rome until his martyrdom under Nero.

THE READERS OF 1 PETER

1. IDENTITY

The epistle is addressed "to the elect who are sojourners of the Dispersion in Pontus, Galatia, Cappadocia, Asia, and Bithynia" (1:1). That the readers are Christians is evident from the term "the elect" as well as the entire contents of the epistle. But opinion has been divided on the question whether Peter intended to address Jewish churches or Christians generally in those provinces. From the time of Origen the view has been current that Peter wrote to Jewish Christians. Did he not speak of them as "sojourners of the Dispersion"? The designation is held to be similar to that in James who directed his epistle to Jewish Christians in the Dispersion. The Jewish character of the readers is implied in the frequency of Old Testament quotations and allusions. The readers are described entirely in terms taken from the Old Testament (2:9). Finally, it is held that this view is in accord with the position of Peter as minister to the circumcision.[25]

23. Philip Schaff, *History of the Christian Church*, 1:252.
24. See Cullmann, p. 37, note 14. It is not pressed by J. P. Kirsch, "Peter, Saint, Prince of the Apostles," in *The Catholic Encyclopedia*, 11:747b-51b.
25. See elaboration of view in Bernhard Weiss, *A Manual of Introduction to the New Testament*, 2:137-44. Briefly in G. F. C. Fronmüller, "The Epistles General of Peter" in Lange's *Commentary on the Holy Scriptures*, pp. 7-8. Tom Westwood, *The Epistles of Peter*, pp. 1, 4-6.

Admittedly the epistle is written from a Jewish background, but it does not follow that the readers are thereby proved to be Jewish Christians. Peter, unlike James, does not call his readers "the twelve tribes"; he rather uses the term "the Dispersion" in a figurative sense to denote the Christians in their minority position as strangers scattered in an alien land. The proposed division of labor agreed upon by Paul and Barnabas with James, Peter, and John (Gal 2:9) was a general working agreement and must not be pressed too literally. As apostles to the Gentiles, Paul did not feel it inconsistent with the agreement to begin preaching in the Jewish synagogue in a new place. Nor can we believe that Peter would exclude Gentile Christians from his ministry because he was the apostle to the circumcision.

There are statements in the epistle which forbid the view that the readers were exclusively Jewish Christians. Thus the readers are addressed as those who have been called "out of darkness into his marvelous light" (2:9), who once "were no people, but now are the people of God" (2:10). Their unconverted days are described as "the time of your ignorance" (1:14), a term suited to Gentile readers. They are reminded of and warned against their old heathen practices from which they have been delivered (4:1-4). Certainly the heathen would not have thought it "strange" (4:4) if Jews abstained from partaking in those practices. The women are represented as having *become* through their conversion the daughters of Sarah (3:6). These things point definitely to Gentile Christians.

The correct interpretation of the facts requires a combination of both views. As in the case of most churches outside of Palestine, their membership was of mixed racial origin. They were composed of both Jewish and Gentile Christians, with perhaps the Gentiles in the majority in most churches. Peter thinks of them not as Jews or Gentiles but as all members of one Body in Christ. As Selwyn aptly remarks,

> The abounding grace and salvation of which the Apostle speaks have already flowed over any Judaeo-Gentile controversies that may have existed; and there is something in the Epistle for each and for all, whatever their spiritual past had been.[26]

26. Selwyn, p. 44.

2. LOCATION

The readers are mentioned as residing in "Pontus, Galatia, Cappadocia, Asia, and Bithynia" (1:1). The question has been raised whether these names are to be taken in the sense of Roman provinces or as designations of old geographical areas. If the former meaning is accepted, then all of Asia Minor, except Cilicia, is included in the address of the epistle; if the latter view is adopted, then a lesser area is intended. Zahn points out that not a single old geographical name is mentioned which is not also a Roman province; this indicates that the Roman provincial nomenclature is being employed.[27] The exclusion of Cilicia seems intentional, since the churches in that area were closely related to Syria in origin and supervision. Lycia and Pamphilia were not organized as provinces until the year A.D. 74; they stood in close relation to the province of Galatia.

That all the Christians in these areas were addressed seems clear from 5:14. "You all that are in Christ" naturally includes all believers in that area. That they were organized churches is evident; they are under the care of their elders, they are the flocks of Christ in that region (5:1-3). The epistle is thus an encyclical addressed to the scattered Christian congregations throughout Asia Minor.

3. ORIGIN

As far as the New Testament record goes, these churches owed their origin either directly or indirectly to the instrumentality of the apostle Paul. In Acts we have information about the work of Paul only in the provinces of Galatia and Asia. Yet the record makes it clear that churches were founded far beyond the immediate efforts of Paul. Luke informs us that as the result of Paul's work at Ephesus "all they that dwelt in Asia heard the word of the Lord, both Jews and Greeks" (Ac 19:10). We have no details of the work thus indicated. The Colossian church offers an illustration; it was founded by Epaphras, apparently a convert of Paul's during his Ephesian ministry. In writing to the Corinthians Paul mentions these Asian churches as sending greetings to the Corinthian Christians (1 Co 16:19). Thus apparently Paul had some contacts with them.

We have no record of any work by Paul in the other provinces mentioned. That a considerable number of congregations early

27. Zahn, 2:134.

sprang up in these regions need not surprise us. It was the natural outcome of the self-propagating nature of Christianity. The glowing missionary zeal of the early Christians caused the Good News to spread rapidly.

That Peter himself had visited these churches is entirely probable in itself, but there is no evidence in the New Testament to prove it. The assertion of early Christian writers that Peter visited these churches before going to Rome seems to be merely an inference drawn from this epistle. Selwyn makes the interesting suggestion that on the second missionary journey Paul was forbidden to enter the province of Bithynia (Ac 16:7) because missionary work under the supervision of Peter was already in progress there, thus preventing Paul from building on another man's foundation.[28] The hypothesis is attractive but cannot be proven. Whether these churches were of Pauline or Petrine origin, Peter would see no grounds for any hesitancy in writing to them in their hour of need.

THE OCCASION FOR 1 PETER

The immediate occasion for the writing of 1 Peter was the information received by the apostle that the Christians addressed were beginning to experience sharp opposition and persecution because of their faith (1:6; 3:13-17; 4:12-19). A recent unfavorable change in the situation of the readers had taken place. While there are no hints of actual martyrdom or bloodshed, or even of imprisonment or confiscation of their goods, they were being subjected to a "fiery trial" (4:12). The persecutions were in the form of vile slander and calumnious attacks upon them because they were Christians (4:14-15). They were being hated and suspected because of their withdrawal from the licentious practices and amusements of their pagan neighbors (4:4-5). Apparently there also were charges of disloyalty to the state (2:13-17).

It may be inferred that Peter also had information concerning certain evil tendencies within the churches which needed to be checked. The apostle's warnings may imply that there was a tendency on the part of certain members to yield to the temptation to fall in with the heathen ways of living (2:11-12, 16). The words directed to the elders may also imply a greedy and domineering tendency among

28. Selwyn, p. 45.

them which needed to be corrected (5:2-3). Yet these warnings may have been simply prophylactic in intent.

Aware of the needs of these churches, Peter, in fulfillment of the charge given him by the risen Lord to tend His sheep (Jn 21:15-17), addressed this epistle of exhortation and testimony to the believers in Asia Minor.

THE PLACE AND DATE OF 1 PETER

1. PLACE

The place of composition is indicated in the words of the epilogue, "She that is in Babylon, elect together with you, saluteth you; and so doth Mark my son" (5:13). Much controversy has centered around the meaning of this verse. Three different interpretations have been advanced as to the meaning of "Babylon"; namely, that it means the city by that name in Egypt, or Babylon on the Euphrates, or that it is a cryptic designation for Rome.

A few have held that the reference was to the Babylon in Egypt, located near the present Cairo. It was a military center with a considerable population gathered around it. The Coptic Church has a tradition dating from remote antiquity that this was the Babylon from which Peter wrote. While tradition does connect the name of Mark with Egypt, there is no evidence that Peter even went to Egypt. It seems highly improbable that we should find Peter, Mark, and Silvanus all there at the same time. Besides, if he had written from this Babylon, it seems likely that some word to distinguish it from the other Babylon in Mesopotamia would have been given. Moorehead remarks, "Few beside the Copts of Egypt entertain this view."[29]

The choice lies between the Babylon on the Euphrates and Rome. The former has been the choice of a large number of Protestant scholars.[30] In favor of this view is the natural meaning of the word "Babylon" as a proper place designation. Its sole mention in the epilogue in a matter-of-fact way seems to point to its literal meaning. Advocates of this view feel that the use of such a cryptograph to designate Rome in this epistle seems to be out of harmony with Peter's direct and nonfigurative style.

29. William G. Moorehead, *Outline Studies in the New Testament, Catholic Epistles—James, I and II Peter, I, II, III John, and Jude*, p. 36. An exception among modern scholars is A. F. Klijn, *An Introduction to the New Testament*, pp. 157-58.
30. So Calvin, Bengel, Neander, de Wette, Weiss, Alford, Harman, Bleek, Lange, Fronmüller, Huther, Keil, Wordsworth, Kerr, Caffin, Barnes, Moorehead, Thiessen, and others.

Since Babylon was the chief center of the Jews of the Dispersion, adherents of this view feel that it would only be natural for Peter, the apostle of the circumcision, to make a visit to that city. That there were large numbers of Jews in the region of Babylon is well known, and considerable numbers of Jews with whom Peter might be working may still have resided in the city in spite of the misfortunes of the colony there some twenty years before.

There are, however, serious difficulties to this view. There is the fact that no tradition associates Peter with Babylon. But it must be admitted that tradition is full of blanks. While tradition does associate the name of Thomas with the evangelization of the Parthians, there is no tradition that connects Peter with the East. The early Syrian tradition connects Peter with Rome rather than Babylon. Also the Babylonian view was not advanced until the time of the Reformation, apparently because the old view seemed to favor the papal claims. Calvin's strong party spirit caused him to reject the old view,[31] but Luther maintained the old view lest it would give his bitter enemies a vantage ground in the conflict.

Against the Babylonian view is urged the fact that the early records of Christianity are absolutely silent concerning the existence of a Christian church in Babylon. If there ever was a church there it must have been swept away without leaving a trace of its existence. And the view that there was a large Jewish colony in Babylon to whom Peter might go to preach, it is pointed out, is beset with difficulty. Up to the time of Caligula the Jews formed a large and very influential colony there. But Josephus informs us that in the fifth decade severe misfortunes befell the Jews there. Pestilence and persecution caused them to leave the city of Babylon for Seleucia; and later hostilities caused them to flee from there.[32] Thus, urge the opponents to the Babylonian view, it seems very improbable that there were enough Jews in Babylon at this time for Peter to establish a church among them. But, it is replied, there is no reason to doubt that in the twenty years since that period they had again returned to their old quarters. The Jews were expelled from Rome under Claudius but soon returned in great numbers.

31. In his comment on 5:13 Calvin tartly remarks: "This comment the Papists gladly lay hold on, that Peter may appear to have presided over the Church of Rome: nor does the infamy of the name deter them, provided they can pretend to the title of an apostolic seat." *Commentaries on the Catholic Epistles*, p. 154.
32. Flavius Josephus *Antiquities Of The Jews* 18. 9. 8-9.

The order in which the provinces are named in the salutation (1:1) is sometimes appealed to for evidence. It is generally assumed that the order in which they appear indicates the order in which the messenger would travel with the letter. Under either view the order is difficult, yet the order tells more heavily against the Babylonian view. If Peter was in Babylon, it is difficult to see why Pontus should be mentioned first; the natural thing would have been to begin with Cappadocia, since it was nearest Babylon. If the writer was in Rome, the messenger could easily take a ship to some Pontic seaport and begin the overland journey from there. Yet if the messenger came from Rome the logical place for him to disembark would have been at Ephesus, hence beginning with Asia. Why Pontus heads the list is not obvious.[33]

Proponents of the Roman view are confronted with the problem of the cryptographic designation of Rome. It is urged that such a figurative meaning for "Babylon" was unknown before the writing of Revelation. It is natural to find it in such a symbolical book as Revelation (chaps. 17-18), but would Peter have used it thus? Does not its use in the conclusion of the epistle rather point to a literal interpretation?

Advocates of this view hold that the term is an appropriate metaphorical designation of Rome, the great successor of Babylon as the world center of power and vice. Van Der Heeren thinks that "no other metaphor could so well describe the city of Rome, rich and luxurious as it was, and given over to the worship of false gods and every species of immortality."[34] Indeed, the metaphor may have been in common usage even before the day of Peter. Zahn boldly concludes, "The name did not originate either with Peter or John, both of whom assumed rather that their contemporaries and fellow-believers were familiar with the Babylon of the present."[35]

The entire sentence in which the expression occurs, it is pointed out, has a figurative tone. Certainly Mark was not the literal son of Peter; "my son" must be interpreted spiritually. And the expression, "she that is in Babylon, elect together with you," when occurring in

33. Bigg suggests that the order is due to the fact that the mission contemplated had originated in the Pontic churches, hence it was fitting that the envoy would first go to them (pp. 69-70).
34. A. Van Der Heeren, "Peter, Epistles of Saint," in *The Catholic Encyclopedia,* 11:735*b.*
35. Zahn, 2:178.

a greeting to a series of churches, seems best to be intended as a mystic designation of the Christian community from which the epistle was written. In the original construction a feminine noun, either church or wife, must be supplied. While a number of scholars hold that Peter has reference to his wife, it seems most in harmony with the passage to refer it to a church.[36]

In favor of Rome is the fact that this is the earliest tradition and goes back to the beginning of the second century. Eusebius apparently quotes this as the view of Clement of Alexandria (*c.* 155-215) and Papias (*c.* 80-155) (*Eccl. Hist.* 2. 15). If the epistle was written from Babylon it is difficult to see how the view could have arisen and gained such general acceptance. At that time the exaggerated claims for the Roman church had not yet been advanced.

Admittedly the question is beset with difficulties, yet the preponderance of evidence points to Rome as the place of composition. It is the view maintained by almost all Roman Catholics and by numerous Protestant scholars.[37]

2. DATE

The date of 1 Peter must be some time in the sixties of the first century. That it was written during the latter part of Peter's life is obvious. It cannot have been written after A.D. 68, the year of the death of Nero, since tradition asserts Peter's martyrdom under Nero. The exact date assigned to the epistle will be determined by the interpretation given to the state of affairs portrayed in the epistle. Many scholars, especially impressed with the statement in chapter 4 about the readers being made to "suffer as a Christian" (4:16), hold that it was written after the outbreak of the Neronian persecution in the fall of A.D. 64. Then the date must be given as the very last months of A.D. 64 or later.

More probable to us seems the view that it was written shortly before the actual outbreak of the Neronian persecution. There is no evidence in the epistle that the persecutions have actually resulted in martyrdoms. The sufferings were rather such as were being experienced by Christians generally (5:9). They were being hated and

36. The word *church* is found in Codex Aleph, the Peshito-Syriac, the Vulgate, and the Armenian versions.
37. So Grotius, Whitby, Macknight, Olshausen, Wiesinger, Sieffert, Hengstenberg, Ewald, Schaff, Horne, Davidson, Salmon, Cook, Farrar, Lenski, and others.

maligned because of their stand for Christ (4:16). This hatred was fanned by their refusal to participate in the pagan practices of their neighbors (4:3-4). They were being suspected of being enemies of the state, but there was the hope that by their good conduct this charge could be refuted (3:15-16). If Christianity had already been officially charged with being an enemy of the state, this hope could not have been entertained. But the obvious trend of events made it clear that more ominous things were ahead (4:17-18).

Instead of being due to systematic governmental action, their present sufferings were rather the result of outbursts of fanatical pagan hatred against the Christians. As Zahn points out, shortly before the outbreak of the Neronian massacre in Rome the opinion was "held by the vast majority of the populace that the Christians were a band of dangerous criminals, whose extermination would be for the good of the State and of society."[38] It was this attitude toward the Christians that made it possible for Nero to use them as the scapegoat upon whom he could unload the false charge of incendiarism at Rome. The trial and acquittal of Paul before the imperial court in Rome, terminating his first Roman imprisonment (Ac 28:30; Phil 2:23-24), had established in the thinking of governmental leaders that there was a clear distinction between the church and the Synagogue. Previously the governmental leaders had been prone to regard Christianity as a Jewish sect and had viewed the conflicts between Jews and Christians as intra-Jewish controversies (see Ac 18: 12-17). With the official establishment of that distinction, discerning Christian leaders, aware of the hostile feelings and false charges being made against believers, recognized the rumblings of the coming storm. Peter foresaw the possibility of hate-inspired mob actions and even locally inspired official action against the house of God (4:17-18).

We conclude that the epistle was written on the eve of the outbreak of the Neronian persecution. The date then assigned to it must be in the summer of A.D. 64.

THE PURPOSE OF 1 PETER

The purpose of the epistle is clearly stated in the words, "I have written unto you briefly, exhorting and testifying that this is the true

38. Zahn, 2:185.

grace of God: stand ye fast therein" (5:12). The purpose is thus seen to be twofold, to exhort and to testify.

1. EXHORTATION

The hortatory character of the epistle is its prominent feature. It is almost entirely hortatory. It is not a doctrinal treatise but a powerful appeal to courage, purity, and faithfulness to Christ amid the sufferings which they are experiencing. It is full of that "comfort which only a true Christian, rich in faith and rich in love, can give to the suffering."[39]

The grand doxology, setting forth the glories of our great salvation (1:3-12), which opens the epistle, at once strengthens their faith and brightens their hope. The remainder of the epistle is given over to an elaboration of three grand exhortations. In 1:13—2:10 we have an exhortation to live a life befitting this great salvation, Godward as well as toward the brethren. In 2:11—3:12 he presents an exhortation to submission in view of our position in the world, while 3:13—5:11 gives a powerful exhortation in view of Christian suffering. A brief epilogue closes the epistle (5:12-14).

2. TESTIMONY

Peter's exhortations, earnestly urging them to stand fast in the faith they have received, constitute his testimony to the fact that "this is the true grace of God" (5:12). The epistle assures the readers that they are fundamentally right in spite of the opposition and hatred which they are experiencing. In encouraging them to remain true to their faith Peter makes an incidental but forceful reference to his own experience (5:1).

THE CHARACTERISTICS OF 1 PETER

1. STYLE

The language of the epistle is vivid and energetic yet marked by tenderness and sympathy. His words are forceful but simple and to the point. In the words of Caffin,

> He speaks with the authority of an apostle, but with the gentleness of one who knew the power of temptation and the difficulty of

39. B. C. Caffin, *The First Epistle General of Peter,* The Pulpit Commentary, p. xi.

steadfastness, with the humility of one who well remembered how he himself had fallen.[40]

The epistle reveals a strong character, a man of warm affection and strong assurance of the rightness of his faith.

Being hortatory in nature, the epistle is characterized by the frequent use of the imperative. Tenney points out that, following the opening doxology, Peter uses thirty-four imperatives in the letter (1:13—5:9) and adds, "These numerous imperatives give the epistle a directness and an informality which resembles a preaching style. Peter was speaking from his heart, not writing a formal essay."[41]

2. CONTENT

There is but little of the autobiographical element in the epistle. It contains almost nothing that is merely local or temporary in interest. "There is in his Epistle very little of the subjective side of Christianity. Truth is presented objectively and practically."[42]

The epistle does not manifest that logical development and close sequence of thought which characterize the letters of Paul. The writer rather has a few leading thoughts and these he enforces in different ways with great earnestness and intensity.

Although the air of the epistle is eminently practical, its contents are yet of great theological importance. The magnificent doxology with which the epistle begins sets forth a thrilling view of our great salvation and is full of doctrinal significance (1:3-12). Peter's statement about the means of our redemption, both negatively and positively, has inextricably woven itself into our theological terminology (1:18-19). The exalted conception of the Church in 2:9-10 is set forth in terms which were once applicable only to Israel but terms which the apostle now realizes to have a true fulfillment in the Church of Christ. The statement of 2:24 is important as a doctrinal summary of the significance of the cross. The noted passage in 3:18-22, about Christ preaching "unto the spirits in prison," is one of the most difficult in all Scripture. Almost every word in the passage has received varying interpretations. What is said in the second epistle concerning Paul's epistles would apply to this passage, for certainly it contains "some things hard to be understood" (2 Pe 3:16).

40. Ibid., p. iv.
41. Merrill C. Tenney, *The New Testament, An Historical and Analytic Survey,* pp. 365-66.
42. Herbert L. Willett and James M. Campbell, *The Teachings of the Books,* p. 285.

The epistle is characterized by its close connection with the Old Testament. This is evident not only from its numerous quotations from the Old Testament but also in the language of the epistle as a whole. It is said that proportionately there are more quotations from the Old Testament in 1 Peter than in any other book of the New Testament. The epistle also reveals remarkable affinities in thought and expression with Romans and Ephesians. Yet it bears evidence of sturdy independence and originality. "It exhibits a wealth of thought, a dignity, a fervour, a humility and love, a believing hope, a readiness for the advent of Christ, in exact harmony with the individuality of the Apostle."[43]

The prominent feature of the epistle is its elaboration of the theme of Christian suffering. It contains numerous references to the matter, and various terms are employed to indicate the Christian position. The apostle admonishes the readers to expect suffering (4:12), and he exhorts them not to be troubled by it (3:14) but rather to bear it patiently (3:9), yea, even to rejoice in it (4:13). They are reminded that suffering for Christ is the common lot of all believers (5:9), that suffering may be the will of God for them (4:19), and that it has beneficial results (1:6-7; 2:19-20; 3:14; 4:14). Warning them against suffering as an evildoer (2:20; 4:15), he reminds them of the sufferings of Christ (1:11; 2:21, 23; 4:1). He holds up before them the suffering Christ as the Example to follow (2:2). In their suffering there is the sustaining power of a living hope (1:3-8).

The thought of the future is prominent in the epistle. It is ever before the mind of the writer, both in reference to his readers (1:6-9, 13; 2:2, ASV; 4:13; 5:10) and to himself (5:1). As the sufferings of Christ pointed to His coming glory (1:9), so the possession of a living and sure hope (1:3, 13) inspire the follower of Christ worthily to live out his redemption in a hostile world. But it is a hope that rests not on man but on the living God, who raised up Christ from the dead and gave Him glory, so that our faith and hope might be in Him (1:21). Amid the sorrows and sufferings of this present world the believer is sustained by the assurance that he has awaiting him at the end of life's journey "an inheritance incorruptible, and undefiled, and that fadeth not away" (1:4).

43. Fronmüller, p. 6.

AN OUTLINE OF 1 PETER

I. The Introduction, 1:1-12

A. The salutation, vv. 1-2

B. The thanksgiving for our great salvation, vv. 3-12

1. The description of this salvation, vv. 3-5

   a) The source of the salvation, v. 3*a*

   b) The explanation of the salvation, v. 3*b*

   c) The nature of the salvation, vv. 3*c*-4

   d) The certainty of the salvation, v. 5

2. The experiences with this salvation, vv. 6-9

   a) The contrasting nature of the experiences, vv. 6-7

   b) The sustaining power amid the experience of trials, vv. 8-9

3. The magnification of this salvation, vv. 10-12

   a) The magnification by prophetic search, vv. 10-12*a*

   b) The magnification by apostolic proclamation, v. 12*b*

   c) The magnification by angelic inquiry, v. 12*c*

II. Exhortations in View of Our Salvation, 1:13—2:10

A. The life arising out of this salvation, 1:13—2:3

1. The life of the saved in relation to God, 1:13-21

   a) A life sober in hope, v. 13

   b) A life holy in conduct, vv. 14-16

   c) A life reverent in attitude, vv. 17-21

      (1) The basis for reverence, v. 17*a*

      (2) The call for reverence, 17*b*

      (3) The motivation for reverence, vv. 18-21

2. The life of the saved in relation to the brethren, 1:22-25

   a) The experience of purification, v. 22*a*

   b) The call to mutual love, v. 22*b*

   c) The new birth as the basis for brother-love, vv. 23-25

3. The life of the saved in relation to personal growth, 2:1-3

   a) The hindrances to personal growth, v. 1

   b) The call to spiritual growth, v. 2

   c) The argument for spiritual growth, v. 3

B. The reasons for such a life of the saved, 2:4-10

1. Because of the work of God with believers, vv. 4-8

    a) The believer's approach to Christ, v. 4
    b) The character and function of believers, v. 5
    c) The character and effect of Christ the cornerstone, vv. 6-8
   2. Because of the nature of believers, vv. 9-10

III. Exhortations in View of Our Position in the World, 2:11–3:12
  A. The appeal for appropriate individual conduct, 2:11-12
  B. The duty of submission to the state, 2:13-17
    1. The statement of the duty of submission, v. 13*a*
    2. The scope of the duty of submission, vv. 13*b*-14
    3. The motivation for submission, v. 15
    4. The character of those submitting, v. 16
    5. The sphere of well-doing, v. 17.
  C. The duty of submission in household relations, 2:18-25
    1. The statement of the duty of submission, v. 18
    2. The reasons for submissive suffering, vv. 19-21
      a) The acceptableness with God of suffering for conscience' sake, vv. 19-20
      b) The challenge from the example of Christ's suffering, v. 21
    3. The elaboration of the example of Christ, vv. 22-25
      a) His exemplary sufferings, vv. 22-23
      b) His vicarious death, vv. 24-25
  D. The duty of believers in marital relations, 3:1-7
    1. The submission of the wives, vv. 1-6
      a) The statement of the duty, v. 1*a*
      b) The purpose in the submission of the wife, vv. 1*b*-2
      c) The adornment of the submissive wife, vv. 3-4
      d) The examples of godly submission, vv. 5-6a
      e) The outcome of the submission, v. 6*b*
    2. The obligation of the husband, v. 7
  E. The appeal for becoming corporate conduct, 3:8-12
    1. The description of the desired conduct, vv. 8-9
    2. The enforcement of the conduct from Scripture, vv. 10-12

IV. Exhortations in View of Christian Suffering, 3:13–5:11
  A. The experience of suffering for righteousness, 3:13-17
    1. The unnaturalness of suffering for doing good, v. 13

2. The blessedness of suffering for righteousness, v. 14*a*
3. The reaction to suffering for righteousness, vv. 14*b*-16
4. The assurance amid suffering for well-doing, v. 17

B. The example of Christ as suffering for righteousness, 3:18-22
 1. The character of His suffering, v. 18*a*
 2. The consequences of His suffering, vv. 18*b*-21
 3. The culmination of His sufferings, v. 22

C. The equipment for suffering as Christians, 4:1-11
 1. The necessary equipment in view of present suffering, vv. 1-6
  a) The call to be equipped with the proper attitude, vv. 1-2
  b) The motivation for being properly equipped, vv. 3-6
   (1) The motivation from past sinfulness, v. 3
   (2) The motivation from present opposition, v. 4
   (3) The motivation from future judgment, vv. 5-6
 2. The necessary conduct in view of the end, vv. 7-11
  a) The motivation from the impending end, v. 7*a*
  b) The description of the necessary conduct in view of the end, vv. 7*b*-11*a*
   (1) The description of personal conduct, v. 7*b*
   (2) The description of social conduct, vv. 8-11*a*
  c) The purpose of such conduct, v. 11*b*

D. The need for steadfastness in Christian suffering, 4:12-19
 1. The necessary attitude toward Christian suffering, vv. 12-13
 2. The evaluation of Christian suffering, v. 14
 3. The causes for suffering, vv. 15-16
  a) The causes for suffering excluded for believers, v. 15
  b) The cause for suffering approved for believers, v. 16
 4. The judgment of God exercised in suffering, vv. 17-18
 5. The exhortation to Christian sufferers, v. 19

E. The appeals to the church in view of Christian suffering, 5:1-11
 1. The appeal to the elders, vv. 1-4
  a) The person making the appeal, v. 1
  b) The duties of the elders, v. 2*a*
  c) The motives for the work of the elders, vv. 2*b*-3
  d) The reward of the work of the elders, v. 4
 2. The appeals to all church members, vv. 5-9
  a) The appeal for humility, vv. 5-6

    b) The appeal for trustfulness, v. 7
    c) The appeal for watchfulness, vv. 8-9
  3. The final encouragement amid suffering, vv. 10-11
    a) The glorious promise to Christian sufferers, v. 10
    b) The concluding doxology, v. 11

V. The Conclusion, 5:12-14

  A. The indication of the messenger, v. 12*a*
  B. The characterization of the message, v. 12*b*
  C. The concluding greetings, vv. 13-14*a*
  D. The benediction of peace, v. 14*b*

A BOOK LIST ON 1 PETER

Barclay, William. *The Letters of James and Peter.* 2d ed. The Daily
Study Bible. Philadelphia: Westminster, 1960.
    Prints the author's own translation. Barclay defends Petrine au-
    thorship of 1 Peter but not of 2 Peter. Valuable for its numerous
    helpful word studies and background material. Barclay holds that
    Christ's descent into Hades gave those who there heard Him a sec-
    ond chance.
Beare, Francis Wright. *The First Epistle of Peter.* 3d rev. ed. Ox-
ford: Blackwell, 1970.
    Greek text. An important critical commentary by a noted liberal
    scholar. Rejecting Petrine authorship, Beare dates the epistle A.D.
    111-12. Contains a thorough bibliography on 1 Peter. Important
    for the discerning student.
Best, Ernest. *I Peter.* New Century Bible. London: Oliphants, 1971.
    A scholarly study by a leading New Testament scholar, based upon
    a careful examination of the original text. Best denies Petrine au-
    thorship. Presents the theme of the letter as encouragement to Chris-
    tians undergoing persecution. Liberal in its theology.
Bigg, Charles. *A Critical and Exegetical Commentary on the Epistles
of St. Peter and St. Jude.* 2d ed. International Critical Commentary. Edinburgh: T. & T. Clark, 1902.
    Greek text. Lengthy and informative introductions, setting out
    the ancient testimony to each of these epistles. Bigg holds that Peter
    cannot have written 1 Peter directly but worker through an aman-
    uenisis. He is favorable to the traditional authorship of 2 Peter and

Jude. A most thorough and rewarding commentary on the Greek text.

Brown, John. *Expository Discourses on the First Epistle of the Apostle Peter.* 3 vols. Marshallton, Del.: National Foundation for Christian Education, n.d.

Prints author's own translation. An exhaustive exposition by a conservative interpreter which has stood the test of time. Important for the expositor of 1 Peter.

Clark, Gordon H. *Peter Speaks Today. A Devotional Commentary on First Peter.* Philadelphia: Presby. & Ref., 1967.

A devotional and practical commentary by a well-known conservative American scholar. Clark deals with the passages into which the letter is divided not only in relationship to the immediate context and the epistle as a whole but in the light of the entire Bible. There are frequent detours to show the unity of the biblical message and to set forth its doctrinal message.

Cranfield, C. E. B. *The First Epistle of Peter.* London: SCM, 1950.

A brief, critical exposition defending Petrine authorship as aided by Silvanus and dating the epistle at A.D. 63-64. Reflects interaction with recent critical views.

English, E. Schuyler. *The Life and Letters of Saint Peter.* New York: Publication Office "Our Hope," 1941.

The first half treats the high points of Peter's life, while the second half gives a devotional running exposition of his epistles. A warm treatment of these epistles by a well-known evangelical Bible teacher.

Ferrin, Howard W. *Strengthen Thy Brethren.* Grand Rapids: Zondervan, 1942.

A popular, devotional exposition of 1 Peter by a conservative Bible teacher. Contains many apt illustrations.

Fronmüller, G. F. C. "The Epistles General of Peter." In *Lange's Commentary on Holy Scripture.* Translated from the German with additions by J. Isidor Mombert. Reprint. Grand Rapids: Zondervan, n.d.

A careful interpretation of these epistles with a mass of material of a practical and homiletical nature.

Hart, J. H. A. "The First Epistle General of Peter." In *The Expositor's Greek Testament,* vol. 5. Reprint. Grand Rapids: Eerdmans, n.d.

Greek text. A technical commentary providing grammatical information and important word studies. Often cites rabbinic sources. Defends Petrine authorship and dates the letter at A.D. 64.

Hunter, Archibald M.; and Homrighausen, Elmer G. "The First Epistle of Peter." In *The Interpreter's Bible*, vol. 12. New York: Abingdon, 1957.

> Introduction and exegesis by Hunter, exposition by Homrighausen. A significant liberal exposition. Defends Petrine authorship and date the letter A.D. 62-64.

Jowett, John Henry. *The Epistles of St. Peter*. Grand Rapids: Kregel, 1904; reprint, 1970. Also reprinted under the title, *The Redeemed Family of God.*

> A series of twenty-nine sermons eloquently expounding the Petrine epistles section by section. A practical and devotional exposition; critical problems are not dealt with.

Kelly, J. N. D. *A Commentary on the Epistles of Peter and of Jude*. Harper's New Testament Commentaries. New York: Harper & Row, 1969.

> A scholarly, critical commentary. Prints the author's own translation. Kelly accepts Peter's connection, directly or indirectly, with the first epistle but rejects Petrine authorship for the second. Frequently refers to the Qumran literature and to early Christian writers. A critical work fully cognizant of recent critical theories.

Kelly, William. *The Epistles of Peter*. Reprint. London: Hammond, n.d.

> Two volumes in one. The wordy exposition of a leading Plymouth Brethren scholar of the past century. Contains clear reflections of the doctrinal and ecclesiastical views of his circle. The difficulties of these epistles are dealt with in a clear and conservative manner. The author's death terminated the exposition of the second epistle at 3:7.

Leighton, Robert. *A Practical Commentary upon the First Epistle General of Peter*. Reprint. Grand Rapids: Kregel, 1972.

> A warmly devotional commentary by an Anglican bishop of a past century. While often quoting from the early Church fathers, the eloquent bishop provides his readers with the results of his vast learning in a very readable form. A thorough, conservative exposition.

Lenski, R. C. H. *The Interpretation of the Epistles of St. Peter, St. John and St. Jude*. Columbus, Ohio: Lutheran Book Concern, 1938.

Prints the author's own literal translation. A masterly exposition of these epistles by an accomplished, conservative Lutheran scholar. Richly rewarding for careful interpretation of these letters.

Lumby, J. Rawson. "The Epistles of St. Peter," in *The Expositor's Bible*, vol. 6. Reprint. Grand Rapids: Eerdmans, 1943.

A full exposition by a conservative scholar of the past century; rich in homiletical usefulness.

Masterman, J. Howard B. *The First Epistle of S. Peter (Greek Text).* London: Macmillan, 1900.

A reverent exposition by a conservative Anglican professor. The volume concludes with additional notes on difficult passages.

Moffatt, James. *The General Epistles—James, Peter, and Judas.* The Moffatt New Testament Commentary. Reprint. London: Hodder & Stoughton, 1947.

Nieboer, J. *Practical Exposition of I Peter Verse by Verse.* Erie, Pa.: Our Daily Walk, n.d.

A practical, heartwarming, devotional exposition by an American Plymouth Brethren minister. Abounds in apt illustrations and applications.

Plumptre, E. H. *The General Epistles of St. Peter and St. Jude.* Cambridge Bible for Schools and Colleges. Cambridge: U. Press, 1893.

A valuable commentary on these epistles for the lay student by a conservative British scholar of the past century. Important introductions and concise notes on the text.

Rees, Paul S. *Triumphant in Trouble. Studies in I Peter.* Westwood, N.J.: Revell, 1962.

A homiletical treatment of 1 Peter presenting an articulate interpretation of the privileges, practices, and perils of the Christian life. The stimulating work of a conservative Christian leader. Uses numerous apt illustrations and quotations from a wide variety of sources.

Reicke, Bo. *The Epistles of James, Peter, and Jude.* The Anchor Bible. Garden City, N.Y.: Doubleday, 1964.

Selwyn, Edward Gordon. *The First Epistle of St. Peter.* London: Macmillan, 1949.

Greek text. A brilliant, exhaustive work on this epistle. Supports Petrine authorship with extensive influence on the epistle by Silvanus. Indispensable for the advanced student. Three-fourths of the volume is given over to the introduction and additional notes and essays.

Stibbs, Alan M. *The First Epistle General of Peter.* Tyndale New Testament Commentaries. Introduction by Andrew F. Walls. Grand Rapids: Eerdmans, 1959.

The introduction by Walls is a masterly survey of the critical problems, offering conservative conclusions. The commentary by Stibbs offers a careful and accurate, evangelical interpretation of the epistle. Both men are leaders in the Anglican church.

Wand, J. W. C. *The General Epistles of St. Peter and St. Jude.* Westminster Commentaries. London: Methuen, 1934.

Accepts Petrine authorship with the collaboration of Silvanus. Wand holds that Christ descended to Hades, and His preaching gave the spirits in prison a "fresh opportunity of salvation." The general theological viewpoint is Arminian.

Williams, Nathaniel Marshman. "Commentary on the Epistles of Peter." In *An American Commentary on the New Testament.* 1888. Reprint. Philadelphia: Amer. Bap. Pubn. Soc., n.d.

Quite full but concisely written; a rewarding exposition by a conservative Baptist scholar of the past century.

Woods, Guy N. *A Commentary on the New Testament Epistles of Peter, John, and Jude.* Nashville, Tenn.: Gospel Advocate, 1954.

A readable, conservative interpretation by a "Campbellite" scholar.

Wuest, Kenneth S. *First Peter in the Greek New Testament for the English Reader.* Grand Rapids: Eerdmans, 1942.

Offers a simplified commentary on the Greek text for the benefit of the English reader by means of exegetical comments, word studies, and an expanded translation.

6

SECOND PETER

An Introduction to 2 Peter

EACH OF THE PETRINE EPISTLES presents its own timely message. In 1 Peter the emphasis is on Christian suffering inflicted by a hostile world; in 2 Peter the stress is on the dangers arising from apostasy within the Church. The first is an exhortation to endurance and loyalty to Christ amid undeserved opposition; the second is an appeal for loyalty to Christ in the midst of subtle heresy. First Peter instructs believers how to react to their external enemies, while the second epistle strengthens believers to resist the internal adversaries of the truth. The first inculcates hope amid suffering, the second accentuates the need of full knowledge as the safeguard against vicious error. Thus the pertinent message of 1 Peter to persecuted believers is supplemented by the equally apt warning against prevalent apostasy in 2 Peter.

The Authenticity of 2 Peter

1. DIFFICULT PROBLEM

The conservative's acceptance of the authenticity of 2 Peter is admittedly beset with serious difficulties, both external and internal. Farrar remarks,

> Common honesty compels us to acknowledge that of all the books of the New Testament it is the one for which we can produce the smallest amount of external evidence, and which at the same time offers the greatest number of internal difficulties.[1]

Second Peter was regarded with doubts in many sections of the early Church. Questions concerning its authenticity were again raised

1. F. W. Farrar, *The Early Days of Christianity*, p. 99.

during the time of the Reformation, and in modern times many otherwise quite conservative critics are either noncommittal or feel that
they must join forces with the negative critics in the rejection of the
Petrine authorship of the epistle. It is fair to say that 2 Peter has
been the most controverted book in the New Testament. Yet the
objections to it are not so conclusive as to silence those who defend
its authenticity.

2. EXTERNAL EVIDENCE

The external evidence for the epistle is meager. In considering this
evidence it will be desirable to begin with the time when the epistle
became fixed as canonical and go backwards.

Toward the close of the *fourth* century the epistle was acknowledged as canonical by the Council of Laodicea (363)[2] and the Third
Council of Carthage (397). But even then it was rejected by the
Syrian Church, where apparently it was not accepted until the sixth
century. Jerome (340-420) admitted it into the Vulgate, but he recorded doubts concerning it, doubts which he based on the difference
in style between the two Petrine epistles. Yet it is evident that
Jerome is only expressing the feelings of the scholars rather than the
general opinion of the members in the Church. In his famous *Ecclesiastical History*, which appeared around A.D. 324, Eusebius of
Caesarea (c. 265-340), recorded his doubts concerning 2 Peter when
he wrote:

> As to the writings of Peter, one of his epistles called the first, is
> acknowledged as genuine. For this was anciently used by the ancient
> fathers in their writings, as an undoubted work of the apostle. But
> that which is called the second, we have not indeed understood to
> be embodied with the sacred books, yet as it appeared useful to
> many, it was studiously read with the other Scriptures (3. 3).

He classified 2 Peter among the disputed books (3. 25), but did not
stamp it as spurious, and he refrained from classifying it with the
extracanonical Petrine literature (*Gospel, Acts,* and *Apocalypse of
Peter*). From his reference to the "many" who accepted 2 Peter, it is
evident that the majority in the Church in his day accepted it as

2. The council requested that only the "canonical" books be read in the churches,
but the 60th Canon giving the list of the N.T. books is doubtless unauthentic.
Cf. Westcott, *A General Survey of the History of the Canon of the New Testament,*
pp. 400-407.

authentic. Evidently the doubts of Eusebius, like those of Jerome, are the doubts of the learned scholars. His doubts concerning 2 Peter arose from two sources: 1) the writers whose opinion he respected regarded it as uncanonical; 2) the older writers, as far as he had consulted their works, did not quote the epistle.

No references to 2 Peter are found in the voluminous writings of Chrysostom (347-407). Theodore of Mopsuestia (*c.* 350-428) rejected it along with the rest of the catholic epistles. It was received as Peter's by the following writers of the fourth century: Athanasius of Alexandria (298-373); Epiphanius, bishop of Cyprus (315-403); Ambrose, bishop of Milan (340-97); Cyril of Jerusalem (315-86); Hillary of Piotiers in Gaul (*c.* 300-367); Gregory of Nazianzus (330-90); Basil the Great (329-79); and Augustine (354-430). Harman observes, "This Epistle obtained a very general recognition among the writers of the fourth century, although they made little use of it."[3]

From the evidence of the fourth century it is seen that although doubts still lingered, it was widely accepted as authentic and apparently won its place by the intrinsic merits of its contents in spite of the scholarly doubts concerning its authorship. Significant is the fact that the councils of Hippo and Carthage recognized it as canonical, although these councils rejected the *Epistle of Barnabas* and *1 Clement*, both of which had a long history of being read in the churches alongside Scripture.

In the *third* century no mention of the epistle is found in the writings of Tertullian (150-222), Dionysius of Alexandria (200-265), or Cyprian (200-258). Near the end of the century Methodius, bishop of Lycis, explicitly quotes 2 Peter 3:8. In A.D. 256 Firmilian, bishop of Caesarea in Cappadocia, in writing to Cyprian *(Epistle 75)*, says that Peter had execrated heretics and warned against them. This can only refer to 2 Peter, since 1 Peter contains no such reference. Plummer cites this as "the first *certain* reference to the Epistle as by St. Peter."[4]

The testimony of Origen (185-253) is somewhat ambiguous. He is the first one to distinguish the two epistles ascribed to Peter. In his *Commentary On John* (5. 3), he says,

3. Henry M. Harman, *Introduction to the Study of the Holy Scriptures*, p. 737.
4. Alfred Plummer, "The Second Epistle General of Peter," in *Ellicott's Commentary on the Whole Bible*, 8:438a.

And Peter, on whom the Church of Christ is built, against which the gates of hell shall not prevail, left only one epistle of acknowledged genuineness. Suppose we allow that he left a second; for this is doubtful.[5]

Origen gave no indication as to the reasons for the doubt concerning the second epistle. Bigg observes, "He says nothing about the style of 2 Peter, though he was a keen critic, as may be seen from his remarks on the Epistle to the Hebrews (Eus. *H.E.* VI. 25. 11)."[6] Yet in the Latin translation of his works by Rufinus, there are several passages where Origen expressly quotes 2 Peter without indicating any doubt. Some have questioned the authenticity of these passages as translated by Rufinus.[7] On this point Salmon asserts,

> On examination of the passages, it does not seem to me likely that Rufinus could have invented them; and I believe the truth to be, that Origen in popular addresses did not think it necessary to speak with scientific accuracy. It is implied in this solution that Peter's authorship was the popular belief of Origen's time.[8]

Origen's acquaintance with 2 Peter suggests that his teacher, Clement of Alexandria (155-215), also knew it. There are, however, no references to it in his extant writings. But Eusebius says that in the *Hypotyposes* Clement gave us "abridged accounts of all canonical Scriptures, not even omitting those that are disputed, I mean the book of Jude, and the other general epistles" (*Eccl. Hist.* 6. 14). This would include 2 Peter. In spite of the conflicting testimony of Cassiodorus, given about three hundred years later, it is generally agreed that Clement knew and accepted 2 Peter as authentic.

There is evidence that an earlier ancestor of Codex B did not contain 2 Peter. This conclusion seems certain from the fact that this manuscript uses two systems of divisions of sections, one older than the other, but the older is missing for 2 Peter, although preserved in the rest of the catholic epistles. But it should be noted that 2 Peter was included in the two great Egyptian versions of the third century, the *Bohairic*, probably originating in the first half of the century, and

5. Also quoted by Eusebius *Ecclesiastical History* 6:25.
6. Charles Bigg, *A Critical and Exegetical Commentary on the Epistles of St. Peter and St. Jude*, International Critical Commentary, p. 201.
7. F. H. Chase, "Peter, Second Epistle of," in Hastings *Dictionary of the Bible*, 3:803b.
8. George Salmon, *An Historical Introduction to the Study of the Books of the New Testament*, p. 485.

the *Sahidic,* apparently going back to the very beginning of the century.[9] In the recently discovered Papyrus 72, of the third century, 2 Peter is accepted as canonical along with 1 Peter and Jude. And the variant text types embodied in this manuscript indicate that the use of these epistles in Egypt extended back over a considerable period.

The evidence of the third century shows that although there was widespread doubts as to its authenticity, there was a general willingness to respect its contents. Although mentioned with questions, Peter's is the only name connected with it.

No extant writings from the *second* century makes any express quotations from 2 Peter. It was not contained in the Old Syrian Version (*c.* 200), nor does it appear to have been in the Old Latin Version (before 170). It is not mentioned in the Muratorian Canon (*c.* 170), but this is incomplete and also does not list 1 Peter although it undoubtedly was accepted in the West. Some have sought to prove allusions to 2 Peter in Irenaeus (140-203), the *Epistle of Barnabas* (*c.* 130), Justin Martyr (100-165), *The Shepherd* of Hermas (*c.* 140), Ignatius (d. 116), and Polycarp (*c.* 69-155). But others, like Chase, have demonstrated the weakness of the asserted allusions. The evidence that use of 2 Peter was made by these writers is vague and inconclusive. Two second-century Gnostic works, the *Gospel of Truth* and the *Apocryphon of John,* recently recovered in Egypt, contain probable quotations from or allusions to 2 Peter, thus showing that already in the second century this epistle was regarded as an authoritative book.[10]

The most important piece of evidence for the use of 2 Peter in the second century is found in the *Apocalypse of Peter,* which Harnack dated as probably 120-40. It contains some striking coincidences with 2 Peter. It is agreed that these coincidences are more than accidental. Scholars like Bigg[11] and Strachan[12] conclude that the *Apocalypse* is dependent upon 2 Peter, rather than vice versa.

The evidence of the second century is quite indefinite and neither proves nor disproves the early existence or authenticity of 2 Peter.

9. Henry Clarence Thiessen, *Introduction to the New Testament,* pp. 56-57.
10. Chase, pp. 799*a*-807*a*. A. Helmbold, *The Nag Hammadi Gnostic Texts and the Bible,* pp. 90-91.
11. Bigg, pp. 207-9.
12. R. H. Strachan, "The Second Epistle General of Peter," in *The Expositor's Greek Testament,* 5:88-90.

The scant evidence makes no mention of the Petrine authorship of the epistle. Salmon summarizes it as follows:

> With regard to second-century testimony, the maintainers and the opponents of the genuineness of the Epistle make it a drawn battle. There is no case of quotation so certain as to constrain the acknowl-edgment of an opponent; but there are probable instances of the use of the Epistle in sufficient numbers to invalidate any argument against the Epistle drawn from the silence of early writers.[13]

As the earliest and most important piece of evidence, taking us into the *first* century, we would point to the epistle of Jude. It is the earliest and strongest attestation of 2 Peter.[14] The force of this posi-tion is dependent upon the view that 2 Peter is prior to Jude. (On the priority of 2 Peter see introduction to Jude.)

The external evidence for 2 Peter, when compared with that for 1 Peter, shows that the second epistle had a much narrower circula-tion than the first, and that it came much more slowly into general recognition than the former. The evidence for the Petrine authorship of 2 Peter increases in volume and definiteness in inverse proportion to the lapse of time. The evidence must be recognized for what it is.

If 2 Peter was written by Peter as it claims, how are we to account for this meager evidence? The fact that it was not expressly quoted during the first two centuries does not necessarily disprove its exis-tence or even the knowledge of it. Why the epistle did not come into earlier recognition if it was written by Peter cannot be demonstrated. But several considerations may be advanced. The nature and short-ness of the epistle may help to account for the lack of quotations from it. For as Bigg says, "It contains very few quotable phrases. It is probably very seldom quoted even in the present day."[15] Many re-ligious books are written today which do not quote or even imply the existence of the epistle.

The silence in the Syrian church concerning 2 Peter may have been intentional, since Jude was also omitted. Green observes, "Jude explicitly, and 2 Peter implicitly, quote the apocryphal *Assumption of Moses*. The Gnostics were notorious for their misuse for sectarian purposes of *haggadah* of this sort, and it is precisely in Syria, where

13. Salmon, p. 489.
14. So Bigg, p. 210; Theodor Zahn, *Introduction to the New Testament*, 2:285.
15. Bigg, p. 211.

the extravangances of Jewish angelology were most notorious, that one would naturally expect to find the most violent reaction against anything that might be adduced in their support."[16]

The slowness with which the epistle, for some reason, came into general circulation would account for the suspicions concerning it. The numerous pieces of pseudonymous Petrine literature, which began at an early date, and flooded the Church during the second and third century, would make the appearance of an epistle by Peter be regarded with suspicion. Every passing year which delayed a general knowledge concerning the epistle would make its acceptance as authentic more difficult.

Plumptre makes the suggestion that the false teachers condemned in the epistle would make an effort to discredit and suppress it as far as lay in their power. He thinks that it would not be strange if their expressions of doubts concerning it should "gain a certain degree of currency and be reproduced even by those who had not the same motive for suggesting them." Harrison further suggests that the scanty notices of 2 Peter during the early centuries may be due to the fact that as a general epistle, "No single congregation was committed to preserving it and making it more widely known."[17]

3. INTERNAL EVIDENCE

The claim to Petrine authorship is stronger in this epistle than in 1 Peter. The writer calls himself Simon Peter (1:1) and identifies himself as a witness of the transfiguration (1:16-18). He places himself on a level with the apostle Paul (3:15), identifies himself as the writer of a previous epistle (3:1), and recalls the Lord's prediction concerning his death (1:14). Yet the contents of the epistle are strongly appealed to by the critics to deny its authenticity. The epistle itself, it is said, reveals that it was written by some second-century imitator of Peter.

The writer tries too hard, it is held, to make himself appear to be Peter. In undoubtedly genuine epistles, it is said, the reference to the reputed author is confined to the address and his personality is not unduly obtruded. But this writer, instead of bringing in incidental

16. E. M. B. Green, *2 Peter Reconsidered*, p. 7.
17. E. H. Plumptre, *The General Epistles of St. Peter and St. Jude,* Cambridge Bible for Schools and Colleges, p. 81. Everett F. Harrison, *Introduction to the New Testament,* p. 415.

memories of the life and words of Jesus, goes out of his way to bring in the story of the transfiguration and the Lord's prophecy concerning his death. The double use of the name in the salutation (1:1) betrays an anxiety to identify himself with the apostle; the apostle would simply have written Peter as he did in the previous epistle.

It may be replied that a writer who wished to assume the personality of Peter would not have aroused suspicion by so obviously departing as he does from his model in 1 Peter. In professing to write to the same people it is unlikely that an imitator would have failed to use the old form of address and have adopted instead the present vague designation. The assertion that the references to the writer's relations to Jesus are foisted in is a matter of personal impression on the part of the critics. Such personal references are quite in accord with Peter's personality. When brought before the Sanhedrin, Peter boldly asserted his personal knowledge of the great Gospel facts (Ac 4:20). The same characteristic is seen in his speech at the Jerusalem Conference (Ac 15:7-11). The reference to the transfiguration (1:17-18) comes in naturally, suggested by the course of thought in the letter. And the delicate way in which the reference to the death of Peter is introduced does not point to a later forgery. In fact, this argument really does not furnish proof either for or against the authenticity of the epistle. As Salmon says,

> In the present case we must own that a forger, no doubt, would be likely to take pains to make the Petrine authorship plain, but it would be absurd to deny that Peter himself might also leave on his work plain traces of his authorship.[18]

It is held that if the epistle were by Peter we should expect to find in it more allusions to words or facts which are found in the gospels, especially since 1 Peter contains a number of such references. But again this argument cuts both ways. As Bigg points out,

> If it is difficult to understand why St. Peter does not quote the words of our Lord, it is far more difficult to explain why a forger, late in the second century, does not. The apostles, as all their letters show, did not feel bound to be constantly quoting. This habit begins with St. Clement of Rome.[19]

18. Salmon, pp. 490-91.
19. Bigg, p. 231.

Yet in 2:20 the author does seem to have an unconscious adoption of Christ's words in Matthew 12:45, Luke 11:26. Compare also 3:10 with Matthew 24:43.

In 3:2 reference is made to "your apostles" (ASV), and in 3:4 mention is made of the death of the "fathers." In these references, it is held, the author betrays the fact that he belongs to a later generation when the apostles were no longer alive. But these passages do not require such an interpretation. From 1:1 it is seen that the writer included himself among the apostles and he might well speak of "your apostles" since all of them were sent for the benefit of Christ's Church. And it is quite natural that as a true apostle the writer "would sink his own personality in the group of his colleagues from a feeling of humility and of delicacy towards those whom he was addressing, especially when they owed their Christianity mainly to other Apostles than himself."[20] Furthermore, as Plummer points out, "the expression 'our beloved brother Paul,' so unlike the way in which Clement of Rome, Ignatius, Polycarp, and Clement of Alexandria speak of St. Paul, is a strong mark of an Apostolic author—a writer of the second century would scarcely find his way back to this."[21]

The reference to the "fathers" who have died may have reference to those Christian leaders who had already died before the writing of the letter by Peter. But it is not even certain that by "fathers" the writer meant Christians at all. The expression may simply mean our past ancestors. But we can accept the view that the reference is to Christians. As a forward-looking prophecy it tells what the scoffers will say, as viewed from their time. While the passage might have a good background in the second century it is not a proof that it did not have a good setting as a prediction of the future in Peter's day.

It is maintained that the skepticism concerning the Lord's return (3:3-4) points to "a time when through long delay the hope of the Second Coming had grown faint."[22] But it is quite groundless to think that this problem did not arise in the first century. From 1 Thessalonians it is clear that the delay in the expected return of the Lord caused deep anxiety and discussion. As Bigg reminds us,

This doubt would arise over the grave of the first Christian; we have

20. Plummer, 8:458*a*.
21. Ibid., p. 440*b*.
22. Arthur S. Peake, *A Critical Introduction to the New Testament*, p. 98.

an interesting and most pathetic case in point in the anguish of Irving over the loss of his son, who was taken away before the dawn of that millennium which the father thought to be so near.[23]

To be sure, in 2 Peter the denial is supported by the argument from the unchanging continuity of the cosmic system. But that this spirit already prevailed in the first century is proved from the fact that Clement of Rome in his *Epistle to the Corinthians* in A.D. 96 censures those who say, "These things we have heard even in the time of our fathers; but, behold, we have grown old, and none of them has happened unto us" (chap. 23).

It is contended that the phrase "the holy mount" (1:18) is a kind of phrase that a later age would use in describing the transfiguration scene, and that it is a very different thing from the simple phrase "a high mountain" in Mark 9:2. But surely this is a straining after argument by one already convinced that the epistle is pseudonymous. How long must Peter be allowed to think about the marvelous transfiguration scene before he would speak of it as a "holy" mount? The epithet "holy" does not indicate a later miracle-loving age. Any Jew would use the term to describe the spot where God had revealed Himself in a special way (cf. Ex 3:5; Jos 5:15). We all speak of the scene of a profound spiritual experience as a hallowed spot.

The claim of Edwin Abbott (*Expositor*, January 1882) that 2 Peter is dependent on Josephus need not detain us. Salmon has sufficiently refuted this assertion.[24] The similarities that exist do not prove that 2 Peter used Josephus.

It is thought that the reference in 1:14 to Jesus' prophecy about Peter's death was drawn from John 21:18-19, and since John was not written until after the death of Peter, the epistle cannot be by Peter. If other indications required a second-century date, such a conclusion would be valid, but the reference does not prove the conclusion. If Jesus said what John records Him as saying, why could not Peter to whom the words were originally addressed have made the statement independently of what John later wrote? The approaching storms of persecution would naturally remind Peter of this prophecy. The passing statement is very natural if written by Peter, but its simplicity is unlike that of a later writer.

23. Bigg, p. 240.
24. Salmon, pp. 496-508.

It has been maintained that the picture of the false teachers condemned in the epistle points to a date later than Peter. It would be a mistake to assume that the epistle presupposes the fullblown Gnosticism of the second century. The picture of the heretics is not specific enough to allow definite historical identification. That similar heresies existed during Peter's lifetime is shown by Colossians and the pastoral epistles. The absence of any reference in the epistle to the more developed heresies of the second century points rather to an early date. Bigg confidently concludes that "every feature in the description of the false teachers and mockers is to be found in the apostolic age."[25]

Of greater weight is the argument drawn from the similarity between 2 Peter and Jude which asserts that 2 Peter copied from Jude. The close connection between the two epistles is obvious. But the argument is based on the uncertain assumption of the priority of Jude. If 2 Peter copied from Jude and *if* Jude wrote after the death of Peter, then 2 Peter cannot be by Peter. But both *if* clauses are open to question. We hold that the balance of probability is decidedly in favor of the priority of 2 Peter.[26]

Adeney contends that "in defending the genuineness of 2 Peter we accuse the great apostle Peter of plagiarising in a remarkable way."[27] This assumes the priority of Jude. But accepting, as we do, that Jude is an inspired work, why should it be thought a discredit to Peter to quote from another inspired writing? Similar examples of dependence of sacred writers on each other may be seen in Scripture. Compare Isaiah 2:1-4 with Micah 4:1-3; Psalm 18 and 2 Samuel 22; 2 Chronicles 36:22-23 with Ezra 1:1-3; the well-known parallels in the synoptic gospels. Salmon expresses himself on the matter as follows:

> Since an Apostle's letters were not prompted by vanity of authorship, but by anxiety to impress certain lessons on his readers, I do not see why he should have thought himself bound to abstain from using the words of another, if they seemed to him most likely to make the impression he desired.[28]

25. Bigg, p. 239.
26. See the introduction to Jude.
27. W. H. Bennett and Walter F. Adeney, *A Biblical Introduction,* p. 449.
28. Salmon, p. 493.

With regard to the mention of Paul's epistles in 3:15-16 Moffatt asserts, "This allusion to a collection of Pauline epistles is an anachronism which forms an indubitable water-mark of the second century."[29] The argument is that the reference shows that the epistles of Paul already formed a collection and that they had already been the object of considerable misinterpretation. It cannot be conceived that Peter would refer to Paul's letters as Scripture.

The phrase "in all his epistles" (3:16) does not tell us how many epistles the writer had in mind; it says nothing about a definite collection of those epistles which were regarded as canonical. That Peter did know several of the Pauline epistles seems evident from 1 Peter. Bigg feels that it is very probable that the apostles kept in close touch with what each taught or wrote. He even goes so far as to suggest that Peter may well have gotten "every epistle that circulated in the Church within a month or two of its publication."[30] That the epistles of Paul were early collected is quite probable. The letters of Cicero were kept together; why not those of Paul?

The fact that the Pauline epistles had already been the subject of much misinterpretation does not demand a second-century date. Such misinterpretations occurred almost immediately. In fact Paul found it necessary to correct a misinterpretation of a former letter when writing 1 Corinthians (1 Co 5:9-11). Romans 3:8 reveals the fact of willful perversion of his teaching. Paul early found it necessary to safeguard the teaching of his epistles against forgers by the use of his own signature as the sign of their authenticity (2 Th 2:2; 3:17; 1 Co 16:21; Gal 6:11). Surely it is not necessary to wait until the second century to find malicious and ignorant distortions of his epistles.

The impression that the passage reflects a second-century setting is offset by the writer's use of the intimate phrase, "our beloved brother Paul" (3:15). He regards Paul as a respected contemporary, not a venerated saint of a past age. The expression is quite unlike the references to Paul in second-century writers. The fact that the writer refers to the epistles of Paul as Scripture does not conclusively prove that he lived in the second century. Would Peter, who acknowledged the divine call and work in Paul (Gal 2:6-9), refuse to recog-

29. James Moffatt, *An Introduction to the Literature of the New Testament*, pp. 363-64.
30. Bigg, p. 241.

nize the writings of Paul as inspired? Paul repeatedly asserted his own inspiration (1 Co 2:13; 14:37; 1 Th 2:13). In 1 Timothy 5:18 Paul applies the term "scripture" to words which could be a quotation from Luke 10:7. Why, then, should it be thought impossible that Peter could speak of Paul's epistles as Scripture? From the very first Paul's letters were read in the churches, side by side with Moses and the prophets (cf. 1 Th 5:27; Col 4:16). That they were highly venerated and closely scrutinized is certain. Accepting the divine commission of the apostles, the early Christians would have little difficulty in accepting as inspired the epistles of the apostles. Plummer comments,

> The high authority claimed by Apostles for their own words makes this passage, although unique in the New Testament, quite intelligible. (Comp. Acts 15:28; I Cor. 5:3, 4; I Thess. 2:13). Perhaps the nearest parallel is I Peter 1:12, where evangelists are placed on the same level with the Old Testament prophets, a very remarkable coincidence between the two Epistles.[31]

The critics who do not believe in the inspiration of these epistles feel that such an evaluation of them can only be postapostolic. Cartledge remarks, "Radical criticism needs time to account for the evolution of a belief in inspiration for books that it does not consider inspired. Conservative criticism has no such gap to bridge."[32]

Critics have relied heavily upon the fact of the difference in style between the two epistles ascribed to Peter. That they do reveal differences in style and thought has long been recognized, as seen from the comment of Jerome. Yet the differences are not as vast as is sometimes made out. To the fact of the differences must be added the fact that there are definite similarities between the two epistles.

In regard to the difference between the two epistles, Robertson says, "The most outstanding difference between 1 Peter and 2 Peter is in the vocabulary."[33] Bigg counts 361 words in 1 Peter not in 2 Peter, while 2 Peter has 231 not in 1 Peter.[34] This is indeed a remarkable situation. But the truly remarkable fact is, as Ebright points out, that both epistles have a vocabulary differing much from

31. Plummer, 8:440.
32. Samuel A. Cartledge, *A Conservative Introduction to the New Testament*, pp. 143-44.
33. A. T. Robertson, *A Grammar of the Greek New Testament in the Light of Historical Research*, p. 125.
34. Bigg, p. 225.

the rest of the New Testament. "There are seven times as many rare
words in 1 Peter as in the New Testament taken as a whole, and ten
times as many in 2 Peter. . . . The noticeable difference therefore, is
not between the two Petrine epistles, but between these epistles and
the rest of the New Testament."[35] And add to this the fact of the
definite similarities in the two epistles. Thus Robertson says,

> Both use the plural of abstract nouns; both have the habit, like James,
> of repeating words, while Jude avoids repetitions; both make idio-
> matic use of the article; both make scant use of particles, and there
> are very few Hebraisms; both use words only known from the ver-
> nacular koine; both use a number of classical words . . . both use
> picture-words; both seem to know the Apocrypha; both refer to
> events in the life of Christ; both show acquaintance with Paul's
> Epistles, and use many technical Christian terms.[36]

Yet there are differences in the epistles.. First Peter is generally
smooth Greek while 2 Peter has a certain roughness of style and is
more labored and awkward Greek. The language phenomenon in
these epistles leads Robertson to remark, "As Peter was full of im-
pulses and emotions and apparent inconsistencies, the same heritage
falls to his Epistles."[37]

Attempts to make a comparative evaluation of the style of the two
epistles have resulted in conflicting pronouncements. Thus Bleek
concluded, "The language of the first epistle is somewhat rough and
Hebraizing, while that of the second is more elegant and better
Greek; the style of the second is more periodic, while in the first the
connection of sentences is simple, and even clumsy."[38] But Adeney,
with whom most scholars would agree, says, "The style of I Peter is
excellent; that of II Peter most awkward."[39] Obviously judges differ in
their evaluations of style and taste. To attempt to determine authorship solely on the basis of style is always precarious.[40] A man's style

35. Homer Kingsley Ebright, *The Petrine Epistles, A Critical Study of Authorship,*
    p. 121.
36. Robertson, p. 126.
37. Ibid., p. 125.
38. Friedrich Bleek, *An Introduction to the New Testament,* 2:179-80.
39. Bennett and Adeney, p. 449.
40. "Mark Twain once resolved to write a serious book, so he wrote 'Personal Recol-
    lections of Joan of Arc,' and had Harpers publish it anonymously, and for two
    years he kept all the greatest scholars of the world guessing but no one ever
    dreamed of attributing it to Mark Twain, not even his closest friends—it was not
    Mark Twain's style. Just so it was when Spurgeon published 'John Ploughman's
    Talks.'" T. J. McCrossan, *Jesus Christ as a Higher Critic,* p. 11.

varies with his mood, his subject, his purpose, and his sources. Gloag quotes Reuss, who on other grounds rejects the epistle, as saying,

> We lay no stress on the linguistic differences between the two Epistles which modern criticism has so much emphasized. The two Epistles are too short, have to do with wholly different circumstances, and there are no direct contradictions to be found. Only when the spuriousness has been proved on other grounds may this point be taken into account.[41]

This difference in style between the two epistles may perhaps be satisfactorily acounted for by the assumption of Peter's use of an amanuensis for 1 Peter. Scholars are generally inclined to the view that Silvanus had a hand in the shaping of the language of 1 Peter, but 2 Peter may well be Peter's own writing, since no mention is made of a scribe in it.

A weighty argument in favor of the authenticity of 2 Peter is its acknowledged superiority to all other known pseudonymous writings. Although Farrar rejects the direct Petrine authorship of 2 Peter, he well remarks,

> Who will venture to assert that any Apostolic Father—that Clement of Rome, or Ignatius, or Polycarp, or Hermas, or Justin Martyr, could have written so much as twenty consecutive verses so eloquent and so powerful as those of the Second Epistle of St. Peter?[42]

Fronmüller maintains that the denial of the Petrine authorship presents us with "an insoluble psychological riddle." He asks,

> Is it possible that a man animated through and through with the spirit of Christianity, who expressly renounces all cunning fabrications, should have set up for the Apostle Peter, and have written this Epistle in his name? Intentional fraud and such illumination—who is able to reconcile them?[43]

All must admit that the moral tone and impact of the epistle are entirely consistent with its claim to apostolic authorship. We must agree with the dictum, "Its inspiration if tested by its moral value stands unquestioned."[44]

---

41. Paton J. Gloag, *Introduction to the Catholic Epistles*, p. 216.
42. Farrar, p. 115.
43. G. F. C. Fronmüller, "The Second Epistle General of Peter," in Lange's *Commentary on the Holy Scriptures*, p. 5.
44. Herbert L. Willett and James M. Campbell, *The Teachings of the Books*, p. 286.

4. CONCLUSION

The external evidence, adverse though it is to any categorical claim to apostolic authorship, is not conclusive. The evidence from the first two centuries is very weak and offers no direct support for the traditional authorship. But its authoritative reception in the fourth century, after full doubt and debate, lends favorable support to that position. The internal evidence makes a strong claim to Petrine authorship, yet the features of the epistle have given rise to strongly diverse opinions. It is but natural that diverse conclusions have been reached. Three positions have been assumed on the question of the authorship of 2 Peter.

There are those who reject the claims of the epistle and ascribe it to some unknown writer in the second century (usually around A.D. 150) who cleverly sought to gain acceptance for his work under the name of Peter. Consistency in such a view requires the assumption that

> The real author of any such work had to keep himself altogether out of sight, and its entry upon circulation had to be surrounded with a certain mystery, in order that the strangeness of its appearance at a more or less considerable interval after the putative author's death might be concealed.[45]

Such a position assumes a certain amount of misrepresentation on the part of its real author. These critics may decry the application of the term "forgery" to such a production. But regardless of the ethical standards of the age, if there was intention to deceive, it is inconsistent with the lofty ethical demands of Christianity. Such a work is best termed a "pious fraud" and merits no place in the New Testament canon. The contents and the lasting impact of 2 Peter make highly improbable such an evaluation of it.

Others, influenced by the fact of its meager external attestation, as well as the difficulties of the internal evidence, hold that Peter is not the author *directly*, but that it was apparently written by an associate or disciple of Peter in his name, perhaps even after his death. This view, first broached by Jerome, was adopted by Calvin,[46] and in mod-

---

45. Quoted with approval from Dr. V. H. Stanton, *Journal of Theological Studies,* 2:19 by Moffatt, *The General Epistles—James, Peter, and Judas,* The Moffatt New Testament Commentary, p. 174.
46. John Calvin, *Commentaries on the Catholic Epistles,* pp. 363-64.

ern times has found the support of a few scholars, such as Farrar, W. H. Simcox, and Selwyn.

Thus Michaels suggests that 2 Peter should be regarded as the testament of Peter and that it was composed of "genuine Petrine material put together in testamentary form by one or more of the apostle's followers after his death."[47] As a compromise this view is not improbable, yet it fails to do full justice to the explicit claim of Petrine authorship.

The conservative position is that the Petrine authorship is not without rational explanation, and that it furnishes the best and least confusing solution to the difficult problem. This view receives at face value the claims of the epistle and eliminates all implications of deception in the personal references in the epistle. We accept this as the best working solution. We concur in the conclusion of Ebright:

> When we discover an epistle which has the dignity and originality and high ethical character of II Peter, in which are no anachronisms that the most searching investigation can discover, and in which are found no absurd miracles or foolish legends or heretical teaching contrary to the spirit and character of Peter, but in which there are touches that remind one of the fiery apostle described in the Acts and the Gospels, and in the very body of which there are claims of Petrine authorship, and which commended itself in the course of years to the general body of Christians when tested in the crucible of experience, then it is a fair conclusion that we have here a genuine message of the Apostle-Preacher Peter, and the world of the twentieth century can profit greatly by heeding his threefold message.[48]

THE UNITY OF 2 PETER

A few critics who have been much influenced by the claims for a late origin and yet are unwilling to admit that the epistle is pseudonymous, have resorted to the hypothesis that the present epistle contains interpolated material. In view of the absence of any evidence, internal or external, for such a claim, such a proposal is always a last desperate resort. The interpolation hypothesis can show no support from any manuscript, version, or early writer of any kind. The internal evidence is equally against it. "The thought is emi-

47. Glenn W. Barker, William L. Lane, J. Ramsey Michaels, *The New Testament Speaks*, p. 352.
48. Ebright, p. 149.

nently consecutive throughout, the style is uniform, and the writer frequently glances back at what he has said before or anticipates what is coming."[49] Further, the lack of any agreement among the critics where the supposed interpolations begin or end is strongly against the advocates of such disintegration of the epistle. Some argue that only the second chapter is an interpolation from Jude. Others think the interpolation extends from 1:20 to 3:3. Others think only the first chapter is authentic, while another would retain only the first eleven verses and the doxology. The epistle shows a definite logical unity as it stands and there is no warrant for such attempts to expurgate the epistle. The author's twofold purpose of warning and exhortation runs through the whole and gives it unity and coherence.

THE READERS OF 2 PETER

The readers of this epistle are nowhere expressly designated. The statement in 1:1 is quite general: "To them that have obtained a like precious faith with us." In 3:1 a further indication is given of the readers in the words, "This is now, beloved, the second epistle that I write unto you; and in both of them I stir up your sincere mind by putting you in remembrance." The Greek is literally, "This is already a second epistle I am writing to you," thus implying that the second came soon after the first.

This latter reference has commonly been accepted to mean that this epistle was addressed to the same churches as 1 Peter. Yet the general way in which the readers are addressed in 1:1 seems to indicate that Peter did not have them exclusively in mind. The reason for this Caffin conceives to be as follows:

> The dangers to be apprehended from the false teachers threatened other Churches beside those of Asia Minor; therefore the apostle gives his letter a more general character, probably intending it for a wider circulation.[50]

The contents of the epistle are such that they would be readily applicable to believers generally.

The view is advanced by a few scholars that 2 Peter 3:1 cannot refer to the letter we know as 1 Peter. It is held that 2 Peter was really written before our 1 Peter and that the reference is to a lost

49. Plummer, 8:437*a*.
50. B. C. Caffin, *The Second Epistle General of Peter*, The Pulpit Commentary, p. xiv.

letter by Peter. It is asserted that the implied character of the letter mentioned in 3:1 does not correspond to the nature of our 1 Peter. Thus Dana holds that this lost letter was "a reminder; that is, of the same general nature as 2 Peter, a message of instruction and correction. First Peter is a message of exhortation and comfort."[51] It is quite true that 1 Peter does not contain the very words found in 2 Peter 3:1-7, yet it does contain the substance, and that is all that is necessary. He says that in both epistles he is *stirring up their minds,* and certainly 1 Peter has this hortatory character.

Zahn holds that the readers were Jewish Christians in Palestine and Syria won through the ministry of Peter and others of the twelve.[52] But in describing his readers as those who "have obtained a like precious faith with us" (1:1) the natural implication is that they were Gentile Christians in distinction from himself and other Jewish Christians. But in the Petrine epistles this distinction between Jewish and Gentile Christians is not pressed. No conclusive proof concerning the background of the readers can be drawn from the designation. If 2 Peter was not primarily intended for the churches of Asia Minor, then we have no information concerning the location of the readers.

THE OCCASION FOR 2 PETER

The occasion for the writing of 2 Peter apparently was the information conveyed to the apostle of an outbreak of heresy among the churches addressed. After he had written 1 Peter, intended to strengthen them amid their sufferings from without, he learned that an even more serious danger had arisen in the presence of heretical teachers within the bounds of the churches. It was this latter danger that called forth this epistle.

A general view of the character of these false teachers may be gathered from the epistle. They denied the Lord that bought them (2:1), were daring and irreverent (2:10*b*, 12), and scoffed at the promise of the Lord's return (3:3-4). They lived immoral lives (2:13), seduced unstable souls (2:14, 18), and by their influence caused the way of truth to be evil spoken of (2:2). They made great promises of liberty to their followers but were themselves the slaves of sin (2:19). They were characterized by insubordination to estab-

51. H. E. Dana, *Jewish Christianity*, p. 160.
52. Zahn, 2:207-9.

lished authority (2:10c, 12). It is apparent that these false teachers were already at work in certain places (2:11-12, 17, 18, 20; 3:5, 16), but with prophetic insight Peter saw that the evil would become much more widely operative (2:1-2; 3:3).

This false teaching was characterized by antinomianism with its resultant immoral tendencies. It was marked by immortality, irreverence, and insubordination. Zahn thinks that they were men who were twisting the Pauline doctrine of justification by faith to their own harm.[53] And Bigg regards them as men given to immoral disorder similar to those Paul rebuked at Corinth, who were now spreading over the churches of Asia Minor.[54] Others think that the error was more than simple antinomianism and that it was some form of incipient Gnosticism. Thus Strachan says, with reference to 2 Peter and Jude,

> In these Epistles it can scarcely be doubted that we are in the presence of an incipient Gnosticism, and the two directions in which the Gnostic tendency led, *viz.* Intellectualism and Antinomianism, are clearly marked.[55]

But the error faced in this epistle is not a systematic philosophical error, and historical identification of it cannot be made.

The Date and Place of 2 Peter

1. DATE

Those who deny the Petrine authorship generally place the epistle in the middle of the second century. But in accepting the Petrine authorship we cannot date it later than A.D. 68, the year of Nero's death. If it was written after 1 Peter, as we believe, it must be placed as near the end of Peter's life as possible. But the year of Peter's martyrdom is uncertain. Some would place his death shortly after the outbreak of the Neronian persecution, in the latter part of A.D. 64. Others feel that it may be as late as A.D. 67 or even 68. It would seem, however, that Peter met his fate before Paul. When Paul wrote 2 Timothy, Peter could no longer have been in Rome. Apparently Peter's execution had already taken place. We may accordingly date 2 Peter in the early part of the year A.D. 65.

53. Ibid., p. 228.
54. Bigg, pp. 237-39, 316.
55. Strachan, 5:116.

2. PLACE

No hint of the place of composition is given in the epistle. If 1 Peter was written from Rome, as seems probable, it seems natural to conclude that 2 Peter was also written from there. Those who hold to Babylon as the place from which 1 Peter was written generally hold that this epistle was written on the way to Rome or even in Rome.

THE PURPOSE OF 2 PETER

While the aim of the epistle is not directly declared, it is evident that the last two verses summarize the twofold purpose which runs through the whole.

One phase of his purpose is *warning*—"Beware lest, being carried away with the error of the wicked, ye fall from your own steadfastness" (3:17). His desire is to put them on their guard against the false teachers so that they will not be misled by these lawless ones. The warning against their moral perversions (chap. 2) is followed by admonitory instructions concerning the skeptical denial of the Lord's return (chap. 3).

The other phase of his purpose is *exhortation*—"But grow in the grace and knowledge of our Lord and Saviour Jesus Christ" (3:18). Their ability to resist these errors will best be insured by their personal growth in grace and Christian knowledge. Their steady growth will assure them an abundant entrance into the eternal Kingdom (1:11). In chapter one he seeks to promote this growth by reminding them that the Christian life is a matter of personal growth, founded upon a reliable foundation. The epistle is a hortatory memorial to the truth in which they are already established (1:12).

THE CHARACTERISTICS OF 2 PETER

The keynote of 2 Peter is knowledge. A prominent place is given to it. The words *know* or *knowledge,* in their varied forms, occur sixteen times in the epistle. Six times the intensive form, signifying *full knowledge,* is used.[56] In view of this emphasis Robertson remarks,

I call the Second Epistle of Peter the True Christian Science (knowl-

---

56. The Greek words and their occurrences are as follows: *oida* occurs in 1:12, 14; 2:9; *ginōskō* in 1:20; 3:3; *gnōsis* in 1:5-6; 3:18; *gnōrizō* in 1:16; *proginōskō* in 3:17; *epiginōskō* in 2:21 twice; and *epignōsis* in 1:2-3, 8; 2:20.

edge) in contrast with the false so-called Christian Science of the Gnostics and of Mrs. Eddy whose "Christian Science" is neither "science" (knowledge) nor Christian.[57]

This emphasis upon true knowledge is very timely today. It is the Christian's safeguard against all heresies. The believer today, confronted with a multiplicity of heretical cults, urgently needs this knowledge.

> Christians should know the truth and the whole truth; they should be able to detect error, and recognize the times in which they live; they should know the dangerous world that surrounds them and that ever seeks to poison their minds, debase their affections, neutralize their testimony, and paralyze their faith.[58]

This knowledge springs out of a living faith in Christ and the promises of God (1:2-4), is characterized by continuing growth and development (1:5-11), and is anchored in the certainty of the apostolic testimony and the divine inspiration of the prophetic revelation (1:16-21).

The primary doctrinal contribution of 2 Peter is its statement about the origin of prophecy (1:20-21). Its origin, negatively and positively, assures the inspiration and entire trustworthiness of Scripture. The passage unites with 2 Timothy 3:16 in setting forth the origin and nature of the Holy Scriptures.

A remarkable feature of this epistle is Peter's passage about the three worlds in 3:5-13. Here Peter divides history into three vast cosmic epochs and indicates something of the characteristics of each. There was the antediluvian world, the world destroyed by the Flood (vv. 5-6); there is the present cosmic system, "the heavens that now are, and the earth" (v. 7), which will come to a fiery apocalyptic consummation; then there is the future order, the "new heavens and a new earth" (v. 13) wherein righteousness shall be at home. In the light of our own atomic era this prophetic passage in 2 Peter has suddenly taken on striking relevance. Until well within the twentieth century the skeptics continued to say, "All things continue as they were from the beginning of the creation" (3:4). But with the bursting of the atomic age it is becoming frightfully evident that

57. A. T. Robertson, *Epochs in the Life of Simon Peter*, p. 297.
58. William G. Moorehead, *Outline Studies in the New Testament, Catholic Epistles—James, I and II Peter, I, II, III John, and Jude*, p. 73.

Peter's picture of the destruction of this present world system by means of a universal conflagration is not just an impossible fantasy but offers evidence that gives a sober picture of prophetic revelation.

AN OUTLINE OF 2 PETER

I. The Salutation, 1:1-2

II. The Nature of the Christian Life, 1:3-21
   A. The impartation of divine life, vv. 3-4
   B. The growth in the Christian life, vv. 5-11
      1. The stages of growth, vv. 5-7
      2. The incentives to growth, vv. 8-9
      3. The exhortation to effort, v. 10*a*
      4. The results of growth, vv. 10*b*-11
   C. The authoritative ground for the Christian life, vv. 12-21
      1. The personal concern of the apostle, vv. 12-15
         a) His determined purpose, v. 12*a*
         b) His commendation of them, v. 12*b*
         c) His motivation, vv. 13-14
         d) His provision, v. 15
      2. The objective certainty of Christian truth, vv. 16-21
         a) The apostolic testimony concerning Christ, vv. 16-18
         b) The character of the prophetic revelation, vv. 19-21

III. The Warning Against False Teachers, 2:1-22
   A. The prediction concerning the false teachers, vv. 1-3
      1. The character of these false teachers, v. 1
      2. The success of these false teachers, vv. 2-3*a*
      3. The doom of the false teachers, v. 3*b*
   B. The examples of divine judgment, vv. 4-10*a*
      1. The examples of divine judgment in the past, vv. 4-8
         a) The example of the fallen angels, v. 4.
         b) The example of the antediluvian world, v. 5
         c) The example of the cities of the plain, vv. 6-8
      2. The conclusion concerning future judgment, vv. 9-10*a*
         a) The conclusion as to the godly, v. 9*a*
         b) The conclusion as to the ungodly, vv. 9*b*-10*a*

C. The description of these false teachers, vv. 10*b*-22
1. The graphic picture of the false teachers, vv. 10*b*-17
2. The seductive influence of the false teachers, vv. 18-19
3. The tragic status of the false teachers, vv. 20-22

IV. The Certainty of Christ's Return, 3:1-18*a*

A. The denial of Christ's return, vv. 1-7
1. The purpose of the apostle in writing, vv. 1-2
2. The denial of Christ's return by the mockers, vv. 3-4
3. The fallacy of the mockers, vv. 5-7
   a) The past judgment by water, vv. 5-6
   b) The future judgment by fire, v. 7
B. The correct view concerning Christ's return, vv. 8-13
1. The true explanation of the delay, vv. 8-9
2. The coming of the day of the Lord, v. 10
3. The Christian life in view of the future, vv. 11-12*a*
4. The results in the coming day, vv. 12*b*-13
C. The exhortations in view of the future hope, vv. 14:18*a*
1. The exhortation to maintain personal purity, v. 14
2. The exhortation to a reverent attitude to Scripture, vv. 15-16
3. The exhortation to beware of falling, v. 17
4. The exhortation to continued growth, v. 18*a*

V. The Doxology, 3:18*b*

A Book List on 2 Peter

Barclay, William. *The Letters of James and Peter.* 2d ed. The Daily Study Bible. Philadelphia: Westminster, 1960.

Barnett, Albert E.; and Homrighausen, Elmer G. "The Second Epistle of Peter." In *The Interpreter's Bible*, vol. 12. New York: Abingdon, 1957.
> An interpretation of 2 Peter from the liberal position. Introduction and exegesis by Barnett, exposition by Homrighausen. While holding that the epistle is not from the actual hand or immediate dictation of Peter, it is accepted as Petrine in character and spirit.

Bigg, Charles. *A Critical and Exegetical Commentary on the Epistles of St. Peter and St. Jude.* 2d ed. International Critical Commentary. Edinburgh: T. & T. Clark, 1902.

Blair, J. Allen. *Living Faithfully.* New York: Loizeaux, 1961.
A devotional study of 2 Peter by a noted evangelical Bible teacher.
Clark, Gordon H. *II Peter. A Short Commentary.* Nutley, N.J.:
Presby. & Ref., 1972.
A vigorous, conservative interpretation with emphasis upon the
grammar and theology of the epistle. Strong Calvinistic emphasis.
The treatment is not always verse by verse but a summary of the
teaching.
English, E. Schuyler. *The Life and Letters of Saint Peter.* New York:
Publication Office "Our Hope," 1941.
Fronmüller, G. F. C. "The Epistles General of Peter." In Lange's
Commentary on Holy Scripture. Translated from the German with
additions by J. Isidor Mombert. Reprint. Grand Rapids: Zondervan, n.d.
Green, E. M. B. *2 Peter Reconsidered.* London: Tyndale, 1961.
———. *The Second Epistle General of Peter and the General Epistle
of Jude.* Tyndale New Testament Commentaries. Grand Rapids:
Eerdmans, 1968.
An outstanding, conservative interpretation of these epistles by a
leading evangelical scholar in England. The forty-page introduction
handles critical problems with rare ability. The unfolding of the text
of the epistles is based on a detailed exegesis and able applications
of the teaching to the present time.
Jowett, John Henry. *The Epistles of St. Peter.* 1904. Reprint. Grand
Rapids: Kregel, 1970.
Kelly, J. N. D. *A Commentary on the Epistles of Peter and of Jude.*
Harper's New Testament Commentaries. New York: Harper &
Row, 1969.
Kelly, William. *The Epistles of Peter.* Reprint. London: C. A. Ham-
mond, n.d.
Lenski, R. C. H. *The Interpretation of the Epistles of St. Peter, St.
John and St. Jude.* Columbus, Ohio: Lutheran Book Concern,
1938.
Lumby, J. Rawson. "The Epistles of St. Peter," in *The Expositor's
Bible,* vol. 6. Reprint. Grand Rapids: Eerdmans, 1943.
Mayor, J. B. *The Epistle of St. Jude and the Second Epistle of St.
Peter.* London: Macmillan, 1907.
This massive volume contains an unsurpassed accumulation of

details concerning these two epistles, setting forth parallels to the
language from all Greek literature. The work of a painstaking liberal
scholar, the volume is a mine of information for the diligent, discerning student.

Moffatt, James. *The General Epistles—James, Peter, and Judas.*
Moffatt New Testament Commentary. Reprint. London: Hodder
& Stoughton, 1947.

Nieboer, J. *Practical Exposition of II Peter Verse by Verse.* Erie, Pa.:
Our Daily Walk Publishers, 1952.

> A companion volume to Niebor's work on 1 Peter, adhering to the
> same pattern.

Plumptre, E. H. *The General Epistles of St. Peter and St. Jude.* Cambridge Bible for Schools and Colleges. Cambridge: U. Press, 1893.

Reicke, Bo. *The Epistles of James, Peter and Jude.* The Anchor Bible.
Garden City, N.Y.: Doubleday, 1964.

Strachan, R. H. "The Second Epistle General of Peter." In *The Expositor's Greek Testament,* vol. 5. Reprint. Grand Rapids: Eerdmans, n.d.

> Greek text. Rejects Petrine authorship and dates the epistle A.D.
> 100-115. The brief comments on the Greek text are technical and
> most helpful to the advanced student.

Wand, J. W. C. *The General Epistles of St. Peter and St. Jude.*
Westminster Commentaries. London: Methuen, 1934.

Williams, Nathaniel Marshman. "Commentary on the Epistles of
Peter." In *An American Commentary.* 1888. Reprint. Philadelphia: Amer. Bapt. Pubn. Soc., n.d.

Woods, Guy N. *A Commentary on the New Testament Epistles of
Peter, John, and Jude.* Nashville, Tenn.: Gospel Advocate, 1954.

Wuest, Kenneth S. *In These Last Days. II Peter, I, II, III John, and
Jude in the Greek New Testament for the English Reader.* Grand
Rapids: Eerdmans, 1954.

> A simplified commentary on the Greek text for the benefit of the
> English reader by means of exegetical comments, word studies, and
> an expanded translation.

7

JUDE

An Introduction to Jude

THE VIGOROUS LITTLE EPISTLE of Jude is without a parallel in the New Testament for its vehement denunciation of libertines and apostates. While displaying affectionate concern for true believers, it burns with fiery indignation and vivid pronouncements of judgment upon religious sensualists. Standing, as it does in our English Bibles, just before the book of Revelation, it forms a fitting introduction to the concluding book of the New Testament.

The Authenticity of Jude

1. EXTERNAL EVIDENCE

In view of its brevity and the polemical character of its contents, the impression that the epistle of Jude made on the early Church is indeed remarkable. It has stronger attestation than 2 Peter.

Some supposed early allusions to Jude in Polycarp (*c.* 69-155), *The Shepherd* of Hermas (*c.* 140), *The Epistle of Barnabas* (*c.* 130), and Clement of Rome (*c.* 30-100) are too vague and uncertain to be insisted on. Zahn thinks that there is evidence that the *Didachē* (*c.* 120) used Jude 22-23.[1] Chase also thinks that in it some tangible signs of the influence of Jude may be traced.[2] Athenagoras (*c.* 177) in his *Plea For The Christians* (chap. 24) speaks of the fallen angels in a manner which suggests acquaintance with Jude 6. Theophilus of Antioch (d. 180) seems to refer to Jude 13 when he speaks of the planets as a type of fallen man, since the figure occurs only in Jude (*To Autolycus* 2. 15).

The epistle of Jude was included in the Muratorian Canon (*c.* 170)

1. Theodor Zahn, *Introduction to the New Testament*, 2:259.
2. F. H. Chase, "Jude, Epistle of," in Hastings *Dictionary of the Bible*, 2:799b.

This may be taken as representative of the opinion of the Western Church soon after the middle of the second century. Although direct proof is lacking, it seems to have been in the Old Latin version (before 170). Tertullian of Carthage (150-222) spoke of the apostle Jude as the author of the epistle, termed it Scripture, and argued that its quotation from *Enoch* upheld the authority of that book (*On The Apparel Of Women* 1. 3). His language implies that Jude was an acknowledged part of the canon in North Africa.

Clement of Alexandria (155-215) several times quotes Jude in his works. And Eusebius informs us that Clement in his work called *Hypotyposes* made "abridged accounts of all the canonical Scriptures, not even omitting those that are disputed, I mean the book of Jude, and the other general epistles" (*Ecc. Hist.* 6. 14). Origen (185-253) quite frequently quotes Jude in his works and seems to have set a high value on it. Thus in his *Commentary on Matthew* he remarks, "And Jude, who wrote a letter of few lines, it is true, but filled with the healthful words of heavenly grace, said in the preface, 'Jude, the servant of Jesus Christ and the brother of James'" (10. 17). Origen himself had no doubts concerning the epistle, yet he knew that there were doubts concerning it.

The most serious item in the external evidence against the epistle is the fact that it is absent from the Old Syriac version (*c.* 200). There are a few quotations from Jude in the Latin translations of Ephraem the Syrian, the most distinguished name in the Syrian church in the fourth century. But there is little or no evidence of its use in the Asiatic churches before that time. It was excluded from the canon drawn up by Lucian of Antioch (d. 312). Nor is there any mention of it in all the writings of Chrysostom (347-407).

Eusebius (265-340) in his *Ecclesiastical History* classified Jude among the *Antilegomena* (2. 23) and remarks, "Among the disputed books although they are well known and approved by many, is reputed that called the Epistle of James, and that of Jude" (3. 25). His reason for classifying Jude as disputed was the fact that few of the ancient writers had mentioned the epistle, although he admitted that some of them had done so and that it was regarded as genuine by very many in the Church.

Concerning Jude, Jerome (340-420) wrote, "He left a short Epistle, which is one of the seven Catholic Epistles. And because testimony from the apocryphal Book of Enoch is used in it, it is rejected by very many persons; nevertheless, it has acquired authority by antiquity and use, and is reckoned among the sacred Scriptures" (*Cat. Script. Eccles.*, chap. 4). Didymus (d. 398), head of the Catechetical School at Alexandria, commented on Jude and defended its authority against those who rejected it because of its quotations from apocryphal books.

The external evidence shows that the epistle of Jude quite early won acceptance in the Western Church, being known in Italy, North Africa, and Egypt by the middle of the second century. But the Syrian churches long rejected it. It was little known there until the fourth century.

The shortness of the epistle and the nature of its contents may well account for the silence of many about it. The available evidence shows that there was little, if any, question concerning the authorship of the epistle. The doubts were rather concerning its canonicity. Did the author have the required authority for a canonical book? Did the quotations from apocryphal books invalidate its canonical status?

The epistle won a recognized place in the canon in the face of these questions. It was recognized as canonical by the Councils of Laodicea (363) and Carthage (397). The pronouncements of these councils were universally accepted in the churches. There was an awareness of the difficulties concerning it, yet the evidence for its canonicity, after full and ample testing, was considered to be adequate.

2. INTERNAL EVIDENCE

The epistle claims to be written by "Jude, a servant of Jesus Christ, and brother of James" (1:1). In verse 17 the author seems to distinguish himself from the apostles. The fact that the writer takes this humble position tells heavily for its authenticity. If the epistle was a forgery of the second century, the forger would doubtless have chosen the name of some person of greater fame and authority in the Church than the asserted writer of this epistle.

The epistle, however, has been seriously controverted on the basis of internal evidence. The critics contend that certain features within the epistle unmistakably point to a time outside the possible lifetime of the Jude to whom the epistle is traditionally ascribed.

It is held that the appeal to contend for "the faith" (v. 3) points to a creedal development in Christianity later than the first century. That Jude does have in mind an objective, divinely delivered faith which must be preserved is clear, but the statement does not necessitate a formalized creed. The "faith" is simply the body of Christian belief to which true Christians adhere as divinely given and authoritative. Paul has this objective use of the word "faith" in the pastorals, and even as early as Galatians (cf. Gal 1:23; 3:23). Compare also Acts 6:7.

It is asserted that the allusion to "the apostles of our Lord Jesus Christ" (v. 17) betrays the writer as belonging to a later time. Thus Scott holds that "the 'Apostles of the Lord' are mentioned reverently as men of a former age who had foretold what is happening now (17-18)."[3] Certainly this reference to the teaching of the apostles is spoken of as past, but it is supposed to be in the memory of the readers not as a mere tradition but what they had heard themselves. While Jude does thereby distinguish himself from the apostles he does not thereby place himself in a later generation. There is nothing in the expresison to prove that the writer considered himself considerably removed in time from the apostles.

It has been maintained that "the type of Gnosticism attacked in the Epistle is one which came into existence considerably after Apostolic times."[4] The force of this argument depends entirely upon the evaluation being placed upon the error combated in the epistle. If it is held that the epistle deals with the developed Gnosticism of the second century, then the epistle must of necessity be postapostolic. But any assumption that full-blown Gnosticism is in view in the epistle is quite groundless. It cannot be proven that Jude has in view definite Gnostic sects of the second century, such as the Cainites or Ophites. It is generally conceded that the error in Jude is essentially the same as that in 2 Peter. It is now commonly agreed that "every feature in the description of the false teachers and mockers is to be found in the apostolic age."[5] Salmon, in maintaining a first-century dating for Jude, remarks,

On the whole, I conclude that the evils under which Jude's Epistle

---

3. Ernest Findlay Scott, *The Literature of the New Testament*, p. 226.
4. Ibid., p. 226.
5. Charles Bigg, *A Critical and Exegetical Commentary on the Epistles of St. Peter and St. Jude*, International Critical Commentary, p. 239.

reveals the Church to be suffering are not essentially different from those the existence of which we learn from Paul's Epistles.[6]

The similarity to the troublers in the pastorals is evident. The argument that this similarity points to a late date holds only for those who use the errors combated in the pastorals as a ground for denying the Pauline authorship of the pastoral epistles.

The fact that Jude apparently quotes from apocryphal books offers a definite difficulty. Jerome pointed out the fact that these apparent quotations occasioned questions concerning the epistle. The reference in verse 9 concerning the contention between Michael the archangel and the devil about the body of Moses was held to be a quotation from the *Assumption of Moses*, while the prophecy of Enoch in verses 14-15 was regarded as a quotation from the *Book of Enoch*. At first this fact was not considered a barrier (compare the view of Tertullian), but as the Church became apocrypha-shy this fact became a serious obstacle. That the canonicity of Jude triumphed over such feelings can only be accounted for as due to the strong reasons for its acceptance.

Some scholars, like Lenski, vigorously deny that Jude actually quoted from these books.[7] All that can be proven is that the testimony of the ancient writers says that Jude *confirms* a statement in the *Assumption of Moses* and that he used language very similar to that found in the *Book of Enoch*. Jude may have quoted from tradition. Paul in 2 Timothy 3:8 gives us the names of Jannes and Jambres; since these names are not found in the Old Testament, he must have gotten them from some noncanonical source which he accepted as reliable.

But even if we grant that Jude did use these apocryphal books, that need not discredit Jude's epistle. Fronmüller feels that we should "rather admire the reserve with which the author of our Epistle uses the book of Enoch, which contains so much that is fantastic, and recognize in the reserve a leading of the Divine Spirit."[8] The use of a quotation from an uninspired source need not imply that he approved

6. George Salmon, *An Historical Introduction to the Study of the Books of the New Testament*, p. 477.
7. R. C. H. Lenski, *The Interpretation of the Epistles of St. Peter, St. John and St. Jude*, pp. 610-12; 650-52.
8. G. F. C. Fronmüller, "The Epistle General of Jude," in Lange's *Commentary on the Holy Scriptures*, p. 4.

of the whole book. Modern authors often quote with approval a sentence or illustration from a book with which as a whole they do not agree. Moorehead, in granting the possibility of a quotation in both places, observes:

> Paul cites from three Greek poets: from Aratus (Acts 17:28), from Menander (I Cor. 15:33), and from Epimenides (Tit. 1:12). Does anyone imagine that Paul indorses all that these poets wrote? To the quotation from Epimenides the apostle adds, "This testimony is true" (Tit. 1:13), but no one imagines he means to say the whole poem is true. So Jude cites a passage from a non-canonical book, not because he accepts the whole book as true, but this particular prediction he receives as from God.[9]

If it is felt necessary to accept the claim that Jude does actually quote from these apocryphal books, we feel that such a view of the problem is satisfactory.

3. CONCLUSION

When we remember the brevity of the epistle, its nonapostolic authorship, its polemical character, and its apparent use of apocryphal sources, the external evidence is remarkably strong and early. That the early Church accepted it as canonical, after full questioning and debate, reveals its strength. The internal evidence is summarized by Salmond in the following words:

> Its direct and unaffected style, the witness which it bears to the life of the Church, the type of doctrine which it exhibits, and, above all, the improbability that any forger would have selected a name comparatively so obscure as that of Jude under which to shelter himself, or indeed would have thought of constructing an Epistle of this kind at all, have won for it general acceptance as genuine.[10]

We accept the epistle of Jude as an important part of the New Testament canon.

THE AUTHOR OF THE EPISTLE

1. IDENTITY

The author identifies himself as "Jude, a servant of Jesus Christ,

---

9. William G. Moorehead, "Jude, The Epistle of," in *International Standard Bible Encyclopaedia*, 3:1771*b*.
10. S. D. F. Salmond, *The General Epistle of Jude*, The Pulpit Commentary, p. vi.

and brother of James" (v. 1). The name *Jude* or *Judas*,[11] was a common name in New Testament times. It had been popularized through the exploits of Judas the Maccabee. It remains to determine who the Jude was who wrote this epistle. There are some six men in the New Testament who bear this name. Two of the apostles were named Jude or Judas.

The author's designation of himself as "brother of James" is unique. No other New Testament writer thus identifies himself by his family connections. The designation at once limits the scope of possibilities to two different men. One of these is "Judas (not Iscariot)" (Jn 14:22), one of the twelve, who also seems to have been called Lebbaeus or Thaddaeus (cf. Mt 10:3, Mk 3:18 with Lk 6:16, Ac 1:13). The other Jude is one of the Lord's brothers mentioned in Matthew 13:55 and Mark 6:3. From the position of his name in these lists he was either the youngest or the next to the youngest of these brothers. The attempt is sometimes made to identify these two Judes, but this position is untenable.

That the apostle Jude was the author seems highly improbable and has few advocates.[12] The author's identification of himself as "the brother of *James*" at once suggests that his brother was a noted individual in the Church. If the author is the apostle Jude, then his brother must have been James the son of Alphaeus (Lk 6:16; Ac 1:13). But this James was not such a noted individual as is implied. In fact he seems to have been not at all outstanding; he is unknown to us outside of the appearance of his name in the lists of the twelve.

It is not even certain that the apostle Jude had a brother named James. To be sure, the King James Version in Luke 6:16 and Acts 1:13 reads "Judas *the brother* of James." But we believe this is an unwarranted translation. The words "the brother" are properly in italics and indicate that they were supplied by the translators. The Greek is simply "Judas of James" leaving the exact relation to be supplied from the context. In Luke 6:15-16 and Acts 1:13 we have just preceding an identical construction in the Greek which the King James Version translates "the son of." Why should it not be translated "the son of" in both places? This is the rendering in the American Standard Version and in most recent translations.

11. *Jude* and *Judas* are simply English variants from the one Greek form *Ioudas*.
12. So J. Sidlow Baxter, *Explore the Book*, 6:292-93, 313.

The common view is that the author was Jude "the Lord's brother."[13] He did have a famous brother named James, the leader of the Jerusalem church (Gal 1:19; Ac 12:17; 15:13-21; 21:18). He was the most famous James in the middle of the first century among Christians. The author's reference to this James would immediately establish his identity. This agrees with the fact that the author refrains from calling himself an apostle; he even seems to be careful to distinguish himself from the apostles (v. 17). The statement in John 7:5 that "his brethren did not believe on him" points to the same position. And the mention of His "brethren" in Acts 1:14 occurs in a sentence which is so framed as to emphasize the distinction between the apostles and "the Lord's brethren."

That Jude, like his brother James, does not allude to his being the brother of Jesus is accounted for by the fact that the ascension of Jesus had altered all of Christ's human relationships, and His brethren would naturally shrink from claiming kinship after the flesh with His glorified body. "This feeling," Lumby observes, "would be the stronger in them because they had so long rejected the teaching of Him to whom in humility they now both alike call themselves bond-servants."[14]

2. ACTIVITIES

Of the life and activity of Jude but very little is known. During the ministry of our Lord he was not a believer in Him (Jn 7:3-8). "For a long time he was staggered by the Messianic claims of Jesus, and not until after His resurrection and His personal manifestation to His brother James did Jude come within the circle of the believers (Ac 1:14)."[15] From 1 Corinthians 9:5, reading in the light of a later story preserved by Hegesippus, we learn that Jude was married and apparently traveled considerably as an evangelist. Beyond this the Scriptures are silent concerning him.

Plumptre conjectures that our author may be identified with "Judas surnamed Barsabas," who was reckoned as among the "chief men among the brethren" (Ac 15:22) and was a prophet (Ac 15:32).[16]

13. For the significance of the term see the introduction to James under "Relation to Jesus."
14. J. R. Lumby, "Jude," in *The Speaker's Commentary. New Testament,* 4:384a.
15. Herbert L. Willett and James M. Campbell, *The Teachings of the Books,* p. 313.
16. E. H. Plumptre, *The General Epistles of St. Peter and St. Jude,* Cambridge Bible for Schools and Colleges, pp. 85-86.

The view presupposes that the name Barsabas was not a patronymic but simply an epithet descriptive of character, like Barnabas. This hypothesis would explain the prominence of our author in the Church as implied from the epistle. Although the suggestion is not impossible, there is nothing beyond the common name to warrant the assumption.

Tradition maintains almost complete silence concerning Jude. As Farrar observes, "So little, indeed, is known of St. Jude, that even tradition, which delights to furnish particulars respecting the Apostles and leaders of the early Church is silent about him."[17] The apocryphal gospels do not mention his name. The apocryphal gospels do not mention his name. The only story connected with his name which has come down to us is that told by Hegesippus and preserved by Eusebius in his *Ecclesiastical History* (3. 19, 20). He tells us that informers attempted to excite the jealousy of Domitian against two grandsons of Jude, "said to have been a brother of the Saviour according to the flesh" (3. 19). Upon being questioned by the emperor they answered that their wealth consisted of a small farm of thirty-nine acres which they themselves cultivated, showing him their horny hands in confirmation thereof. As to the Kingdom of Christ which they were accused of expecting, they assured the emperor that it was no earthly kingdom, but a heavenly and angelic one, which would appear at the end of the world. Thereupon they were dismissed with disdain as harmless peasants. These men were afterwards honored in the churches as witnesses to Christ and as being near of kin to the Lord.

3. CHARACTER

This brief letter offers practically the only material available for an evaluation of the character of Jude. The epistle reveals him to have been possessed of keen mental abilities. It shows that he was "a man of clear perception, vivid imagination, intense sensibility, and strong will."[18] He had the ability to give clear and forceful expression to his thoughts. His metaphors are vivid and incisive. He was a man of resolute purpose and strong desires. He had profound convictions and the courage to contend for those convictions.

17. F. W. Farrar, *The Early Days of Christianity*, p. 123.
18. Nathaniel Marshman Williams, "Commentary on the Epistle of Jude," in *An American Commentary*, p. 3.

The impression left by the epistle is that Jude was a man of stern and unbending character. Yet he may well have been of a more tender nature than the epistle would suggest. In dealing with the insidious errors which were rearing their heads within the churches, loyalty to Christ demanded an uncompromising opposition which found expression in vehement denunciation. His love for the truth of God and the souls of men compelled him to speak forth in fiery denunciation against the destructive influences of the false teachers. But when addressing the brethren, there are glimpses of an affectionate nature and a tender spirit. Thrice he addresses the readers as "beloved" (vv. 3, 17, 20). He has a heart concern for those who have been ensnared in the evils being combated and counsels a compassionate and saving attitude toward them (vv. 22-23).

The Relation to 2 Peter

1. PHENOMENA

Even a casual reading of 2 Peter and Jude makes it obvious that there is a close relation between the two epistles. This relation is confined to 2 Peter 2:1–3:4 and Jude vv. 4-18. The rest of 2 Peter bears no resemblance to Jude. In both there is a discussion of false teachers, of an antinomian type, whose character and influence threaten the Church. The similarities in thought and structure are so remarkable that they cannot be merely accidental. For points of resemblance between the two compare Jude 7 with 2 Peter 2:6; Jude 8 with 2 Peter 2:10; Jude 9 with 2 Peter 2:11; Jude 10 with 2 Peter 2:12; Jude 16 with 2 Peter 2:18; and Jude 17-18 with 2 Peter 3:2-3.

But it is equally clear that the two epistles reveal remarkable differences. Obviously one is not merely a copy of the other. Whichever was written later was penned by a writer who maintained his own independence throughout. He adds to, leaves out, and rearranges the material being used in accordance with his own purpose. Thus Jude mentions the cause of the fall of the angels (vv. 6-7); Peter simply states the fact that they sinned (2:4). Both mention the fate of Sodom and Gomorrah (2 Pe 2:6); but Jude describes the sin of the inhabitants which caused that overthrow (v. 7). Peter dwells on the deliverance of Lot from Sodom (2:7-9), but Jude makes no mention of it. Peter speaks of the destruction of the world by the Flood

(2:5), while Jude instead uses the illustration of the destruction of the Israelites in the wilderness (v. 5). Peter cites the case of Balaam as an Old Testament illustration (2:15-16), but Jude mentions three instances from the Old Testament (v. 11). Jude cites the prophecy of Enoch at length (vv. 14-15), while Peter makes no mention of it. Peter cautions his readers against being led astray by the example of these false teachers (2:20-22), but the warning is not in Jude.

How are the phenomena to be explained?

2. ALTERNATIVE VIEWS

Four different answers have been proposed.

1. That Peter and Jude both wrote independently under the inspiration of the Holy Spirit, for both were confronted with the same situation. Although possible, this view seems improbable. We fully accept the inspiration of these epistles, but the sacred Scriptures were yet written by men, each writer using his own style and diction and revealing his own personal characteristics. This human element in the Scriptures may be judged by the ordinary rules of literary criticism. Only a mechanical view of inspiration which eliminates the intervention of human means could thus seek to explain the phenomena.

2. That both Peter and Jude drew from a common source. It is favored by Green but has not won many advocates. It should be regarded as a possible option, but it complicates the matter by predicating a third writing, wholly unknown, whose origin and authority remain unaccounted for. Peter and Jude were both capable of originating this material.

3. That Jude took much of his material from Peter. This view presupposes the priority of 2 Peter.

4. That Jude was used by Peter in the writing of his epistle.

3. ARGUMENTS

Accepting the view that one writer made use of the epistle of the other, the question is debated as to which one was first. There is no agreement on the question, even among those who accept the authenticity of both epistles.

The following considerations are alleged in favor of the priority of Jude:

1. It is more likely that 2 Peter as the longer of the two would incorporate the contents of the shorter than the other way.

2. If Jude used 2 Peter it is strange that he should use only the second chapter and leave the rest of the epistle unnoticed.

3. It is more probable that 2 Peter should omit from Jude what seemed hard to understand and was likely to give offense than that Jude should insert such things.

4. The indefinite reference to the angels in 2 Peter 2:11 is hardly intelligible without the fuller statement in Jude.

5. Jude is the stronger and more vehement of the two; it is more probable that the fervid epistle was the original and that Peter softened some of the sterner language of Jude.

In favor of the priority of 2 Peter the following considerations are advanced:

1. Jude himself tells us that he wrote under pressure to meet an emergency; therefore he would be more likely to use materials already at hand than one who was under no such a necessity.

2. That Jude should quote from 2 Peter is in accord with his known practice of quoting; 2 Peter hardly quotes at all, while Jude has definite quotations.

3. Jude reveals a number of instances which are best explained as examples of expansion on the statement of Peter. The contrary process of Peter abbreviating Jude's letter is difficult to conceive.

4. The picture of the evil is darker and more sinister in Jude than in 2 Peter, so naturally suggests a later date.

5. It is more probable that Jude should borrow from Peter, the prince of the apostles, than that Peter should borrow from one who was not an apostle at all.

6. The studied arrangement of the material into triplets, which prevails in Jude, looks more like a second writer working up old material than a writer working under no influence from a predecessor.

7. Peter simply warns against the wicked workers; Jude on the other hand gives definite directions on how to deal with those who have become the victims of these wily foes (vv. 22-23). Thus Jude implies a later time than 2 Peter, a time when the evil has already wrought its havoc.

It is apparent that these opposing arguments are rather subjective in nature and several of them are capable of a double interpretation.

None of them seems to be decisive one way or the other. There are, however, two further arguments for the priority of 2 Peter which are of a more objective nature.

8. Second Peter is essentially predictive, while in Jude the evil is a painful present reality. Peter uses three strategically placed future tenses: "Among you also there *shall be* false teachers" (2:1); "And many *shall follow* their lascivious doings" (2:2); "In the last days mockers *shall come*" (3:3). Peter is predicting. Jude records the fulfillment of the prophecy: "For there are certain men crept in privily" (v. 4). Jude's aorist tense records the fact. The force of this argument cannot be overthrown by simply pointing out that Peter also uses present tenses. To be sure, Peter does use some descriptive present tenses (2:10, 17-18; 3:5), but this is the natural tense to use in describing the situation. His present tenses do not cancel out his future tenses in the strategic places. But Jude never uses a future tense; his aorist (v. 4) points to a definite historical event. Only if Jude wrote later can these facts be given their natural meaning. Moorehead well says,

> If as Peter wrote he had lying before him Jude's letter, which presents the corrupters as already within the Christian community and doing their deadly work, his repeated use of the future tense is absolutely inexplicable. Assuming, however, that he wrote prior to Jude, his predictions become perfectly intelligible. No doubt the virus was working when he wrote, but it was latent, undeveloped; far worse would appear; but when Jude wrote the poison was widely diffused, as vs. 12, 19 clearly show.[19]

9. Jude quotes from 2 Peter 3:3-4 when he writes, "But ye, beloved, remember ye the words which have been spoken before by the apostles of our Lord Jesus Christ; that they said to you, In the last time there shall be mockers, walking after their ungodly lusts" (vv. 17-18). The words for "mockers" (*empaiktai*) occurs in the New Testament only here and in 2 Peter 3:3. The passage in Jude is an acknowledged quotation, while Peter gives the warning as his own. Yet Jude makes his quotation more general by speaking of the apostles as having given this warning. The apostle Peter had given the warning in his second epistle; Paul was another apostle who had predicted similar things (Ac 20:29-30; 1 Ti 4:1-3; 2 Ti 3:1-5). Thus

19. Moorehead, 3:1769*b*.

Jude bids his readers remember the prophecies of Peter and Paul. We seek in vain for such a prophecy in the Old Testament or even in the book of Enoch, but the words of 2 Peter suit exactly.

It may be replied that Jude must be referring to the Old Testament since in verse four the expression "of old" (*palai*) points back to remote times. But the contention is quite groundless. The word *palai* is an adverb denoting past time, whether long ago or quite recent. It simply looks back from the present to a point of time in the past.[20] In Mark 15:44 Pilate asks whether Jesus died *palai*, "any while dead." In 2 Corinthians 12:19 this word is translated "all this time" and must have a time limit of only a day or two. If two or three years elapsed between the writing of these two epistles, a time during which things definitely grew worse, that would give ample time to justify Jude's use of the term.

4. CONCLUSION

The scholars will doubtless continue to argue the problem and each will decide according to the factors which impress him most. We conclude that the preponderance of evidence is definitely in favor of the priority of 2 Peter.

THE READERS OF JUDE

Jude's comprehensive designation of the readers in the salutation marks it as a general epistle. It is devoid of any geographical limitations. The readers are given a threefold description, "To them that are called, beloved in God the Father, and kept for Jesus Christ" (v. 1). While it is obvious that the address embraces all Christians without distinction, it is yet very probable that the author had some particular circle in view which occasioned the letter. The definiteness of the terms used strongly supports the position that he had a definite group of churches in mind when he wrote. If so, the identity of these churches is left completely to conjecture.

Some think that the intended readers were Jewish Christians. This is concluded from the fact that the author makes reference to himself as the brother of James who was highly esteemed by all Jewish Christians, from the Jewish tone of the epistle, as well as from the author's use of Jewish illustrations and Jewish tradition. Those who

20. See under *palai* in William F. Arndt and F. Wilbur Gingrich, *A Greek-English Lexicon of the New Testament and Other Early Christian Literature*, p. 610.

accept this view are inclined to identify the readers with those addressed by his brother James. But it must be said that the Jewish coloring of the epistle simply proves the Jewish background of the author and does not necessarily demonstrate the Jewish background of the readers.

Others feel that the readers were more likely predominantly Gentile in origin and are inclined to locate them in Asia Minor, thus identifying them with the readers of the Petrine epistles. In favor of this view Salmond holds that "the evils dealt with are of a kind to which converts from heathenism would be more liable than converts from Judaism."[21] Also in favor of this view is the likelihood that Jude and 2 Peter are combating the same error.

The problem of the racial background of the readers of Jude cannot be dogmatically settled. The probability is that the groups involved included both Jewish and Gentile Christians. The address of the epistle includes all Christians regardless of their racial extraction. In most churches outside of Palestine the distinction between Jewish and Gentile converts was not maintained; both were united in Christ, in whom there was neither Jew nor Gentile.

THE OCCASION FOR JUDE

The occasion for the epistle is clearly in verse three. Jude had been contemplating the writing of a general doctrinal treatise when the distressing information about an alarming situation among the readers compelled him to write at once on the urgent topic of this epistle. His deep concern for the welfare of the saints forced him to write. He must seek at once to stem the work and influence of these evil men and endeavor to strengthen the true believers against their insidious onslaughts. How he came into possession of the information concerning the distressing situation we are not informed.

It is commonly accepted that the adversaries whom Jude opposes are essentially the same as those encountered in 2 Peter. They were daring and licentious intruders who shamelessly abused the liberties of the Gospel. Professing to be Christians, they engaged in evils worse than the heathen. In the words of Farrar,

> They were doing the deeds of darkness while they stood in the noonday. They claimed higher prerogatives than the Jews, yet they lived

21. Salmond, p. vii.

in viler practices than the Gentiles. The fulness of their knowledge aggravated the perversity of their ignorance; the depth of the abyss into which they had sunk was only measurable by the glory of the height from which they had fallen.[22]

That these "ungodly men" (v. 4) were libertines is obvious. Some have thought that they were libertines pure and simple who were corrupting the Church simply by their evil practices. But statements like those in verses 4, 10, 16, 17, 18 imply that they were also false teachers. They were libertines whose licentious lives were rooted in their perverted views of divine grace and Christian liberty. They were heretical teachers in that they denied the Lord Jesus as Master and Lord, but their teaching was of a licentious tendency, "turning the grace of our God into lasciviousness" (v. 4). But it is obvious that they were not the developed heretical sects of the second century as some critics would think.

THE PLACE AND DATE OF JUDE

1. PLACE

There is no material in this brief letter to help decide the question concerning the place of its composition. Alexandria in Egypt and Palestine, especially Jerusalem, are generally suggested. If Jude, like James, made Jerusalem his headquarters, it may well be that it was written from there. But as a traveling evangelist (1 Co 9:5) there is no evidence that Jude felt himself bound to the Jerusalem church.

2. DATE

Those who regard the epistle as pseudonymous generally place it around A.D. 150. But even among those who accept its authenticity the date assigned to it varies widely. The dates range all the way from A.D. 64 to 80. There are, however, some indications which may help us arrive at a more definite date. If it is true, as we believe, that 2 Peter was written first, then the date for Jude cannot be earlier than A.D. 65. On the other hand, it seems highly improbable that the epistle should be dated later than the destruction of Jerusalem. If that catastrophe had already taken place it is difficult to see how Jude could have failed to use it among his examples of the destructions which befell the ungodly. Some two or three years may have passed

22. Farrar, p. 127.

since the writing of 2 Peter, thus allowing sufficient time for the development of the conditions depicted in Jude. We may accordingly date the epistle around A.D. 67 or 68.

THE PURPOSE OF JUDE

The purpose of the epistle as stated in verses 3 and 4 seems to have been both negative and positive. Negatively, Jude writes to warn the true believers against the pernicious activities of the licentious apostates. He roundly denounces these "ungodly men" (v. 4) and points out their inevitable fate. Positively, he writes to encourage the believers "to contend earnestly for the faith which was once for all delivered unto the saints" (v. 3). He does not elaborate the contents of that faith but rather in vivid pictures portrays the doom of apostates. He ends his appeal by giving his readers timely suggestions as to their attitude and action toward those who have been seduced by the heretical libertines (vv. 17-22).

THE CHARACTERISTICS OF JUDE

1. STYLE AND TONE

The style of Jude bears a resemblance to that of James. His language is terse, poetic, and vivid. Like James, much of his imagery is taken from nature. "Its style," says Salmond, "is broken and rugged, bold and picturesque, energetic, vehement, glowing with the fires of passion."[23] The severity of the tone of the epistle is without parallel in the New Testament. It is the outflashing of righteous indignation against blatant evil. Willett says,

> It lashes with a whip of scorpions the libertines who try to conceal their evil deeds under the cloak of religion. Fierce invectives flash out like lurid flames. But the severity is seasoned with Christian compassion. The prophet of judgment has felt the touch of the pity of Christ.[24]

2. CONTENTS

One of the striking features of the epistle is its fondness for triplets of thought. The author misses scarcely an opportunity to give his material a threefold arrangement. There are some ten or twelve such

23. Salmond, p. i.
24. Willett and Campbell, p. 314.

triads in the twenty-five verses of the epistle. In illustration, notice the following:

> "Jude, servant, brother" v. 1; "called, beloved, kept" v. 1; "mercy, peace, love" v. 2; Israelites, angels, cities of the plain vv. 5-8; "Cain, Balaam, Korah," v. 11; "defile, set at naught, rail" v. 8; "on some, some, on some" vv. 22, 23 A.S.V.; "before all time, and now, and for evermore" v. 25.

Such a frequent use of triplets of thought as Jude displays does not have a parallel in any other portion of Scripture of equal length.[25]

The epistle presents one of the most fearful pictures of libertines and apostates in all Scripture. Jude paints in dark hues indeed. In the words of Moorehead, Jude pictures them as

> Surreptitious foes (4), perverters of grace and deniers of Christ (4), censorious and arrogant detractors (8), ignorant calumniators and brutish sensualists (10), hypocrites and deceivers (12, 13), grumblers, fault-finders, pleasure-seekers, boasters, parasites (16), schismatics and sensualists (19).[26]

The concluding doxology (vv. 24-25) is one of the fullest and most beautiful of all the doxologies of Scripture. Touching as it does upon the danger from the apostates and the security of the believer, it brings the epistle to a marvelous conclusion.

That the epistle has not lost its value for our day is evident to those who are seeking to live separated lives while surrounded by the growing apostasy and licentiousness of much of present-day professing Christendom. Fronmüller well remarks,

> The closer we draw to the last times of the Church, the more we ought to lay to heart this Epistle, which is a key-stone and an admonition of the most dangerous sins of the Church, and which, like the Second Epistle of Peter, furnishes us with important disclosures relating to judgment and eternity.[27]

---

25. For a devotional study of Jude, with emphasis upon its triplets, see Herbert Lockyer, "Scripture Summaries, Apostasy in Jude," in *Our Hope*, May 1953, pp. 687-94; June 1953, pp. 749-54.
26. Moorehead, 3:1768*b*-69*a*.
27. Fronmüller, p. 7.

AN OUTLINE OF JUDE

I. The Salutation, vv. 1-2

II. The Occasion for the Letter, vv. 3-4

    A. The indication of the former purpose, v. 3*a*
    B. The nature of the altered purpose, v. 3*b*
    C. The reason for the change in purpose, v. 4

III. The Historical Fate of Apostates, vv. 5-7

    A. The purpose to remind them concerning apostates, v. 5*a*
    B. The examples of the divine judgment on apostates, vv. 5*b*-7
        1. The example of unbelieving Israel, v. 5*b*
        2. The example of the fallen angels, v. 6
        3. The example of the cities of the plain, v. 7

IV. The Description of the Modern Apostates, vv. 8-16

    A. The daring nature of their conduct, vv. 8-11
    B. The figurative description of their character, vv. 12-13*b*
    C. The prophetic indication of their doom, vv. 13*c*-15
    D. The indication of their nature and motives, v. 16

V. The Exhortations to Believers Amid Apostasy, vv. 17-23

    A. The exhortation to have an awareness of apostasy, vv. 17-19
    B. The exhortation to maintain the right spiritual attitude, vv. 20-21.
    C. The exhortation to have a saving attitude toward the deceived, vv. 22-23

VI. The Doxology, vv. 24-25

A BOOK LIST ON JUDE

Barclay, William. *The Letters of John and Jude.* The Daily Study Bible. 2d ed. Edinburgh: Saint Andrew, 1962.
    Prints author's own translation. Most helpful for its word studies and background information for these epistles. For his treatment of the Johannine epistles, Barclay acknowledges his heavy dependence

upon the views of C. H. Dodd. Barclay accepts that the epistle of Jude was probably written by Jude, the Lord's brother.

Barnett, Albert E.; and Homrighausen, Elmer G. "The Epistle of Jude." In *The Interpreter's Bible*, vol. 12. New York: Abingdon, 1957.

> Introduction and exegesis by Barnett, exposition by Homrighausen. Rejecting the traditional authorship, Barnett places the epistle about A.D. 125.

Bigg, Charles. *A Critical and Exegetical Commentary on the Epistles of St. Peter and St. Jude*. International Critical Commentary. 1901. 2d ed. Edinburgh: T. & T. Clark, 1910.

Coder, S. Maxwell. *Jude: The Acts of the Apostates*. Everyman's Bible Commentary. Chicago: Moody, 1958.

> A full and rewarding exposition of Jude by an evangelical Bible teacher.

Green, Michael. *The Second Epistle General of Peter and the General Epistle of Jude*. Tyndale New Testament Commentaries. Grand Rapids: Eerdmans, 1968.

Ironside, H. A. *Exposition of the Epistle of Jude*. Rev. ed. New York: Loizeaux, n.d.

> A popular exposition by a well-known, evangelical Bible teacher of the past generation.

Jaeger, Harry. *Hidden Rocks*. Boston: Fellowship, 1949.

> An informative exposition of the epistle with a timely analysis of the modern religious conditions in Christendom.

Kelly, J. N. D. *A Commentary on the Epistles of Peter and of Jude*. Harper's New Testament Commentaries. New York: Harper & Row, 1969.

Kelly, William. *Lectures on the Epistle of Jude*. New ed. Denver, Colo.: Wilson Foundn., 1970.

> A series of popular expository lectures by a noted Plymouth Brethren scholar of the past century.

Lawlor, George Lawrence. *Translation and Exposition of the Epistle of Jude*. Nutley, N.J.: Presby. & Ref., 1972.

> A full and scholarly treament of Jude by an informed conservative. Uses an English translation but frequently quotes the Greek in the interpretation.

Lenski, R. C. H. *The Interpretation of the Epistles of St. Peter, St.*

John and St. Jude. Columbus, Ohio: Lutheran Book Concern, 1938.

Manton, Thomas. *An Exposition of Jude.* Reprint. Wilmington, Del.: Sovereign Grace Pub., 1972.

> A reprint of a solid, old Puritan volume of deep interpretation. Manton died in 1677. While full and rich in content (370 pages), most modern readers will find the style rather difficult. Rewarding to the diligent student.

Major, J. B. *The Epistle of St. Jude and the Second Epistle of St. Peter.* London: Macmillan, 1907.

———. "The General Epistle of Jude." In *The Expositor's Greek Testament,* vol. 5. Reprint. Grand Rapids: Eerdmans, n.d.

> Greek text. Important for advanced critical study of the epistle. The forty-page introduction supplies much valuable information.

Miller, Ira. *The Message of Jude to the Modern Church. The Apostasy and the Remedy.* Arlington, Va.: Wagner, 1944.

> A series of messages covering almost every verse of the epistle. Makes resounding applications to modern religious conditions.

Moffatt, James. *The General Epistles—James, Peter, and Judas.* The Moffatt New Testament Commentary. Reprint. London: Hodder & Stoughton, 1947.

Plummer, Alfred. "The General Epistle of Jude." In *Ellicott's Commentary on the Whole Bible,* vol. 8. Reprint. Grand Rapids: Zondervan, n.d.

> A concise and informative commentary on the epistle. Gives list of parallels between Enoch, 2 Peter, and Jude.

———. "The General Epistles of St. James and St. Jude." In *The Expositor's Bible,* vol. 6. Reprint. Grand Rapids: Eerdmans, 1943.

Plumptre, E. H. *The General Epistles of St. Peter and St. Jude.* Cambridge Bible for Schools and Colleges. Cambridge: U. Press, 1893.

Reicke. Bo. *The Epistles of James, Peter, and Jude.* The Anchor Bible. Garden City, N. Y.: Doubleday, 1964.

Salmond, S. D. F. *The General Epistle of Jude.* The Pulpit Commentary. Reprint. Grand Rapids: Eerdmans, 1950.

> A valuable interpretation of the epistle with an abundance of homiletical suggestions appended.

Wand, J. W. C. *The General Epistles of St. Peter and St. Jude.* Westminster Commentaries. London: Methuen, 1934.

Williams, Nathaniel Marshman. "Commentary on the Epistle of Jude." In *An American Commentary*. 1888. Reprint. Philadelphia: Amer. Bapt. Pubn. Soc., n.d.
    A suggestive exposition by a conservative Baptist scholar of the past century.
Wolff, Richard. *A Commentary on the Epistle of Jude*. Grand Rapids: Zondervan, 1960.
    The introductory section deals with critical problems from a conservative viewpoint. The verse-by-verse commentary is scholarly but readable, showing wide acquaintance with the literature on the epistle.
Woods, Guy N. *A Commentary on the New Testament Epistles of Peter, John, and Jude*. Nashville, Tenn.: Gospel Advocate, 1954.
Wuest, Kenneth S. *In These Last Days. II Peter, I, II, III John, and Jude in the Greek New Testament for the English Reader*. Grand Rapids: Eerdmans, 1954.

8

FIRST JOHN

AN INTRODUCTION TO 1 JOHN

THE FORCIBLE SIMPLICITY of its sentences, the note of finality behind its utterances, the marvelous blending of gentle love and deep-cutting sternness of its contents, and the majesty of its ungarnished thoughts, have made 1 John a favorite with Christians everywhere. The simplicity of its language makes it intelligible to the simplest saint, while the profundity of its truths challenges the most accomplished scholar. Its grand theological revelations and its unwavering ethical demands have left their enduring impact upon the thought and life of the Christian Church.

THE FORM OF 1 JOHN

In the various catalogs of the books of the New Testament this writing is always classified as a "letter," yet, unlike 2 and 3 John, it does not display the regular features of a letter as seen in the models of contemporary correspondence. It is like Hebrews in that it begins without an opening salutation, but it lacks entirely the epistolary conclusion of that epistle. It concludes as abruptly as the epistle of James, but it is without the formal epistolary opening of James. It contains no formal thanksgiving for the readers as is characteristic of the opening paragraphs of Paul's letters. It does not contain a single proper name (except that of Jesus Christ), nor does it offer a single definite statement, personal, historical, or geographic, concerning either writer or readers. It is destitute of all that is merely local or specific.

This absence of the customary epistolary features has led some writers to regard the title of "epistle" as a misnomer. It is held that it

181

should rather be classified as a "homily" intended for Christendom at large.[1] Although the writing does lack the features generally associated with a letter, its contents yet clearly show that it is not a general treatise intended for the general public. The author deals with an actual life situation and addresses readers with whom he has intimate acquaintance, knowing their history, attainments, dangers, and needs. It springs out of a definite historical situation and is adapted to meet that situation. It glows with the writer's keen interest in and personal concern for his readers. While it lacks the external epistolary marks, the contents of 1 John confirm its epistolary character.

The features of 1 John have caused some to think of it as a sermon, containing the substance of a sermon, or several sermons, written out either before or after delivery. The author's solicitude and paternal feelings toward the readers, expressed in his affectionate appellation "little children," reminds us of one who stands in a pastoral relationship to those whom he is addressing. But the contents show that it is not the transcription of a sermon. Repeatedly the author indicates that the form of communication he is using is that of writing (1:4; 2:1, 7-8, 12-13, 14, 21, 26; 5:13). Only once (5:16) does he allow "I say" to take place of "I write." In origin it is thus clearly marked as being a written communication to a specific audience.

The intimate relationship between the writer and his readers, the pertinence of the hortatory appeals, and the tone and contents of the composition as a whole, justify its classification among the New Testament epistles. But the absence of all that is merely local suggests that it was not intended for a single congregation but rather for a larger circle of congregations within the writer's acquaintance. Westcott's description of it as "a Pastoral addressed to those who had been carefully trained and had lived long in the Faith"[2] fits the spirit and contents of the book.

THE AUTHORSHIP OF 1 JOHN

1. EXTERNAL EVIDENCE

First John is better attested by external evidence than any of the other general epistles. Eusebius was fully justified in placing 1 John

---

1. James Moffatt, *An Introduction to the Literature of the New Testament*, p. 584.
2. Brooke Foss Westcott, *The Epistles of St. John*, p. xxx.

among the *homologoumena,* the acknowledged books,[3] in his list of canonical books (*Eccl. Hist.* 3. 25). Only 1 John and 1 Peter among the general epistles were so classified by him.

The earliest definite trace of this epistle is in Polycarp, bishop of Smyrna (*c.* 69-115). In his *Epistles to the Philippians* (*c.* 115) he writes:

> For whosoever does not confess that Jesus Christ has come in the flesh, is antichrist, and whosoever does not confess the testimony of the cross, is of the devil (chap. vii).

These words seem clearly to have been inspired by 1 John 4:2-3. When we remember that the word "antichrist" occurs in the New Testament only in John's epistles and is not of frequent occurrence in the subapostolic literature, and that "confess," "witness," and "to be of the devil" are characteristically Johannine expressions, the conclusion seems certain. Irenaeus, who had known Polycarp personally as a youth, informs us that Polycarp had known John in his youth.[4] Polycarp suffered martyrdom at the age of eighty-six, hence he must have been a contemporary of the apostle John for some twenty years. The quotation of Polycarp proves the early date of the epistle of John, and if it does not attest the Johannine authorship of the epistle it at least suggests it. In view of Polycarp's relation to John is it possible that he could have been ignorant of its authorship? Would he have used it thus if he had any doubts as to its authoritativeness?

Eusebius tells us that Papias, bishop of Hierapolis (*c.* 80-155), "used testimonies from the First Epistle of John" (*Eccl. Hist* 3. 39). He quotes Irenaeus (140-203) as saying of Polycarp that he was "John's hearer and the associate of Polycarp, an ancient writer" (*Eccl. Hist.* 3. 39; *Against Heresies* 5. 33. 4).

Thus we have two early witnesses to this epistle, both from the province of Asia, well within the first half of the second century. In view of the scantiness of the literature from that period which has come down to us, it is remarkable indeed to have these two early witnesses.

3. From the standpoint of their canonicity, Eusebius classified Christian documents as the Acknowledged (*homologoumena*), the Disputed (*antilogomena*), and the Spurious (*nothoi*). Books put forth by heretics in the names of the apostles apparently formed a fourth class, to be rejected as "absurd and impious." *Eccles. Hist.* 3. 25. But compare Westcott, *A General Survey of the Canon of the New Testament,* pp. 382-93.
4. See Eusebius *Eccl. Hist.* 5. 20 and Irenaeus *Against Heresies* 3. 3. 4.

Eusebius records that Irenaeus (140-203) "also mentions the First Epistle of John, extracting many testimonies from it" (*Eccl. Hist.* 5. 8). In his noted work *Against Heresies* Irenaeus quotes 1 John 2:18-19 and expressly says that he is quoting from John's epistle (3. 16. 5). He also quotes 1 John 4:1-2 and 5:1 and identifies it as from John's epistle (3. 16:8). Irenaeus is the first writer to cite it by name as written by John.

The Muratorian Canon (*c.* 170) includes the epistle and ascribes it to John.

These testimonies are primitive and confirm the early appearance and acceptance of the epistle and its Johannine authorship. It is unnecessary to quote further evidence from the writings of Clement of Alexandria (*c.* 155-215), Tertullian (*c.* 150-222), Origen (*c.* 185-253), Cyprian (*c.* 200-258), and others. In fact all Fathers, Greek and Latin, accept this epistle as being by John. The evidence for the epistle is so early, clear, and strong, that Lücke, following his review of the external evidence, is fully justified in saying, "Incontestably then our Epistle must be numbered among those canonical books which are most strongly upheld by ecclesiastical tradition."[5] Thus the evidence shows that this epistle, undoubtedly one of the latest of the New Testament books to be written, took an immediate and permanent position as an authoritative writing of inspiration.

This strong testimony to the Johannine authorship of the epistle is not weakened by the rejection of it by Marcion and the Alogoi. Marcion rejected it, as he did all the gospels except an expurgated Luke, and all the epistles, except those of Paul, not because he regarded them as spurious, but because they contradicted his peculiar anti-Judaistic views. The obscure sect designated the Alogoi by Epiphanius rejected "the books of John" as spurious and ascribed them to Cerenthus because they distrusted the Johannine teaching concerning the Logos.[6]

2. EVIDENCE FROM EPISTLE

The internal evidence has ramifications beyond the epistle itself. In considering the internal evidence we begin with whatever information about the author can be gleaned from the epistle itself. The epistle is anonymous and furnishes us with no clue whereby we can

5. Quoted in Henry Alford, in *The Greek Testament*, vol. 4, part 2, p. 162 Proleg.
6. Theodor Zahn, *Introduction to the New Testament*, 3:200.

identify the writer, but it gives us sufficient material whereby we may classify him. His relation to his readers is one of intimacy and recognized authority. That intimacy is not argued but taken for granted throughout. His relation to the readers was so well known that it was superfluous for the writer to declare his identity.

As Westcott points out, "The writer of the Epistle speaks throughout with the authority of an Apostle."[7] But there is no passionate claim to apostolic authority; he does not feel it necessary to assert that he possesses such authority. His very consciousness as a recognized apostle of Christ enabled him to write thus. "He claims naturally and simply an immediate knowledge of the fundamental facts of the Gospel (1:1; 4:14), and that special knowledge which was possessed only by the most intimate disciples of the Lord (1:1)."[8] Such a claim can have its natural meaning only as coming from a disciple of Christ. Notice also the bold self-testimony with the impression of evident truth found in 4:16, "And we know and have believed the love which God hath in us."

The impression about the author given by the epistle itself is that of a man who speaks with the knowledge and authority of an apostle. This data from the epistle thus agrees with the external evidence that he was the apostle John.

3. RELATION TO FOURTH GOSPEL

A consideration of the internal evidence concerning the authorship of 1 John at once raises the question of its relation to the fourth gospel. That these two writings are from the same hand seems obvious to the unprejudiced reader. This has generally been the conclusion of scholars who have investigated the question. The evidence in favor of the identity of authorship is strong.

A list of phrases common to both writers is very striking. Brooke lists fifty-one references in the epistle which find a parallel in the fourth gospel.[9] Among these we may compare the following: *to do the truth* (1:6 with 3:21)[10]; *the truth is not in any one* (1:8 with 8:44); *to be of the devil* (3:8 with 8:44); *to be of God* (3:10 with 8:47); *to*

---

7. Westcott, p. xxxi.
8. Ibid., p. xxxi.
9. A. E. Brooke, *A Critical and Exegetical Commentary on the Johannine Epistles,* International Critical Commentary, pp. ii-iv.
10. The first reference is to the epistle; the second to the fourth gospel.

be of the world (2:16 with 8:23); *the Spirit of truth* (4:6 with 14:17); *to be called children of God* (3:1 with 1:12); *to lay down His life* (3:16 with 10:11, 17-18); *to have sin* (1:8 with 9:41); *to have eternal life* (3:15 with 3:16, 36); *to pass from death unto life* (3:14 with 5:24); *to overcome the world* (5:4 with 16:33); *to take away sin* (3:5 with 1:29); *to remain in Him* (2:28 with 6:56); *to speak of the world* (4:5 with 3:31); *to walk in the darkness* (2:11 with 8:12); *to receive the witness of men* (5:9 with 3:33); and others. The connection is obvious, but it is not a stereotyped repetition; there are significant variations in the use of the expressions. As Brooke points out, the explanation lies between an imitator and a writer who uses his phrases with variation, and the latter view seems the more probable.[11]

A comparison of 1 John and the fourth gospel reveals that there are also similarities of style. Thus Brooke notes the infrequent use of the relative, the frequent employment of disconnected sentences, and the union of an affirmative and negative expression of thought. There is, further, the restricted range of vocabulary in both writings, which however, is identical to an extent without parallel in two independent works.[12]

Both works have the interesting practice of setting pairs of opposites over against each other, such as light and darkness, life and death, love and hate, truth and falsehood, the Father and the world, the children of God and the children of the devil, to know God and not to know God. Further, as Law points out, similar views of theology and ethics prevade both works:

> The two writings are equally saturated with that spiritual and theological atmosphere; they are equally characterized by that style of thought which we call Johannine and which presents an interpretation of Christianity no less original and distinctive than Paulinism. Both exhibit the same mental and moral habit of viewing every subject with an eye that stedfastly beholds radical antagonisms and is blind to approximations.[13]

That this similarity between the two writings suggests identity of authorship has been accepted from earliest times. Thus Dionysius of Alexandria (c. 200-265), after enumerating various similarities of the

11. Brooke, p. v.
12. Ibid., pp. v-vii.
13. R. Law, "John, The Epistles of: The First Epistle," in *The International Standard Bible Encyclopaedia*, 3:1716b.

two, concluded by saying, "Throughout, to attentive observers, it will be obvious that there is one and the same complexion and character in the Gospel and Epistle."[14] That able and skeptical critic De Wette remarked,

So much is certain, that both writings, this Epistle and the fourth Gospel, proceed from the same author; for both bear the most definite stamp of relationship, as well in style as in conceptions; both impress upon the reader the same charm of a kind nature.[15]

And Ramsay throws the weight of his scholarship behind this conclusion when he says,

There can be no doubt that the same hand can be traced in the First Epistle and the Fourth Gospel. No two works in the whole range of literature show clearer signs of the genius of one writer, and no other pair of works are so completely in a class by themselves, apart from the work of their own and of every other time.[16]

This similarity of the two writings is all the more remarkable when it is remembered that the nature of the fourth gospel is objective narrative, while the epistle is hortatory and polemical. This conclusion concerning the identity of authorship of the two writings greatly strengthens the evidence for the Johannine authorship of 1 John since tradition with unanimity and emphasis ascribes the fourth gospel to the apostle John.

But this view of the identity of authorship of the two writings has been vigorously assailed by the critics. While freely admitting the similarities, it is held that the differences outweigh the resemblances. The view is advanced that the two works are not from the same author but that they are the product of "the Johannine school" to which both writers belonged.[17] This attack upon the identity of authorship is made along two lines, on the ground of style and language, and the contents.

It is asserted that the style of the two compositions is different. Thus Dodd says,

While the rhythm of both is slow and regular, in the Gospel it is

14. Quoted by Eusebius *Ecclesiastical History* 7:25.
15. Quoted in Henry M. Harmon, *Introduction to the Study of the Holy Scriptures*, p. 597.
16. W. M. Ramsay, *The Church in the Roman Empire Before* A.D. *170*, pp. 302-3.
17. See C. H. Dodd, *The Johannine Epistles*, The Moffatt New Testament Commentary, pp. xlix-lvi.

subtly varied, within the limits imposed by its general character; but in the Epistle regularity often descends to monotony. The language of the Gospel has an intensity, a kind of inward glow, a controlled excitement, which the reader does not feel, or seldom feels, in the Epistle.[18]

Dodd admits that such a criticism is subjective and that matters of style are differently estimated by different minds. Ross counters the view of Dodd by replying,

> We need only say that we have found, and that not seldom, this intensity, this inward glow, in the language of the Epistle, as in the language of the Gospel, and the fact that such a mental reaction is experienced at all in the reading of the Epistle tends to prove that we are all the time in contact with the same mind. And, if it be the case that in the Gospel we have a richness of language that is wanting in the Epistle, may the explanation not be that the Gospel was composed with greater care, as a book intended to bring home conviction of the truth of Christianity to enquiring minds, while the Epistle, written to believers, is composed with greater freedom and simplicity of language?[19]

The apostolic authorship has been objected to on the ground of the alleged "feebleness" of the epistle, as evidenced by the frequency of its repetitions. That there is a certain amount of repetition in the epistle, greater than in the fourth gospel, may be allowed. But closer inspection will reveal that these alleged repetitions always result in a progress of thought. This repetition of thought may be due to old age, as has been thought, but this point must not delude us into the supposition that the underlying thought is not of great value. But granting that this is a mark of old age, this would not furnish an argument against the traditional authorship since it is freely admitted that John must have been of quite advanced age when it was written.

Brooke makes a survey of the alleged differences between the two writings as to words and phrases and concludes:

> On closer inspection a considerable number of the phrases which are actually peculiar to the Epistle remind us so strongly of similar phrases and thoughts in the Gospel that it is again the resemblance

18. Ibid., p. xlix.
19. Alexander Ross, *The Epistles of James and John*, The New International Commentary on the New Testament, pp. 110-11.

rather than the difference that is brought into prominence. . . . The variations in phrase suggest common authorship rather than servile, or even intelligent, copying.[20]

The strongest arguments for the duality of authorship are held to be those based on certain doctrinal emphases and developments in the epistle. It is asserted that the eschatological view of the epistle is more primitive than that found in the fourth gospel. The epistle, it is said, holds out the prospect of a near advent of Christ and the end of the world (2:17, 28), while the fourth gospel gives a profound reinterpretation of eschatology by presenting the judgment not as future but as present (3:18) and thinking of the coming of Christ as happening in the experience of every believer (14:18). But this assertion is erroneous. The gospel also speaks of a final and universal judgment (5:29), refers to "the last day" (6:39, 40, 44, 54; 11:24), and holds to a personal return of Christ (21:22-23).

It is claimed that there is "a real difference in the conception of the Paraclete, who is identified in the epistle (2:1) with Jesus Christ as the Righteous One, whereas, in the gospel, Jesus either sends the Paraclete or is at most a Paraclete himself."[21] But there is no disagreement here. For Jesus in the gospel speaks of the coming of the Holy Spirit as "*another* Paraclete" (14:16), thus implying His own character as Paraclete. The objection rests upon the mere use of the word rather than its meaning in its context. "In the epistle it is not used in the same sense as in the gospel, and is applied to Christ in a sense which does not interfere with or contradict its application to the Spirit."[22] Further, against the identity of authorship it is asserted that while in the fourth gospel the Spirit as Paraclete is developed, in the epistle the function of the Spirit is wholly ignored. It is true that the relation of the Spirit to Jesus is not worked out in the epistle as it is in the fourth gospel. But the expression "the spirit is the truth" (1 Jn 5:7) connects directly with John 14:17; 15:26 and shows that the author of the epistle also regards the Spirit as a Paraclete, even though the term is here applied to Christ.

It is maintained that a modification of the idea of faith is noticeable. Thus Moffatt says, "While in the Gospel faith is equivalent to

20. Brooke, pp. xv-xvi.
21. Moffatt, p. 592.
22. Marcus Dods, *An Introduction to the New Testament,* p. 214.

the coming of a man to the truth and light of God in Christ, or to a reception of the words of Jesus in the heart, the writer of the epistle, though far from being an intellectualist, tends to resolve faith into a confession of Jesus as the Son of God (2:23; 4:2-3; 5:1)."[23] But in the gospel there is an equally definite insistence upon the necessity of accepting the deity of Christ (cf. 5:17; 5:39-40; 8:23-24; 8:55-58). However, the full development of Christological faith, spurred by later heretical perversions, naturally has no place in the gospel which deals with the period when that faith was first being presented and developed.

Again, it is said that the epistle presents Christ's death as propitiatory (2:1), while the propitiatory element is absent in the gospel. Admittedly the gospel does not use the word propitiation as does the epistle ((2:1; 4:10), but the basic idea is there, although not in the developed form of the epistles. The concept is involved in the statement, "Behold, the Lamb of God, that taketh away the sin of the world!" (Jn 1:29). This concept is latent in the teaching of the entire fourth gospel. However, for the writer to have put all of his own theological expressions into the mouth of Him whose teachings he professes to report would have been an anachronism.

The attempt to establish duality of authorship for these two writings is not convincing. That there are differences between them is clear, but these differences do not cancel out the marked similarities. The differences show that the writer was a man of enough versatility to alter his phrases and concepts at will as the occasion demanded. A skillful imitator would not have departed from his model like that. Nor could he have combined elements of likeness and unlikeness in such a manner.

After a careful consideration of the differences between the two writings Brooke concludes, "There are no adequate reasons for setting aside the traditional view which attributes the Epistle and Gospel to the same authorship. It remains the most probable explanation of the facts known to us."[24] Salmon emphatically rejects the attempts to establish duality of authorship:

> I am sure that an unprejudiced judge would decide that while the minute points of difference that have been pointed out between the

23. Moffatt, p. 591.
24. Brooke, p. xviii.

Gospel and the First Epistle are no more than must be expected in two productions of the same writer, the general resemblance is such, that a man must be devoid of all faculty of critical perception who cannot discern the proofs of common authorship.[25]

And Peake summarily concludes that "it is hypercriticism to deny the identity of authorship."[26]

We accept without hesitation the traditional view that John was the author of both the gospel and the first epistle.

4. JOHN'S EPHESIAN MINISTRY

The acceptance of the Johannine authorship of 1 John at once raises the problem of John's later life. The apostle John disappears from the story of Acts after chapter 8. In the Pauline epistles he is mentioned only in Galatians 2:9. Does our information about the later life of John agree with the view that he was the author of these writings?

According to persistent Christian tradition the closing years of the apostle John were spent at Ephesus, from which as a center he carried out an extensive evangelistic and pastoral ministry to the regions around. Thus Justin Martyr (*c.* 100-165) in his *Dialogue With Trypho* (chap. LXXXI) wrote: "There was a certain man with us, whose name was John, one of the Apostles of Christ, who prophesied, by a revelation that was made to him, that those who believed in our Christ would dwell a thousand years in Jerusalem." Eusebius in his *Ecclesiastical History* (4. 18) informs us that this dialogue took place at Ephesus.

Irenaeus (*c.* 140-203), bishop of Lyons, but apparently born in Asia Minor, bears explicit testimony to John's Ephesian residence. In his famous work *Against Heresies* he speaks of the testimony of "all the elders . . . who were conversant in Asia with John, the disciple of the Lord," and then adds that John "remained among them up to the times of Trajan" (2. 22. 5). He also says, "Afterwards, John, the disciple of the Lord, who also had leaned upon His breast, did himself publish a Gospel during his residence at Ephesus in Asia" (3. 1.1).

Polycrates, bishop of Ephesus, in his epistle to Victor, bishop of Rome (190-200), says, "And moreover John also that leaned back

25. George Salmon, *An Historical Introduction to the Study of the Books of the New Testament*, p. 192.
26. Arthur S. Peake, *A Critical Introduction to the New Testament*, p. 170.

upon the Lord's breast, who was a priest bearing the plate of gold, and a martyr and a teacher—he lies asleep at Ephesus" (Eusebius *Eccl. Hist.* 5. 24).

Eusebius also quotes Clement of Alexandria (*c.* 155-*c.* 215) as saying of John the apostle:

> When, after the tyrant's death, he returned from the isle of Patmos to Ephesus, he went away upon their invitation to the neighboring territories of the Gentiles, to appoint bishops in some places, in other places to set in order whole churches, elsewhere to choose to the ministry some one of those that were pointed out by the Spirit (*Eccl. Hist.* 3. 23).

Further evidence to the same effect might be given from Origen and Appolonius. Plummer summarizes the evidence for John's residence at Ephesus as follows:

> That S. John ended his days in Asia Minor, ruling 'the Churches of Asia' from Ephesus as his usual abode, was the uniform belief of Christendom in the second and third centuries, and there is no sufficient reason for doubting its truth. . . . S. John's residence there harmonizes admirably with the tone and contents of these Epistles.[27]

Those who reject the apostolic authorship of the fourth gospel and the first epistle feel it necessary to seek to discredit this tradition. Their attack upon the tradition of John's Ephesian residence is made along two lines.

There is, first of all, the argument from silence. It is pointed out that there is nothing in the New Testament to suggest that the apostle John went to Asia. Obviously, the Acts and the Pauline epistles do not do so. But the date for the Johannine residence at Ephesus comes after that time. To those who accept the traditional authorship of the Johannine epistles and the Revelation, the Bible does clearly give such evidence.

More serious is the silence of Ignatius (martyred *c.* 116) whose letters to the various Asiatic churches, written within about twenty years of the supposed death of the apostle John, make no mention of him. Even in his letter to the Ephesians he is silent as to John, although he does mention Paul.[28] This silence is admittedly diffi-

27. A Plummer, *The Epistles of S. John*, Cambridge Bible for Schools and Colleges, p. 11.
28. See Moffatt for further development of this argument from silence, pp. 613-14.

cult to explain. Just why Ignatius did not mention John if he had resided at Ephesus is not known. However, the argument from silence if often a very delusive one and avails little in the face of the strong testimony to the contrary.

The second point of attack on the tradition of the Ephesian ministry of John is found in his supposed early martyrdom. Many scholars think that there is sufficient evidence to show that John was actually martyred at an early date, hence the tradition of his long life and residence at Ephesus must be in error. Moffatt advances three lines of evidence in support of this view.[29]

Attention is called to the prophecy of Jesus that the sons of Zebedee should drink of His cup (Mk 10:39; Mt 20:23). In view of Mark 14:36 it is held that this prophecy implies the martyrdom of both. It is even suggested that John actually died at the same time as his brother James (Ac 12:2). But such an early date for the death of John is in direct conflict with Paul's statement in Galatians 2:9, unless we adopt the improbable hypothesis that the John there mentioned is John Mark. The silence of the New Testament on any martyrdom of John offers a serious obstacle to this contention. The solid tradition of the Ephesian residence is against it. The prophecy of Jesus does not require such a rigid and literal interpretation. Certainly John's experiences of persecution may be accepted as fulfillment of the words of Jesus.

The testimony of Papias that John "was killed by the Jews" is also advanced to support this position. This quotation is given by Georgios the Sinner (ninth century) as being found in the second book of Papias. An eighth-century epitome of the History of Philip of Side (fifth century) says, "Papias says in his second book that John the Divine and James his brother were killed by Jews." This cannot be an accurate quotation since "John the Divine" is a late expression. Philip's reputation as an accurate historian is not high. Papias, to be sure, may have made a statement to that effect. But he may well have used the word *martyr* in its wider sense, or his words may originally have had reference to the martyrdom of John the Baptist. That they prove the actual martyrdom of the apostle John seems doubtful. "Many scholars refuse to credit the evidence of these fragments, in-

29. Ibid., pp. 602-8.

cluding Harnack whose opinion in the matter is disinterested, since he denies that St. John lived at Ephesus."[30]

Evidence from ancient calendars is also brought in to confirm the martyrdom of John. A Syriac fourth-century calendar commemorates as martyrs on December 27 "John and James the Apostles at Jerusalem." A Carthaginian calendar of the sixth century reads for the same date, "St. John the Baptist and James the Apostle." But this is a confusion of persons since John the Baptist is also commemorated on June 24. This evidence has been taken to show that John was still at that date being regarded as having suffered actual martyrdom. But it may well be that these calendars speak of Saint John in a loose sense as a martyr, for they also style Saint Stephen as an apostle.

None of the evidence used to refute the traditional view that John lived at Ephesus rests on very secure ground. There seems to be no compelling reason to discredit the firm tradition as to such a residence. The fact of such a residence seems definitely to lie behind the statement found in John 20:20-23. Without it the report of John not dying is without explanation.

5. THE ELDER JOHN

The figure of "John the Elder" as a person distinct from John the apostle looms large in any discussion of the authorship of the Johannine literature. Opponents of the traditional view generally hold that the tradition has confused two men by the same name. It is thought that John the apostle has been mistaken for another John, resident in Asia, who may have been the real author of the gospel and epistles.

The only evidence for the actual existence of this second John, whom Renan called "a shadow which has been mistaken for a reality,"[31] rests upon the interpretation by Eusebius of certain words which he quotes from Papias. The passage from Papias reads thus:

> I shall not hesitate also to put down for you along with my interpretations whatsoever things I have at any time learned carefully from the elders and carefully remembered, guaranteeing their truth. For I did not, like the multitude, take pleasure in those that speak much, but in those that teach the truth; not in those that relate strange commandments, but in those that deliver the commandments given by the

30. Willoughby C. Allen and L. W. Grensted, *Introduction to the Books of the New Testament*, p. 94.
31. Quoted by F. W. Farrar, *The Early Days of Christianity*, p. 618.

Lord to faith, and springing from the truth itself. If, then, any one came, who had been a follower of the elders, I questioned him in regard to the words of the elders,—what Andrew or what Peter said *(eipen)*, or what was said by Philip, or by Thomas, or by James, or by John, or by Matthew, or by any other of the disciples of the Lord, and what things Aristion and the presbyter John, the disciples of the Lord, say *(legousin)*. For I did not think what was to be gotten from the books would profit me as much as what came from the living and abiding voice *(Eccl. Hist.* 3. 39).

And this is the comment of Eusebius on the passage quoted:

It is worth while observing here that the name John is twice enumerated by him. The first one he mentions in connection with Peter and James and Matthew and the rest of the apostles, clearly meaning the evangelist; but the other John he mentions after an interval, and places him among others outside of the number of the apostles, putting Aristion before him, and he distinctly calls him a presbyter. This shows that the statement of those is true, who say that there were two persons in Asia that bore the same name, and that there were two tombs in Ephesus, each of which, to the present day, is called John's (3. 39).

It is evident that Eusebius learned from Dionysius of Alexandria the possibility of interpreting the words of Papias to mean that there were two Johns (cf. *Eccl. Hist.* 7. 25). Dionysius held that the John who wrote the Revelation was not the apostle John.

The words of Papias are admittedly open to two interpretations. One interpretation, that followed by Eusebius, holds that he makes mention of two different Johns; the other view holds that he makes mention of the same John twice, both times referring to the apostle John. This problem has elicited different views on the part of conservative scholars. Such noted scholars as Lightfoot and Westcott accepted the existence of a presbyter John in Ephesus as distinct from the apostle, while Farrar, G. Salmon, Plummer, Zahn, D. Smith, Lenski, and others have rejected the historical existence of this presbyter John.

Was Eusebius right in his interpretation that there were two Johns at Ephesus? Eusebius had a theological interest in putting this construction upon the words of Papias. It gave him the desired opportunity to get rid of the apostolic authorship of the Revelation which he disliked because of its use by the Chiliasts, a feeling which he shared with Dionysius of Alexandria.

Eusebius in his interpretation is not quite fair to Papias when he says that Papias called this second John "*a* presbyter." Papias did not call him "a presbyter," but "the presbyter," and that may be a different thing. He also overlooks the fact that John of the second clause is given exactly the same designations as the John of the first clause, as one of "the presbyters" and as a "disciple of the Lord." Eusebius makes the term "presbyter" or "elder" mean two different things in the same sentence, which seems very improbable. He also ignores the significance of the change in tense from "said" (*eipen*) to "say" (*legousin*).

Papias tells us that he got his information from two sources. One source was the reports gleaned from the followers of the apostles; the other source was from the lips of Aristion and John himself. He had the advantage of having heard their living voice. This transition from "said" to "say" explains the double mention of John, although Eusebius ignored this point. According to the interpretation of Eusebius here adopted, Papais only got his information from the followers of John, not from John himself. His critical interests led him to discredit the statement of Irenaeus that Papias "was a hearer of John" (*Eccl. Hist.* 3. 39). Hence the second John cannot be the apostle John himself. This causes Farrar to remark,

> In his History he reasons himself into the belief that Papias was only the pupil of 'the Presbyter;' but he had all the writings of Papias in his hand when he wrote the *Chronicon,* and there he says, without any hesitation, that Papias was a pupil of the Apostle. 'John the Presbyter' is the creation of Eusebius' later criticism.[32]

Plummer calls attention to the fact that Irenaeus, who likewise knew the writings of Papias, makes no mention of a second John at Ephesus. Evidently he did not read Papias as Eusebius did.[33] Eusebius does not profess to know anything definite about this second John. He is simply following the lead of the tentative guess of Dionysius of Alexandria about there being two Johns. The reference he makes to the two tombs at Ephesus does not prove the existence of two

32. Ibid., p. 623.
33. Plummer, p. 214.

Johns. They apparently represent two rival claims being made for the burial place of John.

The passage from Eusebius, which forms the sole basis for the very existence of the elder John as distinct from the apostle, is capable of a different interpretation from that given by Eusebius, an interpretation which, in spite of Eusebius, is being held by many today. Concerning this "John the Elder," Salmon says,

> A whole school of critics speak of him with as assured confidence as if he were a person concerning whose acts we had as much information as concerning those of Julius Caesar; but in truth his very existence seems to have been first discovered by Eusebius, and it is still a disputed matter whether the discovery be a real one.[34]

Zahn summarizes his view on the matter with the words, "It is safe to say that the 'Presbyter John' is a product of the critical and exegetical weakness of Eusebius."[35]

The problem of the authorship of 1 John is admittedly beset with many perplexing problems and difficulties. Yet we believe that all the evidence, external as well as internal, is best accounted for by accepting the traditional view. We hold that 1 John is the product of the apostle John.

THE READERS OF 1 JOHN

Any information about the readers of 1 John must be gleaned from the contents of the epistle. That they were primarily converts from heathenism has been inferred from the fact that the epistle contains no quotations from the Old Testament but does carry a definite warning against idolatry (5:21). Yet neither the absence of Old Testament quotations or the warning against idolatry *prove* Gentile readers; the warning need not be restricted to any literal interpretation.

That the readers had been Christians for a long time and were advanced in their knowledge of Christian truth is clear from the contents. Repeatedly the writer declares that he has nothing new in the way of doctrine or exhortation to offer them (2:7, 18, 20, 21, 24, 27; 3:11). There is no intimation that the writer had taken any part in

34. Salmon, p. 268.
35. T. Zahn, "John the Apostle," *The New Schaff-Herzog Encyclopedia of Religious Knowledge*, 6:205b.

their original evangelization. The reference is rather to that which they had heard "from the beginning" (2:7, 24). Yet he writes to them as one who has been intimately acquainted with them for a considerable time and who has been active in their midst as a teacher and leader.

Some have thought that 1 John was directed to a local congregation. Ephesus and Corinth have been suggested. In view of the tradition about John's ministry in Asia and the fact that the earliest testimonies to the epistle come from that province, it seems most natural to locate the readers there. The scope of John's Asian ministry, as well as the absence of all that which is merely local in the epistle, leads to the conclusion that it was addressed to a group of congregations under the supervision of the writer. Zahn holds that the nature of the writer's relation to the readers as well as the false doctrine combated in the epistle point to Asia as the location of the readers.[36] Thus, strictly speaking, 1 John is not a general epistle but was rather directed to a group of churches within John's acquaintance.

The view that this epistle was addressed to the Parthians, although it carries the weight of Augustine's name, cannot be accepted as valid. No other writer, preceding or contemporary with him, lends any support to that view. Various conjectures as to the origin of that view have been made.[37]

The Occasion for 1 John

1. CONDITION OF READERS

The ultimate reason for the writing of 1 John was the spiritual condition of the believers to whom it was addressed. There are no explicit references to persecution in the epistle; words of consolation, such as abound in 1 Peter, are entirely absent. This has commonly been taken to mean that the external conditions at the time of writing were not peculiarly difficult.[38] The Church is indeed hated by the world (3:13), but it is a hatred which arises out of a moral antagonism between the Church and the world.

36. Zahn, *Introduction to the New Testament*, 3:369.
37. See Alford, 4:2:165-67 Prolegomena. Brooke, pp. xxx-xxxii.
38. Ramsay holds that it would be a mistake to argue, from the absence of any explicit reference to persecution, that either this epistle or the Revelation was composed in a time of peace (pp. 304-5).

The real danger lay in the attitude of the readers toward the world and their own Christian faith. "The enthusiasm of the early days of the Faith is no longer theirs. Many of them had been brought up as Christians, and did not owe their faith to strong personal conviction or experience."[39] There had crept in a want of brotherly love, a development of spiritual laxity and internal dissensions, and a lessening of a steadfastness in the fellowship with the Father and the Son. The lessening of a vivid sense of antagonism between them and the world was making them more susceptible to the seductions of worldliness; they must be warned against loving the world (2:15-16). Their readiness to welcome elements of speculative philosophy foreign to the Christian faith had made them less sure of their own position.

2. PRESENCE OF FALSE TEACHERS

Under such conditions the presence of false teachers created a pressing danger and provided the immediate occasion for the writing of the epistle. In proportion as the enthusiasm of earlier days began to cool, doubts and questions as to their own position began to arise. Their uncertainty made them more inclined to lend an ear to the false teachers. They were beset with the temptation to seek to reinterpret their faith "in terms of modern thought." (Such an attitude on the part of Christians is still the source of much confusion and heresy.) In view of these conditions John found it necessary to write to them not only to refute the false teachings which were prevalent but also to exhort them and to establish them in the faith.

THE PLACE AND DATE OF 1 JOHN

1. PLACE

No hint is given in the epistle concerning the place of its composition. Since the latter years of John's life were spent in Ephesus, in the absence of other indications, it seems most natural to hold that it was written there.

2. DATE

There are no indications in the epistle to fix a definite time for its composition. No inference as to the time can be drawn from the statement, "it is the last hour" (2:18); it is a note of spiritual, not ma-

39. Brooke, p. xxviii.

terial time. The tone of the epistle and the writer's attitude toward his readers suggest an old man writing to a younger generation. John must have been at work in Asia already for a number of years when he wrote. There is no hint that he arrived in Ephesus before the death of Paul. Further, the fact that no mention is made of the destruction of Jerusalem seems to suggest that it was written a considerable time after that. If the breaking up of the Jewish world had but recently taken place it seems very probable that some reference would have been made to that momentous change. If the absence of any reference to persecution means that the Church was not being actively persecuted by the state, then the time of composition would most likely be either before the reign of Domitian or at the close of his reign. We would thus get a date of around A.D. 80, or a later date of about A.D. 97. The earlier date seems preferable.

THE PURPOSE OF 1 JOHN

1. PRACTICAL EDIFICATION

We are not left in any doubt as to John's purpose in the writing of this epistle. His basic purpose is the practical edification of his "children" in the true faith and life as Christians. His purpose is given several statements. Thus, "These things we write, that your joy may be made full" (1:4). "My little children, these things write I unto you that ye may not sin" (2:1). "These things have I written unto you, that ye may know that ye have eternal life, *even* unto you that believe on the name of the Son of God" (5:13). The author's practical purpose is apparent. It is his basic desire to ground them in the assurance of their salvation in Christ (5:13). Intimately related with this is the desire that they come to experience victory over sin (2:1), and thus they will share fully the joys of the Christian life (1:4). He is anxious that the joys of the Christian life may not be dimmed in them by the allurements of the world or the seductions of doctrinal error. They must realize that their Christian faith is based on positive, demonstrable, realized facts and that the reception of eternal life in Christ Jesus lays upon them the responsibility of a conduct consistent with their position as children of God.

The statement of purpose in the epistle, as given in 5:13, stands in interesting relation to the stated purpose of the gospel of John.

Many other signs therefore did Jesus in the presence of the disciples, which are not written in this book; but these are written, that ye may believe that Jesus is the Christ, the Son of God; and that believing ye may have life in his name (Jn 20:30-31).

The gospel and this epistle are complementary in purpose. The purpose of the gospel is evangelistic, to lead men to a personal saving faith in Jesus Christ the Son of God; the purpose of the epistle pastoral, to lead believers into a full understanding and assurance of their salvation in Christ Jesus. Both books present the fundamental doctrines of Christianity. "But in the Gospel these are given as the foundation of the Christian's *faith;* in the Epistle they are given as the foundation of the Christian's *life.*"[40] The Christian life that knows the joy of salvation is based upon the assurance of salvation. The epistle advances a series of tests to be applied to Christian profession on the basis of which the believer's assurance of eternal life may be established. The contents of the epistle, we believe, are most advantageously studied in the light of its announced purpose, as given in 5:13.

2. POLEMICAL

That the epistle has a polemical character is obvious. The author is clearly intent upon refuting doctrinal errors which are threatening. But the final aim of the writer is practical. The safety of the readers, whose establishment in the faith in the face of these errors is his chief aim, makes it necessary that these errors be refuted.

The problem of the exact nature and identity of the false teaching being controverted in the epistle has given rise to much discussion and is still a matter of disagreement. Most probable is the view that the heresy in view was some form or forms of Gnosticism. Gnosticism was a philosophy of religion. It professed not to be hostile to the Gospel, but by its attempt to interpret Christian doctrines from a higher philosophical standpoint it in reality disintegrated and destroyed them. By its efforts to reinterpret Christianity in terms of prevailing philosophical thought it introduced elements foreign to it and so destroyed its distinctiveness.

A kaleidoscopic variety marked Gnosticism, but two guiding principles ran through all of its teachings.

The first principle was the supremacy of the intellect and the

40. Plummer, p. 35.

superiority of enlightenment to faith and conduct. These heretics laid claim to a superior knowledge which was the privilege of the few. They were the "knowing ones," as the name implies. "The superior theosophic insight to which they laid claim led naturally to a sense of pride in themselves as the *elite* of Christendom, which fostered an unbrotherly contempt for the unenlightened members of the church."[41] For them spiritual excellence consisted not in a holy life but in a superior knowledge which enabled a man to rise above the earthbound chains of matter into the heavenly apprehension of truth. This not infrequently led to a disregard of the ethical demands of Christianity. Says C. H. Dodd, "Some of the heretics believed themselves to be so far above good and evil that their conduct scandalized even the easygoing censors of Roman Society."[42] In opposition to this dangerous teaching John insisted on the intimate relation between doctrine and conduct. He points out that Christian knowledge, possessed as the result of the anointing from the Holy One (2:20), is a knowledge which involves holiness of life and conduct as well as intellectual enlightenment (1:5–2:5). There is no evidence that all Gnostics were guilty of this scandalous disregard for the ethical demands of Christianity, but apparently the majority of them were. At other times the reaction was toward asceticism.

A second guiding principle of Gnosticism was its view that spirit is good and matter is inherently evil; the two were regarded as being in perpetual antagonism. But if matter is absolutely evil, it followed that there could be no true incarnation of the Son of God. Since it was unthinkable that spirit and matter could unite in any real and vital union, the incarnation of the holy Son of God was impossible. This at once raised Christological problems. The Christian revelation of the incarnation was rejected for a more reasonable view. Two solutions were proposed. One view was that Christ did not have a real human body but only appeared to have one. This theory was known as Docetism, from the Greek verb *dokeō*, to seem, to appear. The other view was known as Cerinthianism, whose chief exponent was Cerinthus, a contemporary of John at Ephesus. Cerinthus separated Jesus from Christ. He denied the virgin birth of Jesus, but recognized that He was preeminent for righteousness, prudence, and wisdom.

41. Moffatt, p. 586.
42. Dodd, p. xx.

He taught that the Christ spirit came upon Him following His baptism, empowered His ministry, but left Him before the crucifixion. The man Jesus suffered and rose again but the Christ, a pure spirit, remained impassible.[43] In thus splitting the person of Jesus Christ, Cerinthus destroyed the reality of the incarnation and the atonement. Apparently both of these forms of error come into view in the epistle.

THE CHARACTERISTICS OF 1 JOHN

1. LANGUAGE AND STYLE

The style of John is strikingly simple. Of John's style Farrar says,

> It is a style absolutely unique, supremely original, and full of charm and sweetness. Under the semblance of extreme simplicity, it hides unfathomable depths. It is to a great extent intelligible to the youngest child, to the humblest Christian; yet to enter into its full meaning exceeds the power of the deepest theologian.[44]

There is a sameness of construction which tends to monotony, yet his apparent repetitions produce an advance in the thought. Although his language is pure Greek, insofar as it is free from solecisms, yet it is as unlike Greek as possible in its periodic structure. He is not given to those long and complicated sentences which characterize the writings of Paul. John's sentences are coordinated by simple conjunctions after the Hebrew model. He makes frequent use of the parallelistic form so common to the Wisdom Literature of the Old Testament. His sentences often assume a triple form. The thought is frequently pressed home by being expressed both positively and negatively.

The language of John has justly been described as being meditative. We feel as if he is engaged in meditation and is allowing us to overhear his thoughts as they arise. His method is not of argument but of categorical affirmation. He speaks with a tone of authority; he sets forth his pronouncements and passes on without stopping to vindicate them. There is a calmness and finality about his words which leaves its inevitable impression on the soul. Fowler says,

> At times there is a lyric quality: Behold what manner of love the Father hath bestowed upon us—it almost sings itself. Always there is the insight of the true poet of the spiritual life.[45]

43. Irenaeus *Against Heresies* 1. 26. 1.
44. Farrar, pp. 520-21.
45. Henry Thatcher Fowler, *The History and Literature of the New Testament*, p. 400.

John has a way of developing his thought in terms of its opposite. Light suggest darkness, life is opposed to death, truth to error, love to hate, God to the devil. "He thinks in terms of ultimates. His colours are white and black; there is no grey."[46]

2. STRUCTURE

Any hurried attempt to set forth in logical outline the contents of this epistle will inevitably result in frustration. The epistle is exceedingly difficult to analyze. It has been seriously questioned whether John had any plan at all in the writing of it. It has been characterized as the ramblings of an old man without system or sequence. Some have thought of it as being merely a series of aphorisms without much sequence or logical connection.

It is a mistake to think that there is confusion and lack of order in its contents. The difficulty lies rather in the nature of its composition. The effort to analyze it is like attempting to analyze the face of the sky. "There is contrast, and yet harmony; variety and yet order; fixedness, and yet ceaseless change; a monotony which soothes without wearying us, because the frequent repetitions come to us as things that are both new and old."[47]

The attempts of commentators to find the outline of the epistle have produced varied results. Moffatt summarizes the results as follows:

> Little success has attended the attempts to analyze it into a double (*God is Light, God is Love:* Plummer; 1:5–2:27; 2:28–5:5: Findlay), triple (1:1–2:11; 2:12–4:6; 4:7–5:21: Ewald; *God is Light, God is Righteous, God is Love:* Farrar), fourfold (1:5–2:11; 2:12-28; 2:29–3:22; 3:23–5:17: Huther), or fivefold (1:5–2:11; 2:12-27; 2:28–3:24a; 3:24b–4:21; 5:1-21: Hofmann) arrangement.[48]

Plummer frankly says, "Probably few commentators have satisfied themselves with their own analysis of this Epistle: still fewer have satisfied other people."[49]

John's method is not that of syllogistic logic. His thought moves in cycles rather than straight forward. Lenski states his view of the structure of the epistle as follows:

46. W. Graham Scroggie, *Know Your Bible, A Brief Introduction to the Scriptures,* Vol. 2, *The New Testament,* p. 346.
47. Plummer, pp. 42-43.
48. Moffatt, p. 584.
49. Plummer, pp. 42-43.

John rises above formal divisions and parts. This letter is built like an inverted pyramid or cone. First the basic apex is laid down in 1:1-4; then the upward broadening begins. Starting with 1:5-10 the base rises and expands, and so continues in ever widening circles, as one new pertinent thought joins the preceding. Here one block is not laid beside the other, so that joints are made. There are really no joints, not even where the new thoughts are first introduced. The line of thought simply spirals in rising widening circles until all is complete. Keeping from idols (5:21) is only the brief, final touch.[50]

It is the point of wisdom to recognize this peculiar characteristic of this epistle's structure. By its very nature, any systematic outline of it must leave much to be desired. Yet for practical study some outline of it is desirable and helpful. An analysis of the epistle in the light of the announced purpose in 5:13 is here followed. It is hoped that it may prove helpful in making clear the basic aim of the epistle. (See the outline.)

3. CONTENTS

The epistle is devoid of all that is merely local. No temporal or individual matters are introduced. Yet, while the epistle is exceedingly impersonal, it is not abstract. Everything is related to the Christian life in the most intimate way. The coloring of the epistle is not local but moral. There is a spiritual and universal tone in it which makes it peculiarly adaptable to the Church today.

One cannot fail to notice the striking fact of the author's gentleness and tenderness of love blended with the most decided sternness and decisive pronouncements of judgment. "The absolute antagonism and incompatibility between the Christian life and sin of whatsoever kind or degree is maintained with a vehemence of utterance that verges at times upon the paradoxical."[51] No other writer in the New Testament uses stronger words in denunciation of sin and error than John. Thus we have a remarkable picture of the "Son of thunder" (Mk 3:17) blazing forth in judgment against sin but mellowed in love and kindness toward those who yielded themselves to our righteous and loving God.

The epistle contains no quotations from the Old Testament and

50. R. C. H. Lenski, *The Interpretation of the Epistles of St. Peter, St. John and St. Jude*, p. 374.
51. Law, 3:1712b.

only one allusion is made to Old Testament history (3:12). There is no mention of any detail of ritual or ecclesiastical organization. There is no mention of circumcision and the controversy which it aroused in the early life of the Church. There is no trace of the conflict between the advocates of the Law and the Gospel, between works and faith. There is no mention of the difference between Jew and Gentile. All these matters have been superseded in the consciousness of one universal Christian brotherhood. The main questions and considerations of the epistle center around the person and work of Christ Jesus and their implications for Christian living.

This is the epistle of love and brotherhood. The word *love* (*agapaō*) and its derivatives occur no less than fifty-one times in 1 John. It is also the epistle of experiential knowledge and Christian assurance. The words for knowledge (*ginōskō* and *oida*) occur forty-one times in the epistle. One of the characteristic ideas of the epistle is that of "witness." Since the received message of Christianity is being questioned by the false teachers, the author sets himself to prove that that message has been fully attested. It is confirmed not only by Christian experience but by the very testimony of God.

4. COMPANION TO FOURTH GOSPEL

That the epistle forms a companion work to the gospel of John is evident. That the two writings are complementary in purpose is clear from the stated purpose found in each.[52] Yet it is uncertain as to just what relation the author intended for the two to have. The view accepted concerning that relationship will be influenced by the view held as to the time of composition of the two. The question as to which was composed first has received opposite answers.[53] Some have held that the epistle was written first, while others maintain that the gospel was written some time before the epistle. Ebrard maintained that "the two documents were strictly simultaneous." He held that both arose out of the same historical situation and that the epistle was intended as a cover-letter accompanying the gospel as it was first sent out. He felt this view explained the absence of the epistolary form of the epistle as well as certain features of its contents.[54] This view that the epistle was a sort of "commendatory post-

52. See under "The Purpose of 1 John."
53. For the evidence on both sides see Brooke, pp. xix-xxvii.
54. John H. A. Ebrard, *Biblical Commentary on The Epistles of St. John*, pp. 24-34.

script" to the gospel is an interesting conjecture but cannot be proved.

Whatever may have been the author's intention as to the relation of 1 John to the gospel, it is clear that there is an intimate connection between the two. Plummer summarizes this as follows:

> The Gospel is objective, the Epistle subjective; the one is historical, the other moral; the one gives us the theology of the Christ, the other the ethics of the Christian; the one is didactic, the other polemical; the one states the truth as a thesis, the other as an antithesis; the one starts from the human side, the other from the divine; the one proves that the Man Jesus is the Son of God, the other insists that the Son of God is come in the flesh.[55]

The first epistle of John is indeed a worthy companion to the fourth gospel and the two may profitably be read together.

5. FAMOUS INTERPOLATION

The *Textus Receptus*, upon which our Authorized Version (1611) is based, contains a famous interpolated passage for which there is no valid textual evidence. The passage reads as follows, the italicized words marking the interpolation:

> For there are three that bear record *in heaven, the Father, the Word, and the Holy Ghost: and* the*se three are one. And there are three that bear witness in earth,* the Spirit, and the water, and the blood: and the*se* three agree in one (5:7-8).

The external evidence against the authenticity of these words is overwhelming. They are found in no Greek uncial manuscripts; no Greek cursive manuscript before the fifteenth century contains them. Only two known Greek cursives contain them (cursive 629 of the fourteenth century and 61 of the sixteenth century; also cursive 635 of the eleventh century has it in the margin in a seventeenth-century hand, and 88 of the twelfth century has it in the margin by a modern hand), and in them they are a manifest translation from a late recension of the Latin Vulgate. No ancient version of the first four centuries gives them. None of the Greek Church Fathers quotes the words. No Latin manuscript earlier than the fifth century contains them. Research has shown that the words had their origin as a gloss.

55. Plummer, p. 36.

on the text of John's epistle and eventually they found their way into the text of the Latin. The internal evidence, likewise, is strongly against them.[56]

In Greek texts the words were first printed in the Complutensian Polygot of 1514. Erasmus did not find them in the Greek manuscripts which he had and did not put them into his first two editions of the Greek Testament. Erasmus rashly promised to insert them into his Greek text if they could be found in any Greek manuscript. When he was confronted with Codex Montfort, cursive 61, he inserted them, although he stated that he suspected that the words had been inserted in the Greek to conform to the Latin. He said that he inserted the words in his text to avoid calumny! No wonder Erasmus never had the courage to embrace the Protestant Reformation. From the text of Erasmus it passed into the editions upon which our Authorized Version is based.

An Outline of 1 John

I. The Introduction, 1:1-4

   A. The eyewitness testimony to the Word of life, v. 1
   B. The historic manifestation of the Word of life, v. 2
   C. The resultant fellowship of believers, vv. 3-4

II. Assurance Through the Test of Fellowship, 1:5—2:17

   A. The basis for fellowship, 1:5
   B. The hindrances to fellowship, 1:6-10
      1. The denial of the reality of sin, vv. 6-7
      2. The denial of the principle of sin, vv. 8-9
      3. The denial of the practice of sin, v. 10
   C. The maintenance of fellowship, 2:1-17
      1. The provision for maintenance of fellowship, vv. 1-2
      2. The signs of the maintenance of fellowship, vv. 3-17
         a) The sign of obedience, vv. 3-5
         b) The sign of imitation, v. 6
         c) The sign of love, vv. 7-11

56. For a full discussion of the evidence see Westcott, pp. 202-9; Plummer, pp. 204-12.
   For this outline I am heavily in debt to Raymond E. Gingrich, *An Outline and Analysis of the First Epistle of John.*

      d) The sign of separation, vv. 12-17
         (1) The grounds for separation from the world, vv. 12-14
         (2) The appeal for separation from the world, vv. 15-17

III. Assurance Through the Conflict of Faith, 2:18—4:6

  A. The conflict between truth and error, 2:18-28
    1. The crisis faced by the believer, vv. 18-19
    2. The resources of the believer, vv. 20-21
    3. The criterion of a true believer, vv. 22-25
    4. The summary of the teaching, vv. 26-28
  B. The conflict between the children of God and children of the devil, 2:29—3:12
    1. The sign of the child of God, 2:29—3:3
      a) The practice of righteousness, 2:29
      b) The realization of present sonship, 3:1-2*a*
      c) The purifying effect of the future hope, vv. 2*b*-3
    2. The revelation from the practice of sin, 3:4-8*a*
      a) The implications of the practice of sin, vv. 4-5
      b) The revelation of the two classes, vv. 6-8*a*
    3. The deliverance from the practice of sin, vv. 8*b*-9
    4. The sign of the children of God and children of the devil, vv. 10-12
  C. The conflict between love and hate, 3:13-24
    1. The evidential value of love and hate, vv. 13-15
    2. The manifestation of love and hate, vv. 16-18
      a) The example and obligation of love, v. 16
      b) The revelation of the lack of love, v. 17
      c) The exhortation to practice true love, v. 18
    3. The assurances from the presence of love, vv. 19-24
      a) The assurance of being in the truth, vv. 19-20
      b) The assurance of answered prayer, vv. 21-22
      c) The assurance of union with Christ, vv. 23-24
  D. The conflict between the Spirit of truth and the spirit of error, 4:1-6
    1. The charge to test the spirits, v. 1
    2. The criterion for testing the spirits, vv. 2-3
    3. The criterion for testing men, vv. 4-6

IV. Assurance from the Evidence of Love, 4:7—5:5

  A. The nature of redeeming love, 4:7-16*a*
    1. The basis for the assurance from love, vv. 7-8
    2. The manifestation of redeeming love, vv. 9-10
    3. The obligation to mutual love, v. 11
    4. The perfecting of Christian love, v. 12
    5. The confirmations of redeeming love, vv. 13-16*a*
  B. The results of love, 4:16*b*—5:5
    1. The result in respect to self, 4:16*b*-18
    2. The result in respect to others, 4:19-21
      a) The principle of love, v. 19
      b) The profession of love, v. 20
      c) The proof of love, v. 21
    3. The result in respect to God, 5:1-5
      a) The revelation of love in saving faith, v. 1
      b) The revelation of love in obedience to God, vv. 2-3
      c) The revelation of love in overcoming faith, vv. 4-5

V. Assurance from the Witness of the Spirit, 5:6-12

  A. The external, historic witnesses, vv. 6-9
  B. The internal witness of the Spirit, vv. 10-12

VI. The Conclusion, 5:13-21

  A. The certainty of salvation as the purpose in writing, v. 13
  B. The confidence of answered prayer, vv. 14-15
  C. The counsel in respect to intercession, vv. 16-17
  D. The certainties of the Christian faith, vv. 18-20
    1. The certainty of the Christian's practice, v. 18
    2. The certainty of the Christian's contrast to the world, v. 19
    3. The certainty of Christ's mission, v. 20
  E. The final warning against idols, v. 21

A BOOK LIST ON THE JOHANNINE EPISTLES

Alexander, Neil. *The Epistles of John.* Torch Bible Commentaries. London: SCM, 1962.

    A brief, critical exposition which attributes the authorship to John the Elder, not the apostle. Does not hesitate to take issue with the position of John and openly denies the authority of the Scriptures.

Barclay, William. *The Letters of John and Jude.* The Daily Study Bible. 2d ed. Edinburgh: Saint Andrew, 1962.

Blaiklock, E. M. *Faith Is the Victory. Studies in the First Epistle of John.* Grand Rapids: Eerdmans, 1959.

Prints author's translation. Brief devotional comments by an evangelical layman. Not a commentary in the ordinary sense, but studies of outstanding themes of the epistle, originally given at a Keswick convention. Contains keen exegetical insights, relevant archaeological data, and significant allusions to persons or customs of the ancient world.

Braune, Karl. *The Epistles General of John.* In Lange's *Commentary on the Holy Scriptures.* Trans. from the German with additions by J. Isidor Mombert. Reprint. Grand Rapids: Zondervan, n.d.

A full exposition with an abundance of doctrinal, ethical, and homiletical material added.

Brooke, A. E. *A Critical and Exegetical Commentary on the Johannine Epistles.* International Critical Commentary. New York: Scribner's, 1912.

Greek text. Important introductory discussion of critical problems. The exegetical treatment of the text is valuable but must be read with theological discrimination. Has an extended treatment of the text on the "heavenly witnesses."

Bruce, F. F. *The Epistles of John.* Old Tappan, N.J.: Revell, 1970.

A popular, verse-by-verse interpretation intended for the general Christian reader. Textual, linguistic, and critical problems are lightly touched on. A conservative exposition which stresses the practical lessons to be learned from these letters.

Burdick, Donald W. *The Epistles of John.* Everyman's Bible Commentary. Chicago: Moody, 1970.

A careful exposition of these letters, well suited for individual study or Bible study classes. Burdick analyzes the first epistle as consisting of three cycles in ascending order to form a spiral. Holds that the apostle John wrote to refute Gnosticism by presenting two basic tests, the Christological and the ethical.

Candish, Robert S. *The First Epistle of John.* Reprint. Grand Rapids: Zondervan, n.d.

A series of forty-six sermon-lectures fervently presenting Christ as the only begotten Son of God and the believer's relationsnip to Him. First published in 1866, it vigorously attacks Romanist doctrine and warns against apostasy. The biographical sketch by Wilbur M. Smith adds to the value of the volume.

Conner, Walter Thomas. *The Epistles of John.* 1929. Rev. ed. Nashville, Tenn.: Broadman, 1957.

A conservative exposition by a Southern Baptist professor. Accepts Johannine authorship and warns against false teaching. Based on a careful study of the original text.

Dodd, C. H. *The Johannine Epistles.* The Moffatt New Testament Commentary. New York: Harper, 1946.

Prints the Moffatt translation. A brief exposition advocating numerous radical views. Dodd holds that the author is unknown, not the apostle John; argues for expiation, not propitiation; and advocates "realized eschatology" in place of John's "crude mythology" in Revelation.

Ebrard, John H. A. *Biblical Commentary on the Epistles of St. John.* Translated by W. B. Pope. Edinburgh: T. & T. Clark, 1860.

A massive (400 pages), technical commentary defending the genuineness of these epistles. The interpretation is based on the Greek and assumes acquaintance with that language. Vigorously conservative in its viewpoint.

Findlay, George G. *Fellowship in the Life Eternal.* Reprint. Grand Rapids: Eerdmans, 1955.

An exhaustive, conservative exposition combining careful scholarship with rare spiritual insight. Emphasizes the doctrinal as well as the practical teaching of the epistles.

Gingrich, Raymond E. *An Outline and Analysis of the First Epistle of John.* Grand Rapids: Zondervan, 1943.

A conservative exposition, originally prepared as a master's thesis. Contains a detailed outline of the epistle of definite value. The exposition brings out in clear form the thought and teaching of the epistle on the basis of the original.

Haupt, Erich. *The First Epistle of St. John. A Contribution to Biblical Theology.* Edinburgh: T. & T. Clark, 1893.

Greek text. While giving careful attention to the grammatical and linguistic side, the emphasis is upon the doctrinal elaboration of the epistle. Valuable for the doctrinal study of 1 John.

Kelly, William. *An Exposition of the Epistles of John the Apostle.* 1905. Reprint. Oak Park, Ill.: Bible Truth Pub., 1970.

Prints author's new translation. Twenty wordy lectures by a noted Plymouth Brethren scholar of the past century. Provides an important study of the text with numerous comments and illustrations of the religious scene from a perspective of intense loyalty to the Scriptures.

Lenski, R. C. H. *The Interpretation of the Epistles of St. Peter, St. John, and St. Jude.* Columbus, Ohio: Lutheran Book Concern, 1938.

Lias, J. J. *The First Epistle of St. John.* London: James Nisbet, 1887.
A full, conservative exposition of 1 John by a British preacher and scholar. At the bottom of each page, in smaller type, is added a homiletical treatment of the epistle.

Moody, Dale. *The Letters of John.* Waco, Tex.: Word, 1970.
Gives the author's own translation of 1 John, printed in strophe arrangement. The epistle, according to Moody, professor of theology at Southern Baptist Theological Seminary, is a polemic against Gnostic Judaism. The exposition reflects interaction with the latest theological theories.

Plummer, A. *The Epistles of S. John.* Cambridge Bible for Schools and Colleges. 1883. Reprint. Cambridge: U. Press, 1938.

————. "The Epistles of S. John, with Notes, Introduction and Appendices." In *Cambridge Greek Testament.* 1886. Reprint. Cambridge: U. Press, 1938.
The former volume is intended for the English student, while the second is an expanded edition for the Greek student. Both have definite value for the interpretation of these epistles.

Ross, Alexander. *The Epistles of James and John.* The New International Commentary on the New Testament. Grand Rapids: Eerdmans, 1954.

Sawtelle, Henry A. "Commentary on the Epistles of John." In *An American Commentary.* 1888. Reprint. Philadelphia: Amer. Bapt. Pubn. Soc., n.d.
A conservative interpretation by a Baptist scholar of the past century. Offers a careful unfolding of the original for the English reader.

Smith, David. "The Epistles of St. John." In *The Expositor's Greek Testament*, vol. 5. Reprint. Grand Rapids: Eerdmans, n.d.
Greek text. Important for linguistic study of the epistles. Defends Johannine authorship. The viewpoint is essentially conservative.

Stott, J. R. W. *The Epistles of John.* Tyndale New Testament Commentaries. Grand Rapids: Eerdmans, 1964.
A valuable, practical exposition by a conservative Anglican minister. The work is a happy blend of Bible teaching and practical theology.

Van Ryn, August. *The Epistles of John.* New York: Loizeaux, 1948.
    A rich, devotional exposition of these epistles by a conservative
    Bible teacher. Exposition based on the American Standard Version
    (1901).
Vine, W. E. *The Epistles of John, Light, Love, Life.* Grand Rapids:
    Zondervan, n.d.
    A strongly conservative exposition based upon a thorough knowl-
    edge of the Greek text. Holds that the first epistle is a defense of the
    true faith against the Ebionites, Docetists, and Cerinthians. The
    author's eschatological viewpoint is premillennial.
Westcott, Brooke Foss. *The Epistles of St. John.* Ed. F. F. Bruce.
    Grand Rapids: Eerdmans, 1966.
    Greek text. Long recognized as a classic commentary on the Johan-
    nine epistles. First published in 1883. Bruce has updated the intro-
    ductory material and provided a summary of the discoveries and de-
    velopments since Westcott's time.
White, R. E. O. *Open Letter to Evangelicals. A Devotional and
    Homiletic Commentary on the First Epistle of John.* Grand Rapids:
    Eerdmans, 1964.
    A neoevangelical interpretation, advocating many of the views of
    C. H. Dodd. Holds that the believer's authority lies not in the words
    of Scripture, but in Christ. Helpful for its illustrations but doctrinally
    weak.
Wilder, Amos N.; and Hoon, Paul W. "The First, Second, and Third
    Epistles of John." In *The Interpreter's Bible,* vol. 12. New York:
    Abingdon, 1957.
    Introduction and exegesis by Wilder, exposition by Hoon. The
    work of two American scholars adhering to the old liberal tradition.
Woods, Guy N. *A Commentary on the New Testament Epistles of
    Peter, John, and Jude.* Nashville, Tenn.: Gospel Advocate, 1954.

9

SECOND AND THIRD JOHN

An Introduction to 2 and 3 John

The two brief letters known as 2 and 3 John have the distinction of being the shortest books in the Bible. Third John is about a line shorter than the second epistle.[1] Their length is such that they would each fill a single sheet of ordinary papyrus paper. Their similarity in length, structure, and style justifies the description of them as "twin-sisters."

The Canonicity and Authorship of 2 and 3 John

1. external evidence

In view of their brevity and the casual nature of these epistles, it is not surprising that they were among the New Testament writings which had the hardest struggle for canonical recognition. Eusebius listed them among the *antilegomena* (*Eccl. Hist.* 3. 25). The external evidence, though scanty, is remarkably weighty.

Irenaeus (*c.* 140-203), in his famous work *Against Heresies*, twice quotes from 2 John. Speaking about certain heretics, he writes, "John, the disciple of the Lord, has intensified their condemnation, when he desires us not even to address to them the salutation of 'good-speed'," and quotes 2 John 11 (1. 16. 3). In 3. 16. 8 he quotes 2 John 7-8 but makes the slip of quoting it as from the first epistle. But this slip of memory all the more strongly shows that he regarded the second epistle equally as the writing of the apostle John.

Clement of Alexandria (*c.* 155-*c.* 215) in his extant works speaks of John's "longer Epistle," thus showing that he recognized at least one other and shorter epistle by John (*The Stromata*, 2. 15). Eusebius

---

1. "Counting the letters, and allowing 36 letters for the ancient line, gives for 2 John 32 lines, for 3 John not quite 31 lines." Theodor Zahn, *Introduction to the New Testament*, 3:382.

tells us that Clement in his *Hypotyposes* gave "abridged accounts of all the canonical Scriptures, not even omitting those that are disputed, I mean the book of Jude, and the other general epistles" (*Eccl. Hist.* 6. 14).

Cyprian, bishop of Carthage (*c.* 200-258) does not quote these epistles himself, but in his account of a council at Carthage (A.D. 256) he says that Aurelius, bishop of Chullabi, quoted 2 John 10-11 with the observation, "John the Apostle laid it down in his Epistle" (*Concerning the Baptism of Heretics*). Alford concludes that this shows that these epistles "were received as apostolic and canonical in the North African church."[2]

The evidence of the Muratorian Canon (*c.* 170) is somewhat ambiguous. First John is mentioned in connection with the fourth gospel, and later on mention is made of "two epistles of the John who has been mentioned before." This has been taken to refer to 1 and 2 John, 3 John being thus omitted. But it seems more natural to refer it to 2 and 3 John. If so, that would show that these two epistles were regarded as canonical at Rome before the end of the second century.

In his extant writings Origen (*c.* 185-*c.* 253) does not quote from these two epistles, but he knew of them. He expresses no personal opinion about them but tells us that "not all agree that they are genuine" (*Eccl. Hist.* 6. 25). Westcott holds that Origen quotes 1 John in such a way as to "shew that the other Epistles were not familiarly known."[3]

Eusebius (*c.* 265-340) conscientiously placed these two epistles among the *antilegomena* in his list of canonical books (*Eccl. Hist.* 3: 25). On the basis of his quotations in his *Demonstratio Evangelica* Alford thinks that Eusebius accepted them as by John.[4]

Jerome (*c.* 340-420), while testifying that the first epistle was universally accepted as by the apostle John, held that the other two were written by "John the Presbyter" instead. The doubts of Jerome are apparently the doubts of the scholar rather than the prevailing view in the Church. The Council of Carthage (A.D. 397) definitely recognized these epistles as canonical.

The epistles were not included in the Old Syriac Version (*c.* 200),

2. Henry Alford, *The Greek Testament*, 4:2:182 Proleg.
3. Brooke Foss Westcott, *A General Survey of the History of the Canon of the New Testament*, p. 331.
4. Alford, p. 183.

but they were included in the Thebaic (*c.* 200) and Memphitic Versions (first half of the third century).

The external evidence for the third epistle is considerably less than for the second. Its contents were less suitable for quotation, so it is less frequently mentioned. Goodspeed, who conceives of 2 and 3 John as covering letters for 1 John, holds that all three originally circulated as a corpus and that consequently the ancients referred to them differently as either one, two, or three letters. He concludes, "These varied testimonies are not to be understood as meaning that one writer had one letter and another two, but that all possessed the full corpus of three letters, one long and two very short, and designated them differently."[5] If this view is correct, it would greatly strengthen the external evidence for both of these epistles.

In summarizing the external evidence Plummer remarks, "It is apparent that precisely those witnesses who are nearest to St. John in time are favourable to the Apostolic authorship, and seem to know of no other view."[6]

That these epistles were tardy in gaining canonical recognition was not without reasons. Their brevity, the comparative unimportance of their contents, as well as the fact that one, if not both, was a strictly private letter, caused them to be less widely circulated and read than letters directed to known churches. When circumstances concerning their origin were forgotten, they came to be looked upon with suspicion. Says Salmon,

> I believe that these hesitations arose from the fact that these Epistles were not included in the public reading of the early Church—a thing intelligible enough from the private nature of their contents.[7]

The nature of their contents as unmarked by special features offered slight occasion to their being quoted. The one passage in them which is distinctive is verses ten and eleven of the second epistle, and it was just this passage which was most often quoted. The fact that they were not quoted more by the ancient Church Fathers does not prove that they did not know them or accept them as authentic. We may say with Law,

5. Edgar J. Goodspeed, *An Introduction to the New Testament*, p. 324.
6. A. Plummer, *The Epistles of St. John*, Cambridge Bible for Schools and Colleges, p. 53.
7. George Salmon, *An Historical Introduction to the Study of the Books of the New Testament*, p. 271.

The fact, therefore, that, in spite of such obstacles, these letters did become widely known and eventually attained to canonical rank is proof of a general conviction of the soundness of the tradition which assigned them to the apostle John.[8]

2. INTERNAL EVIDENCE

The contents of these two epistles proclaim the impression that they are the product of the same pen. This is shown by their close resemblance in structure, style, phraseology, and tone of thought. Both open in the same manner: the writer describes himself as "the elder"; the readers are indicated with the same formula; both give expression to the writer's joy and the reports concerning the readers. Both epistles close in almost identical ways: the assertion about having many other things to write; the promise of an impending visit; the greeting to the readers. Both epistles employ characteristically Johannine expressions. They center in truth and love. Both speak of hospitality, the one of that which is forbidden, the other of that which is enjoined. Brooke concludes:

> The similarity between them is too close to admit of any explanation except common authorship or conscious imitation. It would tax the ingenuity of the most skilful separator to determine which is the original and which the copy.[9]

The relationship of these letters to 1 John further makes it clear that all three must have come from the same hand. Second John bears the closest resemblance to the first. More than half of its contents are also contained in 1 John. Both of these epistles have many phrases which recall, or are identical with those of the first epistle.[10] Both also reveal the characteristic Johannine practice of emphasizing an idea by stating it both positively and negatively (2 John 9; 3 John 11). These similarities shut us up to the alternative choice of a common authorship or a conscious imitation. But the supposition that these brief and comparatively unimportant letters are forgeries places a strain upon credulity. What motive could there be for attempting to pass off such writings as the work of an apostle? Salmon boldly concludes:

8. R. Law, "John, The Epistles of: The Second and Third Epistles," in *The International Standard Bible Encyclopaedia*, 3:1718a.
9. A. E. Brooke, *A Critical and Exegetical Commentary on the Johannine Epistles*, International Critical Commentary, p. lxxiii.
10. Ibid., p. lxxiv.

It is certain that these two letters are no forgeries, but genuine relics of some great Church ruler, preserved after the circumstances which had drawn them forth were forgotten. And if ever the argument from identity of style and matter can be relied on, it is certain also that tradition has rightly handed down the belief that the writer was no other than the author of the First Epistle and the Gospel.[11]

Unlike 1 John, these epistles do contain an epistolary designation of the author. But the writer simply styles himself "the elder" without giving his name. These are the only New Testament epistles which begin with this appellation. But the term is not used to hide the author's identity. He comes boldly forward in his own person; the readers know who he is and know him well. He claims great authority, sends his delegates to an established church, and feels that his presence will be sufficient to put down opposition to his authority. He speaks and acts as one who is conscious of apostolic authority and is aware that his authority is known to them.

It is asserted that the author's description of himself simply as "the elder" distinguishes him from John the apostle. But there is nothing inconsistent in John's use of this term to identify himself. The apostle Peter did not think it inconsistent to speak of himself as an elder (1 Pe 5:1). The absolute use of the term *"the* elder" marks a position wholly exceptional. There is no reason to believe that the term is used in an official sense. An ordinary elder, writing in his own person and not wishing to mislead, would hardly have called himself *"the* elder." Further, "the authority which the author claims is far greater than ever attached to the office of 'Presbyter'."[12] The ministry which "the elder" is seen as engaged in in these epistles—sending out deputies and receiving their reports, supervising a wide circle of churches, visiting them and giving them directions and guidance— is precisely the sort of ministry the apostle John is known to have carried on in his later life from Ephesus.[13]

Just why John did not give his name cannot be said, but his employment of the designation "the elder" is quite appropriate and distinctive. Its use marks out for him a position which would not necessarily have been suggested by the title "an apostle." Toward the close of the first century the term "apostle" had become a common

11. Salmon, p. 272.
12. Brooke, pp. lxxv-lxxvi.
13. See "Introduction to 1 John," under "Authorship."

designation for just such messengers as are mentioned in the third epistle. But this title was more definitive of his true position as the sole survivor of an earlier generation. Concerning the use of this title Smith says,

> The second generation of Christians used it of their predecessors, "the men of early days," who had witnessed the great beginnings. Thus, Papias uses it of the Apostles, and Irenaeus in turn uses it of Papias and his contemporaries. It was therefore natural that St. John, the last of the Apostles, the sole survivor of "the elder men," should be known among the churches of Asia as "the elder."[14]

Thus his use of the term *"the* elder" would at once identify him to his readers.

Humility may have kept John from using either his own name or making a claim to apostolic authority. This is quite in accord with his practice in the gospel and the first epistle.[15] Paul did not always care to use the title of apostle in his letters.

Again, it is objected that the author cannot be an apostle because it is inconceivable that an apostle should have been so opposed and defied as was the author by Diotrephes (3 John 9-10). Certainly, his bold and malicious action is highly astonishing. But the revelation of this surprising action cannot invalidate the evidence for the Johannine authorship of the epistle. The event simply shows us that even apostolic churches were not always examples of worthy Christian conduct and holiness. Paul had his violent opponents; the opposition offered Paul at Corinth should prepare us for an action such as this. As Farrar says, "The history of the Church of Christ, from the earliest down to the latest days, teems with subjects for perplexity and surprise."[16]

3. CONCLUSION

The external evidence is by no means unfavorable to the view that John the apostle wrote these epistles. That was the view of those closest to the time of their composition. Later, as the circumstances

14. David Smith, "The Epistles of St. John," in *The Expositor's Greek Testament,* 5:160.
15. John's use of his name in the Revelation is determined by the fact that the book is modeled after the Old Testament prophetic books where the name of the prophet to whom the prophecy is communicated is always given.
16. F. W. Farrar, *The Early Days of Christianity,* p. 590.

in connection with their composition were forgotten, doubts concerning the identity of the author arose. The preponderance of the external evidence is definitely in favor of the apostolic authorship.

The internal evidence is overwhelmingly in favor of the traditional view. The historical situation reflected in these brief letters harmonizes with our information concerning the closing years of John's life. The contents of the epistles point to the Johannine authorship. We conclude with Salmon that "no account of the matter seems satisfactory but the traditional one, that the writer was the Apostle John."[17]

The Readers of 2 and 3 John

1. SECOND JOHN

The second epistle is addressed to "the elect lady and her children." The exact meaning of this address is enigmatic and has given rise to varied interpretations. The problem that it presents puzzles the scholars. Westcott concludes that "the problem of the address is insoluble with our present knowledge."[18] The diversity of interpretations is by no means of modern origin. These interpretations fall into two general groups. The question is whether the words "elect lady" (*eklektē kuria*) are to be taken figuratively or literally.

Those interpreters who accept the figurative meaning divide into two groups. One view, as old as Jerome, is that this is a catholic epistle addressed to the Church as a whole under the figure of a lady. This view is untenable. It was not addressed to all Christians, for the author knows to whom he is writing and has intimate knowledge of their circumstances. Furthermore, then the reference in verse 13 to her sister is meaningless.

The view of many commentators is that the "elect lady" means a local church. Guesses as to the identity of this local church have included Corinth, Philadelphia, Jerusalem, Ephesus, and Babylon. It was this figurative interpretation which encouraged many early writers to consider the epistle as worthy of a place in the canon. But there is nothing in the epistle which suggests this allegorical meaning for the address. In a highly figurative writing such an interpretation might be fully justified, but the epistle gives no hint of any figurative

17. Salmon, p. 272.
18. Brooke Foss Westcott, *The Epistles of St. John. The Greek Text with Notes and Essays*, p. 224.

interpretation being intended. Rather, "the simplicity of the little letter precludes the possibility of so elaborate an allegory, while the tenderness of its tone stamps it as a personal communication."[19] Further, to make the "elect lady" mean a local church and her children the members of that church is to eliminate the distinction made between the lady and her children; then the two are identical. Also, there is no other instance in the New Testament where a church is addressed in such a figurative manner.

It seems much more natural to take the simple words of the epistle to refer to an actual lady and her children. This view is favored by the simplicity of the letter, the reference to the children of the elect lady (1, 4), the mention of her sister (13), the reference to the elect lady's house (10), as well as the analogy of the third epistle, which certainly is addressed to an individual. It is interesting to notice that the formula of address in both epistles is exactly the same.[20] We conclude the epistle *may* have been addressed to a church but we do not think it probable. We agree with Farrar when he says, "Certainly the *prima facie* impression created by the words would be that they refer to a lady."[21]

But there is no agreement as to the exact significance of the address among those who accept the personal interpretation of the expression "elect lady." The Greek is capable of being differently translated; four translations have been suggested: (1) to *an* elect lady, (2) to *the* elect lady, (3) to the elect *Cyria* (or *Kuria*), (4) to the lady *Electa*. The fourth rendering seems to have been the view of Clement of Alexandria (*c.* 155-215), according to a Latin translation of his writings. Among moderns it is advocated, for example, by Law.[22] But this seems untenable in the light of verse 13. Then we would have two sisters in the family with the strange name of Electa. That the term "elect" is an adjective, rather than a proper name, is suggested by its position without the article in the Greek.

The third rendering has many advocates. It was the view of Athanasius (*c.* 298-373), and it is accepted by many modern scholars.

19. Smith, 5:162.
20. This similarity may be seen by setting out the two as follows:
    "The elder *unto the elect lady and her children* whom I love in truth."
    "The elder *unto Gaius the beloved*　　　　　whom I love in truth."
21. Farrar, p. 578.
22. Robert Law, "Elect Lady," in *The International Standard Bible Encyclopaedia*, 2:925*ab*.

It is the rendering suggested in the margin of the American Standard Version (1901). The name Cyria does occur in ancient documents. The difficulty with this translation is that if it is a proper name, on the analogy of 3 John 1, "Unto Gaius the beloved," the adjective *elect* should stand after the proper name. See also Romans 16:5, 8, 9, 10, 12, 13 (Greek). The name Cyria (*Kuria*) is the feminine of the common word for *Lord* (*kurios*). It is the Greek equivalent of the Hebrew for Martha. This has led some to advance the idea that this lady was Martha of Bethany, or even Mary the mother of our Lord. As Farrar says, to make such conjectures "is to be guilty of the idle and reprehensible practice of suggesting theories which rest on the air, and are not even worth the trouble of a serious refutation."[23]

The renderings "to an elect lady," or "to the elect lady"[24] leave open the question of the identity of the matron to whom the letter is addressed. That the apostle John should write to a Christian lady and her family is nothing extraordinary. Women like Priscilla, Lydia, and Phoebe played an important part in the life of the early church. In Romans 16 Paul sends his greetings to a number of Christian women. It is indicative of the elevating influence of Christianity upon Christian womanhood. That the lady is left unnamed is entirely in accord with the feelings of the day.

Who this lady was we do not know. All we know about her must be gathered from this letter. She was a Christian matron, apparently a widow, known for her exemplary character and Christian hospitality. It is probable that her house was the meeting place of the church in her community, according to the custom of those days when as yet there were no church buildings. She had a family of grown children, at least some of whom John had learned to know as devout Christians. She had a sister, perhaps now deceased, some of whose children were in contact with the apostle as he wrote. Apparently she lived not far from Ephesus and John had previously visited the home.

2. THIRD JOHN

The third epistle is addressed to "Gaius the beloved." About him we know nothing for sure beyond what is found in this brief note. Three other men in the New Testament bear the name of Gaius;

23. Farrar, p. 583.
24. The first is the more literal and seems preferable. The absence of the article in the Greek is perfectly intelligible.

namely, Gaius of Macedonia (Ac 19:29), Gaius of Corinth (1 Co 1:14; Ro 16:23), and Gaius of Derbe (Ac 20:4). Attempts to identify this Gaius with any one of these other men are without a firm basis. The name *Gaius*, which is the Greek equivalent of the Latin *Caius*, was one of the most common names in the Roman Empire. "So common was it that it was selected in the Roman law-books to serve the familiar purpose of John Doe and Richard Roe in our own legal formularies."[25]

Gaius was a man who was greatly beloved by the apostle and received his highest commendation. (Notice the use of the term "beloved" in vv. 1, 2, 5, 11). He was a man of sterling Christian character. His spiritual prosperity reflected itself in active deeds of hospitality toward those engaged in the furtherance of the Gospel. It is not said that he was an official in the church; apparently he was an active lay member who worked in close cooperation with the missionary activities directed by John.

THE OCCASION FOR 2 AND 3 JOHN

1. SECOND JOHN

The writing of 2 John was occasioned by the apostle's knowledge of the persistent efforts of false teachers in the Christian community where this Christian lady lived. He knew that she was a Christian lady given to entertaining itinerant preachers visiting the community. Aware of the efforts of these false teachers to gain entree to such homes, he writes warning her against aiding such false teachers. It also gives him an opportunity to urge the continuance in the teaching which had been received.

2. THIRD JOHN

The third epistle was called forth by the report received by John from his missionaries concerning the high-handed action of Diotrephes in the church to which Gaius belonged. John has sent out messengers of the Gospel to the surrounding territory and had commended them to the churches for hospitality and support. When they arrived at the church where Gaius lived, Diotrephes, an influential member, if not the leader, of the church, refused to receive them, spoke out against the apostle himself, and opposed those who followed John's request. The missionaries were befriended by Gaius

25. Farrar, p. 569.

and upon their return to Ephesus (apparently) made their report before the church. In response John wrote to Gaius expressing his appreciation for his friendly reception of the missionaries and announcing his intention of a personal visit to deal with the trouble.

THE PLACE AND DATE OF 2 AND 3 JOHN

1. PLACE

There is nothing in these epistles which indicates the place from which they were written. The common assumption is that they were written from Ephesus shortly before one of the apostle's tours through the churches of the province. It is possible that the second epistle was written while he was on one of his tours where he met the children of the matron to whom he writes, but the former assumption is more natural.

2. DATE

These letters offer no data to determine the date of composition. Their close affinity to 1 John supports the assumption that they were written near the same time as 1 John. This would suggest an early date of A.D. 80-81, or a later date of A.D. 97-98. The early date seems preferable.

THE PURPOSE OF 2 AND 3 JOHN

1. SECOND JOHN

The primary purpose of this epistle was to give warning against extending indiscriminate hospitality to traveling teachers whose soundness in the Christian faith was questionable. Those who proved themselves to be "progressives" who did not abide in the doctrine of Christ were to be refused aid in their destructive work. A further purpose in writing was to commend the recipients for their loyalty to the truth as preached by the apostle himself and to urge them to continue to walk in love and to keep the Lord's commandments.

2. THIRD JOHN

The primary object of this epistle was further to enlist the good services of Gaius on behalf of the missionaries whom John was sending out. John warms the heart of Gaius by expressing his deep love for him, assures him of his prayers for his prosperity and health, tells him of his joy because of his stand for the truth, and commends him for his hospitality already shown to the visiting missionaries. He is urged to continue the good work. He encourages him with a lesson from the unworthy conduct of Diotrephes and announces that he will come to deal personally with the self-seeking Diotrephes. The letter is in effect a letter of recommendation for Demetrius, who probably was the leader of the missionary party being sent out and the bearer of the letter.

THE CHARACTERISTICS OF 2 AND 3 JOHN

These brief letters show a remarkable likeness in structure, style, and tone of thought. The salutation and the conclusion are very similar. Both epistles move in the realm of truth and love. The word *truth* occurs five times in the second epistle and six times in the third. The word *love* is used four times in the second, while in hte third it is used twice, and *beloved* four times. Both contain the thought of the Christian life as a walk in the truth.

These two writings, the shortest in the Bible, are valuable as offering us a picture of the apostle John in his dealings with individuals. They are valuable illustrations of a free and intimate correspondence between Christians such as must have been very common in the early Church. They are not of any great doctrinal importance, but they do give us a vivid glimpse into the closing years of the apostolic era with its troubles and its triumphs.

The message of the two epistles is complementary. They show the place and importance of Christian hospitality in the early Church. The second warns against false hospitality which would aid and further false teaching. The third commends Christian hospitality to missionary brethren as the inviolable duty of individuals and the churches. It is distinctly the epistle of missionary obligation. In them John provides two safeguards for the Church. "Heresy and schism are the dangers to which it is perpetually exposed. St. John's condemnation of the spirit of *heresy* is recorded in the Second Epistle; his condemnation of the spirit of *schism* is written in the Third Epistle."[26]

The most startling thing in the second epistle is John's directive not to receive heretics into the house, nor to bid them goodspeed. Not

26. W. Alexander, "The Third Epistle of John," in *The Speaker's Commentary, New Testament*, 4:374b. Italics in original.

infrequently this has been felt to be too severe. The advice certainly is not inconsistent with the character of John. It gives us a glimpse of that element in his nature which caused Jesus to call the sons of Zebedee "sons of thunder" (Mk 3:17). But it would be a mistake to attribute it simply to the fiery nature of John. The words of John contain a vitally needed corrective to our modern easygoing tolerance which will tolerate and even fellowship with error for the sake of peace and organizational unity. Alford rightly remarks, "It would have been infinitely better for the Church now, if this command had been observed in all ages by her faithful sons."[27]

The third epistle gives a vivid character portrayal of the three men which appear in it. The etching is made with great psychological skill. Each man appears as a distinct individual; the presentation testifies to the writer's full knowledge behind the picture. The character delineations are life-like and convincing.

AN OUTLINE OF 2 JOHN

I. The Salutation, vv. 1-3

    A. The writer, v. 1*a*

    B. The readers, vv. 1*b*-2

    C. The assurance, v. 3

II. The Message, vv. 4-11

    A. The occasion for the letter, v. 4

    B. The appeal for love and obedience, vv. 5-6

    C. The warning against false teachers, vv. 7-9

        1. The reason for the warning, v. 7

        2. The contents of the warning, v. 8

        3. The statement of the contrasted consequences, v. 9

    D. The prohibition against aiding the false teachers, vv. 10-11

        1. The statement of the prohibition, v. 10

        2. The reason for the prohibition, v. 11

III. The Conclusion, vv. 12-13

    A. The explanation about the brevity of the letter, v. 12

    B. The greeting from the children of her sister, v. 13

27. Alford, 4:2:521*a*.

AN OUTLINE OF 3 JOHN

I. The Salutation, vv. 1-4

   A. The writer, v. 1*a*
   B. The reader, v. 1*b*
   C. The wish, vv. 2-4
      1. The statement of the wish, v. 2
      2. The reason for the wish, vv. 3-4

II. The Message, vv. 5-12

   A. The obligation to support the missionaries, vv. 5-8
      1. The commendation of Gaius for his service to the missionaries, vv. 5-6*a*
      2. The suggestion of his further service to the missionaries, v. 6*b*
      3. The explanation concerning the missionary obligation, vv. 7-8
   B. The temporary triumph of ambitious evil, vv. 9-10
      1. The letter of John to the church, v. 9*a*
      2. The refusal by Diotrephes to receive them, v. 9*b*
      3. The action of John at his coming, v. 10*a*
      4. The account of the activity of Diotrephes, v. 10*b*
   C. The personal lesson from the circumstances, v. 11
   D. The commendation of Demetrius, v. 12

III. The Conclusion, vv. 13-14

   A. The explanation about the brevity of the letter, vv. 13-14*a*
   B. The benediction, v. 14*b*
   C. The greetings, v. 14*c*

A BOOK LIST ON 2 AND 3 JOHN

See the Book List under 1 John

Part 2

THE REVELATION

10

THE REVELATION

AN INTRODUCTION TO THE REVELATION

THE BOOK OF REVELATION[1] is the true capstone of the Bible. It is the only distinctively prophetic book in the New Testament. Other New Testament books contain various prophetic portions, but none of them provides such a sustained prophetic picture of the future as is given in this concluding book of the biblical canon. Without it our Bible would be quite incomplete—like a stirring story without an ending or a drama without its climax. It brings the eschatological expectations of the Church to their fitting conclusion. It "supplies the finishing touch to the whole panorama of the biblical story."[2] It is truly the book of consummation. That which is begun in the book of Genesis is brought to its conclusion in the book of Revelation.[3] It is irreplaceable. For those who have spiritually illuminated eyes, the Apocalypse[4] is one of the most precious and extraordinary writings in the world.

THE APPROACH TO THE REVELATION

The Apocalypse is commonly regarded as being the New Testament book most difficult to understand. Its strange symbolism and grotesque imagery are difficult for the modern reader to envision, leaving the uneasy impression that they are devoid of sober significance. Its sweeping apocalyptic visions of devastating world judgments seem unreal and far removed from the experiences of the com-

1. Not plural "Revelations." This book is not composed of a series of more or less independent revelations; rather, it is a revelation which has its unifying center in Jesus Christ.
2. Everett F. Harrison, *Introduction to the New Testament*, p. 475.
3. See Fredk. A. Tatford, *Prophecy's Last Word, An Exposition of the Revelation*, p. 19, for a thirty-point comparison, drawn from E. W. Bullinger.
4. The terms, *the Revelation*, derived from the Latin, and *the Apocalypse*, derived from the Greek, are synonymous and are used interchangeably.

mon man, striking him as improbable of realization. Although the book presents itself as a "revelation," not a few have felt that it might more appropriately be designated a "concealment." For many readers it remains a closed book. It is unquestionably one of the most misunderstood and misused books of the New Testament.

1. TWO EXTREMES

Two extreme attitudes toward the book of Revelation need to be avoided.

One extreme attitude is that it cannot be understood and should be left alone. Scott, who mentions that some have considered this book "so mysterious that all efforts to understand it must necessarily be futile," quotes an old commentator as saying, "This is a book which either finds a man mad or leaves him so."[5] Due to such an adverse impression of the book, many have deliberately avoided it. It has been the reaction not only of lay Christians but also of ecclesiastical leaders. Smith observes, "Calvin refused to write a commentary on Revelation, and gave it very little consideration in his massive writings. Luther for years avoided its teachings."[6] At the beginning of the modern critical era, the German critic J. S. Semler remarked that " 'the tone of the Apocalypse' was 'displeasing and offensive' to him, and therefore he could not regard the book as inspired."[7] And the modern scholar T. Henshaw wishes "it had not been included" in the New Testament and asserts, "In the last hundred years it has ceased to exercise direct influence on any but eccentric individuals who have no knowledge of modern theological scholarship."[8] While hesitating to express an adverse attitude toward it because it is a part of our Bible, many Christians today seldom read the book and frankly admit that they do not understand it.

Guthrie notes that the modern neglect of the Apocalypse "did not characterize the earliest history of the book."[9] And paradoxically, it has always held a fascination for various individuals. "Down through the ages," says Smith, "it has been like a magnet, irresistibly drawing

5. Ernest Findlay Scott, *The Literature of the New Testament*, p. 275.
6. Wilbur M. Smith, "Revelation," in *The Wycliffe Commentary*, ed. Charles F. Pfeiffer and Everett F. Harrison, p. 1491.
7. Werner Georg Kümmel, *Introduction to the New Testament*, p. 332.
8. T. Henshaw, *New Testament Literature in the Light of Modern Scholarship*, pp. 417-18.
9. Donald Guthrie, *New Testament Introduction*, p. 931.

to its study Christians of every school of thought, laymen, clergy, and professors."[10] Its prophecies have called forth long and intensive study. The steady flow of publications on the Revelation by modern scholars shows that the book continues to challenge attention.

Preoccupation with the Apocalypse can readily lead to a second extreme which should be avoided, namely, the attitude that the interpreter possesses an infallible understanding of every symbol and detail of the book. While we firmly accept that the proper approach to and prolonged study of its contents can give us an intelligible and consistent understanding of the book, it must be admitted that there are many details which will remain uncertain until the actual time of fulfillment. Especially to be avoided is any tendency to use the book to set dates or to employ obscure passages as a basis for promulgating fanciful and spectacular teachings.

2. DEMANDS UPON INTERPRETER

The book of Revelation makes serious demands upon the would-be interpreter. It was originally given to God's "servants" and was communicated to them through "his servant John" (1:1). By its very nature, the Apocalypse cannot be expected to yield its true message to one who lives in the open disregard of God and His will (cf. Rev 22:10-15).

Like other Scriptures, it demands that the interpreter attentively "hear what the Spirit saith to the churches" (2:7). Intellectual acumen and speculative ingenuity are not adequate equipment for the proper unfolding of its message. Spirit-guided receptivity is essential.

For an adequate unfolding of its message, the interpreter needs a knowledge of the rest of the Bible. As the capstone of the biblical revelation, the Apocalypse is rightly to be understood only in the light of that prior revelation. Ideally, the interpretation of the Revelation should constitute the acme of biblical interpretation. Admittedly the book demands prolonged and diligent study. Smith appropriately remarks,

> Because of its symbolism, its saturation with Old Testament passages and themes, the various schemes of interpretation that have developed concerning this book through the ages, and the profundity and

10. Smith, p. 1491.

vastness of the subjects that are here unveiled, I believe that the Apocalypse, above every other book of the Bible, will yield its meaning only to those who give it prolonged and careful study.[11]

THE NATURE OF THE REVELATION

The book of Revelation possesses a unique literary character. Its opening words identify it as a "Revelation" or an "Apocalypse." The latter term, derived from a transliteration of the Greek noun *apokalupsis*, means a disclosure or unveiling of what would otherwise be hidden or unrevealed. But the title and contents of this book establish that it is not an unveiling of truth generally but a disclosure of future or eschatological events which Jesus Christ granted to John.

Only in the opening title (1:1) is this book called an apocalypse. The designation is commonly taken to convey a connection with the genre of writings called "apocalyptic."[12] This type of literature, written in symbolic, pictorial language, employed visions as a means of presenting its message and dealt principally with eschatological events. This type of literature "flourished in Israel from Maccabean times until the final defeat of Bar Kokhba in A.D. 135. As a rule these revelations about the future or about the structure of heaven were not signed by their true authors but were fictitiously attributed to some great man of Israel's past."[13] Examples are *Enoch, Fourth Ezra,* and the *Assumption of Moses.* This literature was rooted in the message of the Old Testament prophets. Conscious that true prophetic revelation had ceased, the apocalyptic writers used their pseudo-predictive writings to seek to strengthen and encourage the suffering people of God with the assurance that He would intervene to punish the wicked, vindicate His cause, and reward His people.

While the title designated his work as an *apocalypse,* John at once proceeded to call his book a "prophecy" (1:3), and reemphasized it in the conclusion (22:7, 10, 18-19). John employed the apocalyptic form in the service of true prophecy. The book is therefore not to be viewed as a Christian equivalent to the Jewish apocalypses which were produced in later Judaism in large numbers. The author is a genuine prophet, who, like the Old Testament prophets, received his

11. Ibid., p. 1500.
12. See George E. Ladd, "Apocalyptic Literature," in *The Zondervan Pictorial Bible Dictionary,* pp. 49-50; Leon Morris, *Apocalyptic.*
13. Glenn W. Barker, William L. Lane, J. Ramsey Michaels, *The New Testament Speaks,* p. 364.

prophetic commission directly when the glorified Christ appeared to him on Patmos and commissioned him to write the message revealed to him (1:19-20). His prophetic consciousness is evident throughout the book. His prophetic work was born out of his own experience as a "seer."

John effectively combined the prophetic and the apocalyptic genre, for they are not mutually exclusive. The latter is rather a development of the former, and some Old Testament prophecy came to take on the characteristics and form of the apocalyptic. This apocalyptic feature of the Old Testament prophets is seen in Isaiah 24–27, Joel, Ezekiel, Daniel, and Zechariah. In combining the two, John communicated his eschatological message through use of the apocalyptic form but preserved the prophetic spirit with his demands for an immediate ethical response.

John further employed the epistolary form to communicate his revealed message. The book begins with the familiar three-point epistolary salutation (1:4-6) and concludes with the epistolary greeting, "The grace of the Lord Jesus be with the saints" (22:21). Goodspeed notes that this combination of the apocalyptic and the epistolary is "something entirely foreign to the apocalyptic type."[14]

Under the guidance of the Spirit, John thus employed a unique combination; he gave expression to his prophetic message in apocalyptic form as peculiarly adapted to the needs of believers under persecution, while using the epistolary form as a practical means of communicating with distant congregations. The strictly epistolary section (chaps. 1-3) serves as the portal to the distinctly apocalyptic portion of the book. The epistolary form "afforded John the medium through which to transmit a specific revelation to each of the seven churches named in the book (cf. 1:11), and at the same time to provide all the churches, not only with analyses of prevailing conditions designed to be mutually instructive, but also with a unifying message of encouragement in the crisis which they were experiencing in common."[15]

THE ATTESTATION TO REVELATION IN THE EARLY CHURCH

The attestation to the book of Revelation in the early Church is

14. Edgar J. Goodspeed, *An Introduction to the New Testament*, p. 243.
15. Elmer E. Flack, "The Revelation of John," in *New Testament Commentary*, ed. Herbert C. Alleman, p. 681.

remarkably strong. Flack asserts, "Evidence of wide recognition at an early period is more abundant for Revelation than for any other book of the New Testament."[16]

The fact that it was addressed as an encyclical to seven churches in the province of Asia (1:11) assured its circulation in that area immediately upon publication. And the timeliness and applicability of its stirring message promoted the early spread of the book far beyond its original destination.

Certain allusions to the terminology of Revelation in Christian writers during the first half of the second century suggest the probability that they were acquainted with the book. Swete thinks it "not incredible" that Ignatius (*c.* 110-17) in his letters to the Ephesian and the Philadelphian churches reflects knowledge of the Apocalypse but thinks that "the coincidences are not such as to justify a definite conclusion."[17] Certain allusions in the *Epistle of Barnabas* (*c.* 130) have been cited as evidence, but they are not sufficiently clear to establish that the author drew from the Revelation.

In the *Shepherd of Hermas* there are several references to the coming great tribulation which recall Revelation 2:10; 7:14, while Hermas's use of a number of parallel images suggests his knowledge of the Apocalypse. Charles holds that there is "a very probable connection" between Hermas and the Apocalypse,[18] but Stonehouse feels that "no conclusive relationship has been proved."[19] It is possible that both writers drew upon a common milieu of thought.

Papias, bishop of Hierapolis (a neighboring city to Laodicea), in the earlier part of the second century, is probably the first writer to make use of the Revelation. Only fragments of his five books have survived, and in none of them does he make mention of the Apocalypse. But Andreas of Caesarea in Cappadocia (d. 614) knew Papias's work and quoted a remark of Papias on Revelation 12 in his commentary on Revelation.

Justin Martyr (*c.* 100-165) traveled widely and knew the tradition of the churches in his day. He accepted the Revelation as a recognized Christian book and in his *Dialogue with Trypho*, written at Ephesus between 155 and 160, he says, "There was a certain man

16. Ibid., p. 678.
17. Henry Barclay Swete, *The Apocalypse of St. John*, pp. cvii-cviii.
18. R. H. Charles, "A Critical and Exegetical Commentary on the Revelation of St. John," in *International Critical Commentary*, 1:xcvii.
19. Ned Bernard Stonehouse, *The Apocalypse in the Ancient Church*, p. 11.

with us, whose name was John, one of the apostles of Christ, who prophesied, by a revelation that was made to him, that those who believed in our Christ would dwell a thousand years in Jerusalem" (chap. 81).

Melito, bishop of Sardis, one of the churches addressed in the book of Revelation, wrote a commentary on the Apocalypse (*c.* 175). The tradition concerning the Apocalypse at Sardis must have been unbroken and strong.

In the *Letter of the Churches of Vienne and Lyons,* written in A.D. 177 and addressed to the churches "in Asia and Phrygia," the book of Revelation is cited or referred to some five times[20] and one of its quotations is introduced by the formula, "that the Scripture might be fulfilled."[21]

Irenaeus (d. 202), bishop of Lyons, lived in Asia and Rome before settling in Gaul. In his noted work, *Against Heresies,* he quoted from nearly every chapter of Revelation, accepted it as Scripture, and attributed it to "John, the Lord's disciple" (4. 11; 5. 26. 1), whom he identified with the John who leaned on Jesus' breast (3. 1. 1). In support of the number 666 in Revelation 13, Irenaeus referred to "the most approved and ancient copies" of the Apocalypse and appealed to the testimony of "those men who saw John face to face" (*Against Heresies.* 5. 30. 1).

Eusebius records that Theophilus, bishop of Antioch (d. 180), in opposing the teaching of Hermogenes appealed to the Apocalypse of John (*Eccl. Hist.* 4. 26. 1). Swete observes that this establishes that "in Asia Minor and in Western Syria the book had clearly become a court of appeal to which Christians of opposite schools could submit their differences."[22]

The Muratorian Canon (*c.* A.D. 170 or a little later) mentions the Apocalypse as a universally recognized book at Rome. Tertullian (150-220) frequently quoted from the book of Revelation and accepted it as the work of John the apostle.[23]

Clement of Alexandria (155-215) followed the common view of the Church in accepting the Apocalypse as Scripture and written by

20. Revelation 14:4; 12:1; 14:4; 19:9; 22:11.
21. Preserved by Eusebius *Ecclesiastical History* 5. 1.
22. Swete, p. cix.
23. See Henry Clarence Thiessen, *Introduction to the New Testament,* p. 317 for references.

John the apostle. Origen (185-253) freely quoted from the Revelation and cited the current tradition which identified the author with John the son of Zebedee.[24]

Thus by the end of the second century the book of Revelation enjoyed wide circulation and was extensively used as Scripture. But its acceptance was not universal.

Marcion, a heretical teacher at Rome, who in A.D. 140 promulgated his own canon of Scripture, rejected the Apocalypse. According to Tertullian (*Against Marcion* 4.5), Marcion objected to it because of its Jewish character and insisted that it did not merit canonical recognition.

The Apocalypse was rejected by the *Alogi,* an Asian sect of the latter part of the second century. This sect was anti-Montanist and rejected the fourth gospel as well as the Apocalypse, because the Montanists appealed to them to support their views. The Alogi insisted that the symbolism of the Apocalypse was unedifying and that it contained errors in matter of fact.[25]

The rejection of the authenticity of the Apocalypse was championed in Rome by a certain presbyter named Caius (or Gaius), who was more or less in sympathy with the Alogi. In writing against the Montanists (*c.* A.D. 210), he assested that the Apocalypse was a forgery written by the heretic Cerinthus who had affixed the name of John to it to gain support for his teaching that Christ would have an earthly kingdom (Eusebius *Eccl. Hist.* 3. 28). But Hippolytus (A.D. 215), a contemporary at Rome, refuted the charge of Caius, and so successfully defended the Johannine authorship of the Apocalypse that from that time on there was no serious question concerning the Revelation in the Western Church.[26]

Dionysius, bishop in Alexandria (A.D. 247-65), was drawn into a discussion concerning the Apocalypse in dealing with the millenarian views of a certain Nepos who appealed to the book in support of his views (Eusebius *Eccl. Hist.* 7. 24-25). Dionysius made a study of Revelation, rejected the radical claim of Caius, accepted the book as the work of "some holy and inspired man" named John, but, on the basis of literary and theological analysis, rejected apostolic authorship. His scholarly reaction toward the Apocalypse had a strong

24. Ibid., pp. 317-18.
25. Swete, *The Apocalypse of St. John,* p. cxii.
26. Charles, *The Revelation of St. John.* 1:ci.

influence on much of the later thinking in the East, where the attitude toward the book was mixed. Cyril of Jerusalem (A.D. 315-86) excluded the Revelation from the canon and forbade its use in public services and even in private devotion.[27] It was not included in the various Syrian versions of the New Testament. Basil the Great (d. 379) and Gregory of Nyssa (d. 394) accepted it, but Gregory of Nazianzus (d. 390), Chrysostum (d. 407), and Theodoret (d. 466) apparently left it unmentioned. Questions concerning the Apocalypse lingered in the Eastern churches for centuries.

THE AUTHORSHIP OF THE REVELATION

1. PICTURE IN BOOK

The author of the Apocalypse four times gives his name as "John" (1:1, 4, 9; 22:8). Although Jewish apocalyptic works were characteristically pseudonymous, there is no indication that this writer is seeking to conceal his identity under the mask of the name "John" in order to secure authority for his literary production. A few radical critics have advanced this claim,[28] but modern scholars reject it.[29] The character and contents of the book are against the claim of pseudonymity. Wikenhauser points to the author's prophetic consciousness throughout the book and his "true prophetic insight in penetrating to the depths of the heart" as demonstrating his genuine prophetic power, and adds,

> Perhaps the strongest proof of the genuinely prophetic character of the book is the fact that the author writes under his own name to definite Christian churches of his own time and castigates them unsparingly. There is nothing similar in the apocryphal apocalyptic writings of Judaism.[30]

The author calls himself a "servant" of Jesus Christ (1:1) and describes himself as a "brother" of the readers and a fellow sharer with them in tribulation (1:9). The implication of 22:9 is that he belongs to the class of "the prophets" (cf. 10:11). He was on the island of Patmos when he received his commission to write his book (1:11, 19).

27. Swete, p. cxvi.
28. Charles B. Williams, *An Introduction to New Testament Literature*, p. 282, lists Volkmar, S. Davidson, Weizsäcker, Wernle, Vischer, Schmiedel, Gunkel, Wellhausen, J. Weiss, Menegoz, Forbes.
29. Kümmel, *Introduction to the New Testament*, p. 321. See also Charles, *The Revelation of St. John*, 1:xxxviii-xxxix.
30. Alfred Wikenhauser, *New Testament Introduction*, p. 545.

The entire book indicates that he had a Jewish background and was thoroughly acquainted with the Old Testament. The messages to the seven churches (chaps. 2-3) show that he was well acquainted with the churches to whom his book was directed. It seems obvious that for a considerable time he had been a leader among them. In 22:8 he asserts that he had personally seen and heard the things recorded in his book.

Who then is this "John," the mere mention of whose name is sufficient to identify him to his readers? Several proposed identifications have been advanced.

2. EVIDENCE FOR APOSTOLIC AUTHORSHIP

The prevailing testimony of early Christian writers identified the author with John the apostle of our Lord. The explicit testimony of Justin Martyr, coming from the middle of the second century, is of vital significance, in view of his wide acquaintance with the traditions of the churches and his extensive teaching activities in the very area where the churches of the Apocalypse were located. Made in the very city where John the apostle spent the closing years of his life, and coming within half a century of his death, Justin's claim would have evoked speedy objection if it was not the accepted view of the early Church.

The testimony to apostolic authorship given by Irenaeus in his important work, *Against Heresies*, written about A.D. 185, is weighty in view of his own background. He wrote his book while bishop of Lyons in Gaul, but he was born in Asia Minor, where as a youth, according to his own testimony, he knew Polycarp, bishop of Smyrna, the personal disciple of the apostle John (*Against Heresies* 3. 3. 4). Polycarp was martyred in A.D. 155, and he had been a Christian for eighty-six years at the time of his martyrdom. There was thus only one link between Irenaeus and the apostolic age. Irenaeus traveled widely and was intimately acquainted with almost the entire Church of his day. He also had the advantage of having been associated with Pothimus, his predecessor in Lyons, who, martyred as a very old man, knew the traditions of the early Christian church in Gaul.

Other Christian leaders, such as Clement of Alexandria, Origen, Tertullian, and Hippolytus, assumed apostolic authorship of the Revelation without question. Guthrie remarks, "So strong is this evidence that it is difficult to believe that they all made a mistake in confusing the John of the Apocalypse with John the Apostle."[31]

A further witness to apostolic authorship, dating from the mid-second century, has recently come from the Gnostic library at Chenoboskion in Egypt. One of the documents, *Apocryphon of John*, of which the library had three variant copies, identifies its author as "John, the brother of James, these who are the sons of Zebedee." Since the document cites Revelation 1:19, its writer presumably purports to be the same person as the writer of the canonical Apocalypse, a view supported by the writer's attempt to imitate the paratactic style of John.[32]

This strong tradition concerning apostolic authorship of the Revelation is consistent with the uniform belief of Christendom, during the second and third centuries, that John the apostle spent the closing years of his life at Ephesus and exercised oversight over the churches in that area.[33]

Advocates of the traditional identification point out that apostolic authorship is most naturally suggested by the fact that the author simply called himself John without qualification. It implies that he was a noted leader of recognized authority who needed no further designation to identify himself to these churches. His manner of dealing with the Asian churches can only be understood if the writer was a man of acknowledged apostolic authority. Ramsay declares,

> It is a psychological impossibility that these letters to the Asian Churches could have been written except by one who felt himself, and had the right to feel himself, charged with the superintendence and oversight of all those Churches, invested with Divinely given and absolute authority over them, gifted by long knowledge and sympathy with insight unto their nature and circumstances, able to understand the line on which each was developing, and finally bringing to a focus in one moment of supreme inspiration—whose manner none but himself could understand or imagine—all the powers he possessed of knowledge, of intellect, of intensest love, of gravest responsibility of sympathy with the Divine life, of commission from his Divine Teacher.[34]

31. Guthrie, p. 935.
32. Andrew Helmbold, "A Note on the Authorship of the Apocalypse," *New Testament Studies* 8, no. 1 (October 1961):77-79.
33. See discussion under the introduction to 1 John, "John's Ephesian ministry," pp. 191-94.
34. W. M. Ramsay, *The Letters to the Seven Churches of Asia,* p. 80.

Church history does not know of any other John in the latter part of the first century who possessed these qualifications.[35]

Guthrie notes that there are some remarkable parallels between the character of the author reflected in the Apocalypse and the portrait of the apostle John in the synoptics. In the synoptics, James and John are called "Sons of thunder" (Mk 3:17), "and the Apocalypse certainly contains its share of stormy descriptions."[36] John's fiery temperament and his readiness to act in righteous anger are seen in the request of the two brothers to be permitted to call down fire upon a Samaritan village (Lk 9:52-55). Guthrie remarks, "Something of this temperament appears in the apocalyptic writer, as is seen in his description of the hostile Jews (ii. 9, iii. 9), of the Beast and all whom he represents, of Rome in the image of the harlot, of the plagues and judgments which will be the expression of the righteous wrath of God."[37] There are also "numerous indications of the loving disciple and saintly soul who delights in fellowship with the Father and with his Son above all other things. That is his conception of eternal Blessedness" (Rev 7:16-17; 21:3, 7-8).[38] The author of Revelation thus displays the same mixture of sternness and tender affection revealed of John the apostle in the rest of the New Testament.

Harrison indicates that in dealing with evidence for apostolic authorship, certain "resemblances between the Apocalypse and the Fourth Gospel deserve to be taken into consideration."[39] Thus the term *Logos* to denote our Lord personally occurs only in the Johannine literature (Jn 1:1, 14; 1 Jn 1:1; Rev 19:13); "Lamb" (*arnion*) as a title for Jesus occurs twenty-eight times in Revelation and elsewhere only in John 1:29, 36 (where a synonymous Greek term is used) and John 21:15 (same term). Only the fourth gospel (19:34) records that the side of Jesus was pierced at His crucifixion, while Revelation 1:7 mentions those "that pierced him"; the same verb is used in both places, but the Septuagint in Zechariah 12:10 uses a

---

35. Theodor Zahn, *Introduction to the New Testament*, says, "The present writer knows no Jew of the Graeco-Roman diaspora with the name of John; whereas, e.g., Jude, Joseph, Jonathan, Samuel, Miriam, and Salome occur in Roman inscriptions. . . . It was not until long after the time of Revelation that the custom arose among the Christians of calling themselves by the names of apostles (cf. Dionysius in Eus. vii. 25. 14)." 3:433, 1.
36. Guthrie, p. 938.
37. Ibid.
38. D. A. Hayes, *John and His Writings*, p. 235.
39. Harrison, p. 468.

different Greek term. The adjective *true* (*alēthinos*) occurs ten times in Revelation, eight times in the fourth gospel, four times in 1 John, but only five times in the rest of the New Testament, three of them in Hebrews. The word *witness,* both as noun and verb, occurs more frequently than in any other New Testament writer. The verb *overcome* (conquer) occurs seventeen times in Revelation, six times in 1 John, in John 16:33, and only four times in the rest of the New Testament. The verb *dwell* (tabernacle) occurs four times in Revelation and elsewhere only in John 1:14. Christ is the Bridegroom in the fourth gospel (3:29) and also in the Revelation (19:7; 21:2; 22:17).

Points of similarity between the Apocalypse and the fourth gospel also extend to the realm of ideas. Westcott presents these similarities as follows:

> Both present a view of a supreme conflict between the powers of good and evil. In the Gospel this is delineated mainly in moral conceptions; in the Apocalypse mainly in images and visions. In the Gospel the opposing forces are treated under abstract and absolute forms, as light and darkness, love and hatred; in the Apocalpse under concrete and definite forms, God, Christ and the Church warring with the devil, the false prophet and the beast. But in both books alike Christ is the central figure. His victory is the end to which history and vision lead as their consummation. His Person and Work are the ground of triumph, and triumph through apparent failure.[40]

The evidence in support of apostolic authorship for the Apocalypse is strong. This is acknowledged by such scholars as Benjamin W. Bacon, who does not accept the traditional view, when he remarks, "One would think the case for apostolic authenticity could hardly be stronger."[41]

3. EVIDENCE AGAINST APOSTOLIC AUTHORSHIP

In spite of the strong evidence pointing to the apostle John as the author of the Apocalypse, that view is rejected by many scholars. Proponents of the traditional view must take into account the contrary evidence which is adduced by those who reject apostolic authorship.

Marcion's rejection of the Apocalypse carries little weight, since

---

40. B. F. Westcott, *The Gospel According to St. John,* pp. lxxxiv-lxxxv.
41. Benjamin W. Bacon, *The Making of the New Testament,* p. 191.

his position was theologically motivated. His doctrinal views were firmly rejected by the orthodox Church.

The radical reaction of Caius, seeking to discredit the Apocalypse by ascribing it to the heretic Cerinthus, was self-defeating. It was obviously an overreaction to the Montanists' appeal to the Revelation in support of their extravagant doctrine about the Millennium. His view was rejected by sober orthodox leaders, such as Hippolytus at Rome and Dionysius at Alexandria.

The work of Dionysius, *On the Promises*, wherein he set forth his grounds for rejecting apostolic authorship of the Apocalypse, is no longer extant, but Eusebius incorporated a lengthy summary of it in his *Ecclesiastical History* (7. 25. 1-27). The summary by Eusebius makes it clear that Dionysius sought to be objective in his criticism and based his conclusions on a comparison of the Apocalypse with the fourth gospel and the Johannine Epistles. He advanced three main arguments: (1) The author of the Apocalypse gives his name at the very beginning, but the author of the fourth gospel and the Johannine epistles does not give his name at all; (2) the gospel and the first epistle of John reveal an entirely different range of thought and terminology than that found in the Apocalypse; (3) the divergence in style between the Apocalypse and the fourth gospel and the epistle is so striking as to preclude common authorship. Since Dionysius accepted the apostle John as the author of the fourth gospel and the Johannine epistles, he concluded that the author of the Revelation must be a different John.

The view of Dionysius greatly influenced the attitude of Eusebius toward the Apocalypse. The essence of his arguments is still employed by opponents of apostolic authorship. Wikenhauser, indeed, observes, "Modern scholarship has not added a single substantially new point."[42] The views of Dionysius call for consideration, along with modern restatements or enlargements.

Dionysius argued against apostolic authorship by calling attention to the fact that the author of the Apocalypse names himself at the very beginning of his book, while the evangelist John never names himself. He concluded that this pointed to nonapostolic authorship for the Apocalypse, otherwise the writer would have described him-

---

42. Wikenhauser, p. 550.

self as "the beloved disciple," or "the one leaning on his bosom," or "the brother of James," or "the eyewitness and hearer of the Lord."

The conclusion which Dionysius drew from the cited facts is a subjective inference. It fails to take into consideration the differences in character and content of the gospel and the Apocalypse. Hayes calls attention to the following facts: "All the historical books of the Old Testament are anonymous, except Nehemiah. All the prophetical books, on the contrary, have the author's name prefixed. Here, then, would seem to be the rule in Hebrew literature, and the writers of our New Testament, being Jews, have followed it. As a historian John suppresses his name. As a prophet he puts his name at the very forefront of his work."[43]

Modern scholars have augmented this argument with the observation that the author of Revelation makes no claim to have known Christ in the flesh.[44] Guthrie counters the force of this argument with the observation that it can be used to cut both ways: "Had the author brought in numerous personal reminiscences, as the author of the *Apocalypse of Peter* does, he would just as certainly have been charged with overdoing his identification, as this author is now charged with underdoing it."[45]

That the original readers knew the identity of the writer is clear. If they had no questions concerning his apostolic identity, there is no reason why in this eschatological work the writer should stress his personal reationship to the human Jesus.

It is maintained that in Revelation 21:14, the author refers to "the twelve apostles of the Lamb" as a group with no indication that he was included.[46] This is held to be firm evidence against apostolic authorship. But it is difficult to see why an apostle could not thus have referred to the apostles collectively in describing the future New Jerusalem. Zahn points out that, in that case, the promise to the twelve in Luke 22:30, which only the twelve heard, "must be the invention of persons who were not apostles."[47] Guthrie well asks, "If an apostolic author has a message to impart which mentions the apostolate, is he to emend the message out of motives and modesty or

43. Hayes, pp. 224-25.
44. Charles, *The Revelation of St. John*, 1:xliii.
45. Guthrie, p. 943.
46. Charles, *The Revelation of St. John*, 1:xliii.
47. Zahn, 3:430.

append a note indicating his own inclusion in the number?"[48] John's reference to the twelve apostles neither proves or disproves his apostolic identity.

A further argument of Dionysius was that the Apocalypse represents a different range of thought and terminology than that found in the fourth gospel and the first epistle of John. The gospel and epistle abound in expressions such as, "the life," "the light," "turning from darkness," "truth," "joy," "the judgment," "the love of God toward us," "keeping the commandments," "the Father and the Son," and others, but the Apocalypse is very different and remote from all this. This argument carries weight. It must be recognized that there are marked vocabulary differences; the two writings do at times use different words for the same ideas, and words and phrases are used with different senses.[49] But there are also remarkable linguistic resemblances.[50] While marked differences in vocabulary and terminology are to be expected in view of the striking differences of subject matter of the Revelation and the gospel and epistle, arresting is the fact there are also marks of close relations between them.[51] Charles acknowledges these resemblances, but he holds that the differences make the assumption of common authorship "absolutely impossible."[52]

In addition to the linguistic evidence, Moffatt also appeals to "the differences of religious thought, christological, spiritual, and eschatological," to support rejection of a common authorship.[53] But Guthrie examines these asserted theological differences and concludes that the differences in emphasis which do exist do not "definitely exclude the possibility that Gospel and Apocalypse were both written by the same author."[54] That differences of presentation and emphasis do exist between these two documents, so radically unlike in their contents, is not surprising. But those who hold to a common authorship must recognize the difficulty that these differences do present.

Dionysius also argued against apostolic authorship of the Apocalypse from the fact that in the gospel and the epistle, the language is

48. Guthrie, p. 943.
49. James Moffatt, *An Introduction to the Literature of the New Testament*, pp. 501-2; Charles, *The Revelation of St. John*, 1:xxxi-xxxii.
50. See pp. 242.
51. Charles, *The Revelation of St. John*, 1:xxxii-xxxiii.
52. Ibid., 1:xxix.
53. Moffatt, pp. 502-3.
54. Guthrie, pp. 943-45.

excellent Greek, but the Greek of the Apocalypse is "not accurate Greek, but that he uses barbarous idioms, and, in some places, solecisms" (*Eccl. Hist.* 7. 25. 26). The existence of stylistic and grammatical irregularities in the Revelation is undeniable: they are more frequent than elsewhere in the New Testament. But Thiessen maintains that "the barbarisms and solecisms have been greatly exaggerated. The solecisms are largely forms of *anacoluthon*[55] (1:5; 2:17; 3:12), attempts on the part of the writer to emphasize certain words and phrases (1:4; 3:3; 9:5; 14:14,—with the latter compare 1:15; 9:7), and constructions according to sense rather than grammar (4:1; 9:13; 11:15; 13:14). If he breaks the rule in one place, he observes it in another."[56] Harrison thinks that some of the irregularities may be due to Semitic influence, but he observes, "No single explanation is probably adequate to explain all the solecisms, although some of these are no doubt deliberate." Moulton, in discussing the Greek of the Apocalypse, holds that "the less educated papyri give us plentiful parallels from a field where semitism cannot be suspected."[57] Some instances of the supposed "bad grammar" in the Apocalypse occur in nonliterary papyri as acceptable by contemporary standards. It may also be valid to suggest that some of the stylistic irregularities were consciously employed to reflect the writer's personal feeling of excitement in recording the amazing revelations made to him. It is well known that under strong emotional pressure, grammatical formulations do not always measure up to formal standards.

Swete's study of the vocabulary, grammar, and style of the Apocalypse confirms the existence of marked differences between the Apocalypse and the fourth gospel, but he concludes that the evidence "creates a strong presumption of affinity between the Fourth Gospel and the Apocalypse."[58] Caird holds that the language differences do not disprove common authorship, although he thinks that the probability is against it.[59] Conservatives who hold that this internal evidence does not overrule the strong external evidence in favor of

---

55. *Anacoluthon* means abandonment in the midst of a sentence of one type of grammatical construction in favor of another construction.
56. Thiessen, pp. 319-20.
57. Harrison, p. 462. James Hope Moulton, *A Grammar of New Testament Greek*, Vol. 1, *Prolegomena*, pp. 8-9.
58. Swete, p. cxxx.
59. G. B. Caird, "A Commentary on the Revelation of St. John the Divine," *Harper's New Testament Commentaries*, pp. 4-5.

apostolic authorship have suggested different explanations to account for the differences between the fourth gospel and the Apocalypse.

Westcott advanced the view that the differences might be explained by assuming that the Revelation was written about twenty years before the gospel, thus allowing John time to improve his Greek sufficiently to write the better Greek of the gospel.[60] But this is a superficial explanation for the irregularities in grammar, since often in the immediate context the author shows that he is well aware of the proper grammatical construction (cf. 1:4). The mixture of correct and incorrect constructions seems to be due to choice rather than carelessness or ignorance.

Zahn suggested that the irregular language of Revelation was probably due to the circumstances under which it was received. He holds that the Apocalypse was strongly influenced by the Old Testament prophetic models which apostolic prophecy followed closely, and since John received his prophecy in an ecstatic state, communicating to him the form as well as the content of the vision, John did not feel wholly free to polish the style of his first draft.[61] For those who accept that this book records a genuine prophetic experience, this suggestion has considerable merit.

Another suggestion is that the differences may be due to the use of an amanuensis. Beckwith regards it as plausible and supports it with a reference to Josephus and the apostle Paul.[62] It is held that the smooth Greek of the fourth gospel is largely due to the aid of the scribe whom John employed in writing it, while the Revelation, written on Patmos, was composed without an amanuensis. While the suggestion lacks historical evidence, it cannot be ruled out. Morris considers this suggestion "the only way in which common authorship of the two writings can be defended."[63]

The majority of modern critics agree that in the light of the differences between them, the John who wrote the Revelation cannot also be accepted as the author of the fourth gospel and the Johannine epistles. For these critics the deciding factor is the internal evidence. But Beckwith remarks, "The phenomenon common in literature of the production by one author of writings differing widely in diction

60. Westcott, p. lxxxvi.
61. Zahn, 3:432-33.
62. Isbon T. Beckwith, *The Apocalypse of John*, p. 356.
63. Leon Morris, *The Revelation of St. John*, p. 39.

and manner must cause hesitation in forming a decision on these grounds alone."[64] The strong external evidence for unity of authorship must not simply be ignored. Edwards calls attention to the fact that "antiquity assigned the whole of the Johannine literature to one man. That judgment ought only to be disturbed on irrefutable grounds."[65] Proponents of apostolic authorship still question whether the actual differences between the Apocalypse and the fourth gospel really provide such irrefutable evidence.

4. ALTERNATIVE SUGGESTIONS

Different proposals have been made as to the possible identity of the author of the Apocalypse by those who reject apostolic authorship.

Perhaps the earliest alternative suggestion was made by Dionysius. He put forth the suggestion that the author might be John Mark, but he himself questioned it on the ground that Mark did not accompany Paul into Asia (*Eccl. Hist.* 7. 25. 15). It is highly unlikely on linguistic grounds that the author of the second gospel was also the author of the Apocalypse. All that we know of John Mark offers no hint that he possessed the prophetic qualities of the author of the Revelation or exercised the position of authority among the Asian churches of its author.

Eusebius of Caesarea (c. 265-340), influenced by the view of Dionysius, advanced the view that the author of the Apocalypse was "John the Elder" (*Eccl. Hist.* 3. 39). Like Dionysius, Eusebius reacted strongly against the chiliasm of his day and was disturbed by the support which its proponents found in the Revelation. Dionysius had conjectured that the Revelation was written by "another John" at Ephesus but could cite no historical evidence in support of his view; he could only appeal to the report of a traveler that there were two tombs at Ephesus bearing the name of John (*Eccl. Hist.* 7. 25. 16). Eusebius found the needed support for this "John the Elder" at Ephesus from the writings of Papias (*Eccl. Hist.* 3. 39). He interpreted the testimony of Papias to mean that there were two Johns at Ephesus, the apostle John and John the Elder.[66] To the latter he

---

64. Beckwith, p. 357.
65. R. A. Edwards, quoted in Morris, p. 33.
66. See discussion under the introduction to 1 John.

attributed the authorship of the Revelation. His view gave him a welcome opportunity to get rid of the apostolic authorship of the Apocalypse, of which he had a very low view. It is obvious that the position of Eusebius, attributing the authorship of the Revelation to John the Elder, was doctrinally motivated. But Eusebius was undecided whether to classify the Revelation with the accepted books of the canon or with the rejected books (3. 25. 2-4). As Stonehouse remarks, "This hesitating attitude can only mean that Eusebius was at odds with the church. Personally he is quite ready to classify it with the spurious works, but in deference to its acceptance as canonic not only in the west but also by the leading teachers of the east, including Origen, he places it also among the undisputed books."[67]

Irenaeus also knew the writings of Papias, but he did not draw from them the view that Eusebius proposed.

The suggestion of Eusebius has played a large part in modern discussions concerning the authorship of the Revelation. Various modern scholars have accepted the proposal and speak of John the Elder as though he were a well-known figure in Church history, but other scholars reject the validity of the "discovery" of Eusebius. If John the apostle and John the Elder both lived at Ephesus and the latter is the author of the Revelation, then he is blameworthy for not making his identity more explicit in view of the obvious tendency of his readers to identify the writer with the more prominent apostle. It is well known that the early Church did make that identification. But if that identification is in error, why did it go unchallenged until the discovery of the mistake by Eusebius? Guthrie concludes, "The Elder theory seems tenable only on the supposition that John the apostle had never lived at Ephesus, and that from the early second century the whole Church mistakenly assumed that he had."[68]

A recent suggestion, proposed by Charles, is that the author was John the prophet.[69] Charles distinguished this John from the apostle as well as the elder. He notes that the writer identifies himself as a prophet (22:9) but refrains from presenting himself as an apostle. Holding that he was a Jew, a native of Galilee, Charles pictures him as "a great spiritual genius, a man of profound insight and the widest

67. Stonehouse, p. 133.
68. Guthrie, p. 947.
69. Charles, *The Revelation of St. John,* 1:xliii-xliv.

sympathies."[70] There need be no objection to the portrait drawn by Charles, but it does not prove the existence of this third John at Ephesus; the portrait could also fit the apostle John. Are we to believe that there were a number of brilliant Christians named John in the Asian Church, so well known that *each* could be assured of correct identification simply by giving his name? Church history has left no trace of such a prophetic genius in the Asian Church, distinct from the apostle John. Harrison points out that the authority which the writer of the Apocalypse "wields over the Asian churches goes beyond anything attributed to prophets in the New Testament."[71]

5. CONCLUSION CONCERNING AUTHORSHIP

The question of the authorship of the Apocalypse is beset with difficulties. Some, like Kiddle,[72] regard it an insoluble problem. Others, like Boismard, prefer to leave the problem open.[73] A failure to identify positively the John who wrote the Revelation does not destroy the spiritual value of it as an inspired part of the canon.

The external testimony for apostolic authorship is solid and early. But the internal evidence admittedly presents serious difficulties to that view. Those scholars who are strongly impressed with the internal difficulties generally conclude that these difficulties overrule the external evidence. But advocates of nonapostolic authorship find it equally or more difficult to identify a John who fits the demands presented by the book. The most certain factor in the confusion of views is the external evidence supporting apostolic authorship. If the apostle John wrote the book, the traditional view has a natural explanation; no other view can satisfactorily explain that tradition. We concur with the conclusion of Hayes.

> We prefer to agree that the tradition of the church is the best authority in the matter, and that this greatest of the New Testament seers and theologians is that apostle of the living heart who lay upon the Master's bosom at the daily meal and came to have the deepest insight into the Master's mind during the life ministry, and then was

70. Ibid., p. xliv.
71. Harrison, p. 471.
72. Martin Kiddle, *The Revelation of St. John,* Moffatt New Testament Commentary, p. xxxiii.
73. M. E. Boismard, "The Apocalypse," in A. Robert and A. Feuillet, *Introduction to the New Testament,* p. 721.

granted the revelation of the Master's ultimate triumph in the visions of the Patmos exile.[74]

The book of Revelation was addressed "to the seven churches that are in Asia" (1:4), that is, the Roman province of Asia. In 1:11 they are specifically identified as the churches in Ephesus, Smyrna, Pergamum, Thyatira, Sardis, Philadelphia, and Laodicea. Since there were churches in other cities of the province, such as Colossae, Hierapolis, and Troas, the recipients are evidently selected. The number seven suggests that they are intended to be representative of all the churches. Ramsay suggested that the selection of the churches was governed by their location which made them strategic centers of communication. "All the Seven Cities stand on the great circular road that bound together the most populous, wealthy, and influential part of the Province, the west-central region."[75] The order may then indicate the circular route of the messenger in delivering the book to the designated churches.

The epistolary section (chaps. 2-3) makes clear that the book had a special message for each of the seven churches addressed. But the repeated call in chapters 2-3, "He that hath an ear, let him hear what the Spirit saith to the churches," makes it equally clear that this section had a message for all the churches. And the distinctly apocalyptic portion conveys a vital prophetic message of significance and value for the entire Church of all ages.

THE PLACE AND DATE OF THE REVELATION

1. PLACE

John received the visions recorded in the Apocalypse while on "the isle that is called Patmos" (1:9), one of a number of islands in the Aegean Sea, off the southwestern shores of Asia Minor. This small, barren, rocky island is located about seventy miles southwest of Ephesus. John says that he was on Patmos "for the word of God and the testimony of Jesus" (1:9). That may mean that he had gone there to evangelize or to find seclusion. More probable is the view that John was banished to Patmos because of his powerful Christian witness at Ephesus. This is in harmony with his self-identification as a

74. Hayes, p. 237.
75. Ramsay, p. 183.

partaker "in the tribulation and kingdom and endurance in Jesus" (1:9, Rotherham), the contents of his book, and the testimony of early tradition. The common view was that John was banished to Patmos by the Emperor Domitian but was released and returned to Ephesus after that emperor's death. Caird points out that it was one of the islands "regularly used for the banishment of political offenders (Tacitus, *Ann.* iii. 68; iv. 30; xv. 71; Juvenal, *Sat.* i. 73; vi. 563f.; x. 170)."[76] The length of John's stay on Patmos is not known.

Did John also write the visions on Patmos, or were they recorded after his return to Ephesus? Ladd holds that the past tense used in 1:9 "suggests that John was no longer on Patmos at the time of writing the book."[77] But Lenski insists that "the visions and John's writing the record of them were simultaneous." He points out that the repeated command to write (1:19; 14:13; 19:9) might leave the question open, but John's own statement in 10:4 "informs us that he was continuing to write, and that the other commands 'Write!' are meant with reference to immediate writing. John is to write 'into a book' (1, 11); in 22, 6-19 we see 'this book' all completed, save for the last few sentences. The angel (22, 7-15), and Jesus (22, 18-19) speak of 'this book' as one already written."[78] Unless these references to his writing are regarded as so many literary devices of an apocalyptic writer, the clear implication seems to be that John wrote as he received the visions given to him, at least took adequate notes of what he saw. Appeal has been made to the rough grammar of Revelation to support the view that it was written on Patmos, but the grammar is not decisive on the point. It may be that John recorded the essence of the book on Patmos but put it into final form at Ephesus.

2. DATE

It was the testimony of the early Church that the Apocalypse was written during the latter part of the reign of Domitian, who was emperor from A.D. 81 to 96. The earliest known witness is Irenaeus who wrote that John saw his visions "no very long time since, but almost in our day, towards the end of Domitian's reign" (*Against Heresies* 5. 30. 3; cf. 2. 22. 5; 3. 3. 4). Irenaeus wrote some eighty-five years after the death of Domitian. Wikenhauser feels that the ex-

76. Caird, p. 21.
77. George Eldon Ladd, *A Commentary on the Revelation of John*, p. 30.
78. R. C. H. Lenski, *The Interpretation of St. John's Revelation*, pp. 5-6.

pression "almost in our day" does not fit Irenaeus well and suggests that Irenaeus is drawing his testimony from the works of Papias, which he dates about A.D. 130. The surviving fragments from Papias do not touch the point.

Victorinus of Pettau (d. 304), the earliest known Latin commentator on the book of Revelation, remarks, "When John said these things he was in the island of Patmos, condemned to the labour of the mines by Caesar Domitian. There he saw the Apocalypse; and when grown old, he thought that he should at length receive his release by suffering, but Domitian being killed, he was liberated" (*Commentary on the Apocalypse* (10:11). Eusebius, in his *Ecclesiastical History* (3. 18), appealed to the testimony of Irenaeus and dated the persecution "in the fifteenth year of Domitian." Jerome (d. 420) in his *Lives of Illustrious Men* (chap. 9) followed this tradition. So do most later writers. But a few isolated voices in antiquity, mostly fairly late, place the date of the Revelation earlier, under Nero or his successor. This early dating is not in accord with the prevailing tradition.

Advocates of an early dating hold that Revelation 11:1-2 indicates that the Temple in Jerusalem is still standing, hence demanding a date before A.D. 70. But there is no necessity to interpret this reference as relating to the historical Herodian Temple. The prophetic character of the passage is against it. Nor can the tense be used to prove a date before A.D. 70.

In his book *Who Is the Rich Man that shall be Saved?* (chap. 42), Clement of Alexandria placed the story of John and the robber chief after John's return from Patmos and pictured the apostle as vigorous enough to run after the fleeing youth. It is held that his picture of John fits the Neronian date, since the Domitian date would make John too old for such vigorous conduct. But obviously the whole picture is unusual and is not impossible under the Domitian dating. History is not lacking in stories of men who remained physically vigorous to old age.

Support for an early date is sought from the first-century myth of "Nero redivivus," which held that Nero was not really dead and would reappear in the East to claim his power. John's statement in 17:10-11 to the effect that five kings have fallen, one is, and one who is an eighth and yet one of the seven would reign for a short time, is held to incorporate this current legend about Nero. Counting from

Augustus, Nero was the fifth emperor, and the argument is that the Apocalypse dates from the time of the end of Nero's reign and the commencement of the following reign. But this view has difficulty in identifying the eighth who is yet one of the seven. Following Nero there were three successive claimants to the throne—Galba, Otho, and Vitellius—none of whom were ever securely established and whose reigns together covered less than a year. If these three are omitted on the ground that their short reigns had no significant bearing on events in the provinces, then the seventh was Vespasian (A.D. 69-79). But his calm reign does not fit the picture, for he did not persecute the Christians. It is highly questionable that the enigmatical reference in chapter 17 can rightly be used to establish any firm dating for the book.

The number of the beast, 666 (Rev 13:18), has also been appealed to in support of a Neronian date. It is held that this is a cryptograph for Nero, since the Hebrew letters for "Neron Kaiser" have that numerical value. But numerous other names have been presented having the same numerical value. Tenney well remarks, "This type of reasoning seems too flimsy to warrant any fixed conclusion, especially when it has no support from external tradition."[79] It cannot be used to settle a chronological question.

The evidence for an early dating does not appear weighty enough to require a rejection of the strong external evidence for a date during the latter part of the reign of Domitian. Internal evidence is consistent with this traditional date.

The Domitian dating is consistent with the condition of the Asian churches, as reflected in the seven letters to the churches. That condition implies that these churches already had a fairly long history behind them. Marked spiritual deterioration has already taken place: Ephesus has left its first love (2:4), Sardis is virtually dead (3:1), and Laodicea is complacent in its repulsive lukewarmness (3:15-18). The Nicolaitan party, of which Paul's epistles to the Ephesians and the Colossians, as well as the letters to Timothy, reveal no certain traces, is now widely distributed and firmly rooted (2:6, 15). The Domitian dating allows sufficient time for this development between

79. Merrill C. Tenney, *The New Testament, An Historical and Analytic Survey*, p. 402.

the founding of these churches during Paul's days and the writing of Revelation.

John's intimate knowledge of the spiritual needs of the churches and his implied authority over them presuppose a fairly long sojourn in the area and a protracted period of activity among them. Since John apparently did not go to Asia Minor until the outbreak of the Jewish War in A.D. 67, the Domitian dating again is the more probable.

As further support for the Domitian dating, M'Clymont points to "the use of the expression 'the Lord's day' (i. 10), instead of the earlier 'first day of the week,' and of the phrase 'synagogue of Satan' (ii. 9; iii. 9), which would scarcely have been employed by a Christian writer previous to the destruction of Jerusalem."[80]

The background of persecution reflected in the Apocalypse seems most consistent with the Domitian dating. The repeated references to persecution (2:10, 13; 3:10; 6:9; 16:6; 17:6; 18:24; 19:2; 20:4) imply a conflict between the imperial power and the Christian Church, centering in the demand of emperor worship. This conflict is personified in the figure of the beast and his image and his demand for universal worship (13:4, 15-17; 14:9-11; 15:2; 16:2; 19:20; 20:4). While the practice of emperor worship was well known before the reign of Domitian, he was the first emperor who demanded the worship of the living emperor. Caird points out that Domitian was personally afflicted by a deep sense of inferiority and had a morbid fear of being supplanted. "It was to offset this sense of insecurity that he began to demand toward the end of his reign that his subjects should worship him as Lord and God."[81] This policy found ready support in Asia where the cult of Caesar flourished most. It set the Roman government on a collision course with the Christian Church. Since Christians recognized but one Lord and God (1 Co 8:5-6), they could not conscientiously conform to this demand. Their refusal as a group called attention to them and marked them for official action. John clearly recognized that a life-and-death struggle with the imperial power lay ahead. This background does not fit Nero's reign.

Further support for the late date has been noted from the history of two of the seven churches addressed. The message to the church

80. J. A. M'Clymont, *The New Testament and Its Writers*, p. 153.
81. Caird, p. 20.

at Laodicea (3:14-22) implies the prosperity of that city. An earthquake destroyed Laodicea in A.D. 62, during the reign of Nero. While the city was soon rebuilt, some time must be allowed for a full recovery. In his letter to the Philippians (chap. 11), Polycarp implies that the believers in Smyrna did not yet know the Lord when Paul wrote Philippians. This implies that the church of Smyrna did not come into existence until after A.D. 63. But Revelation 2:8-11 "presupposes a Church poor in wealth but rich in good works, with a development of apparently many years to its credit."[82] This again does not fit the time of Nero but is fully consistent with a dating under Domitian.

Only two periods for the dating of the Revelation seem historically feasible, a Neronian date of about A.D. 68 or 69 and a date during the latter part of Domitian's reign, A.D. 95 or 96. While the evidence for the latter date is not so conclusive as to exclude consideration for the former, both the external and the internal evidence point to the Domitian dating. If the Revelation really was written at the end of Nero's reign, it is difficult to understand why the early Church developed so strong a tradition relating its composition to the reign of Domitian. We suggest a probable date as A.D. 95 or 96.

THE OCCASION AND PURPOSE OF THE REVELATION

1. OCCASION

John records that he wrote his book at the direct command of the Lord, who appeared to him (1:10-11, 19). This is "the only instance in the New Testament in which a writer gives this as his reason for writing."[83] But obviously, behind the Lord's command to John lay the needs of the churches in that dark hour.

The historical situation was ominous for the Church. Goodspeed observes, "Christians had always been conscious of living on the edge of a volcano."[84] Repeated experience had confirmed that they were constantly subject to persecution on a local level from their traditional Jewish enemies or from hostile pagans and their magistrates. But now the danger had become acute because of the unprecedented demand of Domitian asking divine worship. Domitian's demand and the zeal of the leaders of the imperial cult in Asia had brought the

82. Charles, *The Revelation of St. John*, 1:xciv.
83. Thiessen, p. 321.
84. Edgar J. Goodspeed, p. 242.

churches to a terrible crisis. The prospect had terrifying possibilities for believers, who were well aware of the extermination power of imperial Rome. Needed was a message from God which would strengthen and encourage them to persevere under the impending ordeal and give them assurance that their faith would be vindicated with the return of Christ and His certain victory over all the forces of satanic evil.

Corresponding to this external pressure was a movement within the churches which advocated a little compromise to ease the situation. At Ephesus, Pergamum, Thyatira, and probably elsewhere, the Nicolaitans were advocating participation in pagan feasts and in the quasi-religious practices of the trade guilds in order to make life for Christians easier amid a hostile pagan environment. John recognized that this attitude called for vigorous opposition. It is roundly condemned in the letters to the churches.

2. PURPOSE

The message of the Apocalypse, as a true book of prophecy, is not to be limited to the historical situation that prompted its production. Ladd correctly observes, "The prophecy of the Revelation goes far beyond any known historical situation in the first century."[85] While assuredly its message provided the needed help to the original readers, its contents, in a large measure, deal with events subsequent to the time of its composition. It helped the original readers by enabling them to interpret their own time in the light of the prophetic future.

The divine purpose in giving this revelation to John is declared in the opening sentence, "to show to His bond-servants, the things which must shortly take place" (1:1, NASB). This at once underlines the prophetic character of the book and stresses the sure fulfillment of the divine purpose. Swete comments that *shortly* (*en tachei*) "must be interpreted . . . relatively to the Divine measurements of time"[86] (cf. 2 Pe 3:8). *Shortly* does not mean that the fulfillment of the coming events will begin at once but rather denotes the rapidity of their fulfillment when their execution begins (cf. Lk 18:8; Ac 12:7; 22:18; 25:4; Ro 16:20). The statement inculcates an attitude of confident expectancy.

85. Ladd, *A Commentary on the Revelation of John*, p. 9.
86. Swete, p. 2.

The events that called forth the Revelation were a foretaste of things to come. What the readers were experiencing was a part of the age-long struggle between Christ and His followers and Satan and his followers. Beyond the needs of the local churches addressed, the main purpose was to portray the larger message of Christ's final triumph. The graphic portrayal of the fierce conflict and its glorious outcome was a message of hope suited to counteract their spiritual deterioration, induce repentance and purify their lives, encourage perseverance, fortify them against discouragement and despair, and encourage them with the knowledge of assured ultimate victory.

The blessing pronounced upon those who "hear the words of the prophecy, and keep the things that are written therein" (1:3) underlines that this prophetic unveiling of the future has a practical ethical purpose. The purpose of prophecy is not simply to satisfy curiosity about the future; it is intended to have a sanctifying effect on the daily life of the saints (I John 3:3).

The Characteristics of the Revelation

1. SYMBOLISM

Its symbolism is the most distinctive feature of the book of Revelation. The Apocalypse conveys its message through representative imagery, familiar or grotesque, rather than through formal definition and declaration. The various symbols used are drawn from all areas of life and creation. Some of them "are easily understood, for their meaning shines through the drapery that covers the great thought, but others are so complex, so unearthly, and portentous in their vastness and mysteriousness as to daze, to overwhelm us."[87] At times guidance for interpretation is offered by an indication of the meaning of the symbol; but this is not always the case. As to their interpretation, the symbols of the book may be grouped into three classes: those explained in the book; those explained in other parts of the Bible; those left unexplained.[88] In most instances the writer apparently expected his readers to understand the symbolic significance of the figures he employed; many of them were familiar to the conventional language of the day. A few times the readers are called upon to use their wisdom to understand the picture (13:18; 17:9).

Much of the imagery is taken from the Old Testament. Familiarity

---

87. William G. Moorehead, *Studies in the Book of Revelation*, p. 15.
88. See Merrill C. Tenney, *Interpreting Revelation*, pp. 186-93.

with its symbolism is important for an understanding of the Apocalypse. There are symbolic objects as well as symbolic acts. There is a symbolism of numbers.[89] Thus *four* is the number of the earth or mundane space; *seven* the number of completeness or perfection; *ten* the number of secular organization and power. Other numbers are also used. There is also a symbolism of colors. *White* is preeminently the color of purity and innocence; *red*, the color of war and bloodshed; and *purple*, the color of imperial luxury and ease.

2. BIBLE-BASED

The Revelation is distinctly a Bible-based book. There is not a single direct citation from the Old Testament in the entire book, but its author was thoroughly familiar with it. "John's spirit and style are saturated with the influence of the Old Testament images and allusions, language and thought."[90] But his references to the Old Testament are oblique; he makes free and independent use of the Old Testament material, incorporating it into his own language. All parts of the Old Testament are drawn upon, but Exodus, Psalms, and the major prophets are used most frequently. Views vary as to the exact number of Old Testament references found in the book. Tenney finds 348 identifiable allusions, "an average of more than ten for each chapter in Revelation."[91]

3. ONE WORLD

The concept of one world is strongly presented in the Apocalypse. The fourfold enumeration, "every tribe, and tongue, and people, and nation" (used with variations) suggests the worldwide scope of its theme (5:9; 7:9; 10:11; 11:9; 13:7; 14:6; 17:15). The rulers are spoken of as the "kings of the whole world" (16:14; 17:2, 18; 18:9; 19:9). The economic system of the beast encompasses the whole world (13:16-17). Satan, who is pictured as "the deceiver of the whole world" (12:9), gives worldwide authority to the beast (13:7), resulting in worldwide worship of the beast (13:8). The Babylonian harlot extended her fornications to include "all the nations" (18:3).

89. See John Peter Lange, "The Apocalypse," in Lange's *Commentary on the Holy Scriptures*, pp. 14-41, for various aspects of the symbolism of Revelation.
90. Hayes, *John and His Writings*, p. 287.
91. Henney, *Interpreting Revelation*, p. 101. See chap. 11.

It pictures a one-world condition in ungodliness, a world united in its rebellion against God and His Anointed (cf. Ps 2).

This concept of one world is also presented from the divine perspective. The throne of God (4:1-10) is central to the whole book; He is in control of the whole world. The alternating scenes between heaven and earth picture this control; actions in heaven are determinative of events that follow on earth. The divine control will be openly established on earth when Christ returns as the King of kings; then "the kingdom of the world is become the kingdom of our Lord, and of his Christ" (11:15). And in the eternal state, when fellowship between God and man has been brought to full and final realization, the throne of God and the Lamb is still central (21:3; 22:1-3).

4. JUDGMENT

The Apocalypse is a book of judgment from first to last. The picture of Christ in the first three chapters is that of the Judge in the midst of His churches. The eschatological portion of the book (chaps. 6-16) consists of a series of judgments upon a Christ-rejecting world. Judgment is meted out upon apostate Babylon (chaps. 17-18), judgment falls upon the rebels against Christ at His return in glory, and final judgment is given to the dead at the Great White Throne (chaps. 19-20). It is a book of judgment consummating in victory. But the judgment is righteous, based upon the sharp distinction between righteousness and unrighteousness. The eternal Judge will make no compromise with evil; sin must be punished. "The doctrine of penal retribution is deeply engraved on the Book: and the God whom it honours is a God of judgment."[92]

5. CHRIST-CENTERED

In contrast to Jewish apocalyptic works, the book of Revelation is distinctly a Christ-centered book. It is rich in its Christology.[93] It proclaims itself as the "revelation of Jesus Christ" (1:1). It is a revelation not only from Him but also about Him. His person is central to the book. In the opening chapter, He appears as the glorified Lord communicating His message to His servants. In chapter 5, He is the Lord of the nations, claiming, on the basis of His redemptive

92. Donald Fraser, *Synoptical Lectures on the Books of Holy Scripture, Romans—Revelation,* p. 266.
93. See Tenney, *Interpreting Revelation,* chap. 12.

work, the right to exercise judgment upon all in rebellion against Him as the world's rightful Ruler. In chapter 19, He comes in glory with His saints as the King of kings to consummate His victory and to establish His rule. In the eternal order He is the Bridegroom of His people (19:7; 21:9), ruling over a world united under the eternal "throne of God and the Lamb."

6. SONG AND WORSHIP

As a Christian book, the Apocalypse is characterized by song and worship. While portraying judgment upon sin, a note of joy and praise is heard repeatedly. Some twenty songs of praise and worship are recorded in it. Saints and angels, as well as all nature, are pictured as sharing in the worship of God and the Lamb. The worship is joyous and wholehearted. A number of the songs record the reactions of the witnesses to the just judgments of God being poured out upon an evil world.

It insists that the only proper object of man's worship is God (19:10; 22:9). Both men and angels joyfully unite in their worship of the Lamb of God (5:8-14). The book also shows and denounces wrong worship. It castigates all idolatry and shows that the worship of any man or of Satan will be judged. Worship of the beast and his image is a special object of warning.

7. TIMELINESS

The book of Revelation is one of the most timely writings in existence. It arose out of a troubled age, and it has a vital message for our own age of deepening darkness and spreading fear of impending catastrophe. Its portrayal of human wickedness and the operation of supernatural forces of evil is strikingly relevant today. While painting a realistic picture of evil, the Apocalypse also heralds a ringing message of hope. It proclaims God's overruling presence in the tangled affairs of history and gives assurance that He will bring human affairs to a triumphant conclusion.

Its apocalyptic visions, once regarded as the unrestrained imaginations of speculative fancy, are today beginning to seem less fantastic. Modern developments are forcing the recognition that its prophetic contents do have the possibilities of grim but sober reality. The character and achievements of our own day make it a contemporary book.

THE INTERPRETATIONS OF THE REVELATION

The Apocalypse is the only New Testament book concerning which several different systems of interpretation have been developed. Broadly speaking, interpreters of this book follow one of four main approaches. The debate centers mainly around the distinctly apocalyptic section, chapters 4-20. The system adopted makes a great difference as to what the book is understood to teach.

1. PRETERIST VIEW

Named from the Latin *praeter*, meaning "past," the preterist view confines the meaning of the book to first-century events. It holds that the book is a symbolic portrayal of the conflicts of the Church with its enemies during the author's own day and what he expected to be the outcome of the conflict. Accepting the persecution of Christianity by the Roman Empire as central to the scene, it holds that the author was occupied with that conflict. The writer addressed his message to the believers of his day and had nothing beyond that in view.

This view has the merit of relating the book directly to the historical situation of the original readers. Writers of this school have poured a flood of light on the apostolic age. This approach is essential for a full understanding of the epistolary section of the book (chaps. 2-3). But in limiting the scope of the book to the first century, the view "has the demerit of making it meaningless (except for the information it gives about that early generation) for all subsequent readers."[94] Tenney remarks that this view offers "an interpretation which has a firm pedestal, but which has no finished sculpture to place on it."[95] It squeezes the Revelation into too small a mold and denies the prophetic character of the book. If its advocates are justified in limiting the meaning of the Apocalypse to the first century, it is difficult to see why the Church in subsequent centuries has continued to regard it as prophetic. Christ's eschatological return is the center and goal of the book, not the events of John's own day, and not until Christ returns will its supreme meaning be fulfilled. Gundry points out, "Preterists attempt to salvage the significance of the book for modern times by resorting also to the idealist view."[96]

94. Morris, *The Revelation of St. John*, p. 16.
95. Tenney, *Interpreting Revelation*, p. 144.
96. Robert H. Gundry, *A Survey of the New Testament*, p. 366.

2. IDEALIST VIEW

The idealist view, also known as "the spiritual view," holds that it is not the purpose of the book to predict the future or to foretell precise coming events; rather, it sets forth fundamental spiritual principles which govern the experiences of the Church during the entire period of its earthly pilgrimage. Thus, M'Clymont asserts, "The safest and probably the truest interpretation of the book is to regard it as a symbolic representation of great principles rather than a collection of definite predictions."[97] The book's symbolic language cannot be identified with any definite historical events, past, present, or future, but rather portrays the continuing struggle between good and evil, the Church and the world, and assures that the Kingdom of God will triumph in the end.

This view rightly recognizes the cosmic character of the conflict described in the book. It sees the hand of God in human history and accepts that God is moving toward the triumph of His cause in the world. It focuses attention on the ethical and spiritual values of the book for tested believers.

No one objects to the spiritual truths which this view finds in the Revelation. But the fact that it severs the book from its historical background makes the approach suspect to most students. It is a novel view; until recent times, the book was not so regarded. It has commonly been accepted that its strange symbolism does describe real events and actors. In thus stripping the book of its prophetic character, it contradicts the express claim of the book to be prophecy. Even its advocates admit that the book has a predictive end in setting forth the return of Christ and the resurrection and judgment. This view is inconsistent with the employment of the historical-grammatical method of interpretation.

3. HISTORICIST VIEW

The historicist view, also called the "continuous historical view," holds that the Apocalypse is an inspired forecast of the history of the Western Church from apostolic days to the Second Coming. It is grounded in the observation that the book begins its story in the author's own day and that the story reaches its culmination with the return of Christ; since no clear time break between these two terminal points is declared, the book must describe the continuous

97. M'Clymont, p. 155.

process leading to the consummation of the story of the Church. The Revelation is viewed as setting forth the great turning points of that history.

This theory has had many champions who have sought to work out the interpretation in the light of Church history. Cartledge observes, "Each student works the scheme out so that the end of time falls in his own time. As each new generation rises, it is necessary to work out a new scheme for the identification of events."[98] The great diversity of views among its advocates demonstrates the lack of an objective criterion for identification of the historical events. Walvoord notes, "As many as fifty different interpretations of the book of Revelation" have evolved, "depending on the time and circumstances of the expositor."[99] All this diversity makes the method seem to be arbitrary and hazardous in the extreme. If the Revelation does set forth a continuous history of the Church, surely after more than nineteen centuries of that history, the pattern of fulfillment would be clearly established by now, making it obvious that a definite part of the history has already been fulfilled. But such is not the case.

This view must resort to a thorough use of the allegorizing method in order to identify historical events it professes to see in the Revelation. Advocates of this view generally limit their identification of events to the Western Church and take little cognizance of the spread of Christianity in the East. This view offers no satisfactory explanation why the divine prophetic forecast should be largely confined to the affairs of the Church in the West. Harrison also observes, "It is antecedently doubtful that the Spirit of God would be concerned to inform the apostolic church with a rather detailed picture of events lying beyond their own time and having only a remote bearing on the consummation of the age."[100] If the original readers understood the book according to this theory, it is difficult to see how they could maintain a living hope of the return of Christ. If history is the key to the proper interpretation of the Apocalypse, then a knowledge of ecclesiastical and political history spanning centuries is necessary for an understanding of the Revelation. Then the vast majority of God's common people are cut off from understanding it. Could it be that

98. Samuel A. Cartledge, *A Conservative Introduction to the New Testament*, p. 171.
99. John F. Walvoord, *The Revelation of Jesus Christ, A Commentary*, p. 19.
100. Harrison, p. 463.

a book which is so earnestly commended to their attention would thus be closed to them?

4. FUTURIST VIEW

Adherents to this view generally hold that beginning with chapter 4, the book sets forth end-time events which will be fulfilled in the period immediately preceding and culminating in the return of Christ and the establishment of His millennial kingdom. They hold that chapters 6-19 relate to the end-time period known as "the great tribulation" (7:14) which is generally regarded as a period of seven years (cf. Dan 9:24-27). But there is considerable diversity among futurists as to the probable order of future events, especially the time relationship of the rapture (1 Co 15:51-57; 1 Th 4:13-18) to the great tribulation. While accepting the historical character of the seven churches, some futurists maintain that the seven letters also contain a latent prophetic forecast of the history of the Church.

The futurist view gives due recognition to the prophetic character of the book. It points to the second advent as the central, unifying theme of the book and holds that its interpretation must be understood in the light of that dominating event. "However one may interpret the symbols," says Tenney, "the action of the book leads to and includes the last judgment of earth and the final establishment of the city of God. As the events lead up to this terminus in close succession, one may reason backward and say that the bulk of these events must still be future, since the consummation with which they are associated has not yet been attained and since the symbols seem to call for a rapid succession of acts rather than for a protracted process."[101]

Futurists hold that this view is in harmony with the whole scheme of biblical prediction, which has its two foci in the first and second advents. Building on the historical reality of the first advent, the Revelation looks forward to the time of the second advent. This view does not resort to wholesale allegorizing. While recognizing the use of symbolic language, futurists generally tend to interpret as literally as possible. "The more literal an interpretation that one adopts, the more strongly will he be construed to be a futurist."[102]

Objection is made to the futurist view with the assertion that it

101. Tenney, *Interpreting Revelation*, p. 142.
102. Ibid.

"robs the book of all significance for the early Christians, and indeed, for all subsequent generations right up to the last."[103] This objection assumes that a prophecy can have no meaning for a believer if it does not deal with his own time. Many biblical prophecies are still to be fulfilled, but that does not mean those prophecies are meaningless to the present believer. From 2 Peter 3:10-14, it is obvious that Peter believed a distant prophetic event can have practical significance for the believer. Gundry asserts, "Revelation retains its relevance because of the possibility for each successive generation to see the fulfillment of the book."[104] The point is not the immediate fulfillment of the prophecy but whether its import can be appreciated and valued now in the light of God's future program. Walvoord asserts, "To use the argument that the book must be understood by the first generation of Christians completely as a refutation of the futuristic position is not reasonable nor backed by the study of prophecy in Scripture in general."[105]

Objection to the futurist view is sometimes made with the claim that it relegates too large a portion of the Apocalypse to a relatively very short period relating to the end time. Critics hold it improbable that centuries should be passed over to concentrate on a few brief years at the end. In reply, it must be noted that it is the very nature of basic, far-reaching prophecies thus to look to the end without dealing with the intervening period. Smith pointedly remarks,

> Is not this true of the very first prophecy of the Bible—"and I will put enmity between thee and the woman, and between thy seed and her seed: he shall bruise thy head, and thou shalt bruise his heel" (Gen 3:15)? Is not this a prophecy of Messianic victory which still awaits its final fulfillment? . . . Over and over again in the Book of Daniel, we are told that its prophecies refer to "the end" (7:26; 9:26, 27; 11: 13, 27; 12:8, 13). Does not our Lord's Olivet discourse point directly to the *end* of the age, and Christ's still future Second Advent? (Mt 24:3, 14). So with Paul speaking to the Thessalonians regarding the man of sin; Peter's account of the apostasy of the last days; Paul's great eschatological prophecy in II Timothy 3, and the whole body of prophecy in the familiar resurrection chapter, I Corinthians 15. All these require a futurist interpretation. It is not unreasonable that

103. Morris, *The Revelation of St. John*, p. 18.
104. Gundry, p. 368.
105. Walvoord, p. 21.

the Bible should conclude with a book of prophecies which, for the most part, will be fulfilled at the great final consummation of this age—the end of the revolt against God, and the beginning of that age of righteousness for which all just men long.[106]

Each of these four views contains elements of truth, and impressive names are associated with each. While not accepting all that has been advanced under the banner of futurism, we hold that the futurist view presents the most profitable approach to the interpretation of the Apocalypse.

THE MILLENNIUM IN THE REVELATION

Any study of the Revelation must deal with the question of the Millennium. The term *millennium* is the Latin equivalent of the Greek *chilia* (the basis for the English word *chiliasm*), both simply meaning "a thousand years." The problem centers in Revelation 20:1-10 where the term occurs six times. The crux of the problem is whether the term is to be interpreted literally or figuratively, and whether the Millennium comes before or after the Second Advent of Christ. Although Revelation 20 is the only place where this specific prophetic time designation occurs, the interpretation of the passage is related to what the teaching of the Bible elsewhere on the eschatological future is understood to be. How Revelation 20 is understood will be influenced by the millennial view adopted.

Three views of the Millennium have been advocated.[107]

The *postmillennial* view holds that the return of Christ will be after the Millennium. This view usually interprets the Millennium as figurative, to denote the period of the Gospel's gradual triumph over the nations until a reign of peace results which will endure until Christ comes at the end of history in final judgment.

The *amillennial* view interprets the thousand years as a highly figurative designation and sees no ground for expecting a literal Millennium as a definite time period. Its advocates view the Millennium as representative of the blessedness of Christian experience now, or that it possibly represents the intermediate state of the blessed dead.

---

106. Smith, pp. 1499-1500.
107. Charles Lee Feinberg, *Premillennialism or Amillennialism?*; Loraine Boettner, *The Millennium*; W. J. Grier, *The Momentous Event*; Tenney, *Interpreting Revelation*, chap. 14; Ernest Frederick Kevan, "Millennium," in *Baker's Dictionary of Theology*, pp. 351-55; William G. Moorehead, "Millennium," in *The International Standard Bible Encyclopaedia*, 3:2052-55.

They see no prospect of the conversion of the world through the preaching of the Gospel but rather that an increase of lawlessness may be expected as the end of the world approaches. Christ may return at any time, and that return will usher in the final judgment and the eternal state.

The *premillennial* view accepts the thousand years as a definite chronological period and holds that Christ will return to earth personally in glory to initiate His millennial kingdom. The righteous dead will be raised and rule with Him during the Millennium. This view generally assumes that the Old Testament eschatological teaching must be taken at face value and demands belief in a literal, glorious kingdom on earth in the end time, although its precise duration is nowhere indicated. The millennial period will be terminated with a final Satan-inspired rebellion which will be immediately suppressed; the wicked will be judged, and the eternal state will be ushered in. A regular feature of premillennialism is the view that the Second Advent will be in two phrases, the *rapture*, when the Church will be caught up to meet her Lord and be eternally united with Him, and the *revelation*, when Christ will return to earth in open glory with His Church to establish His millennial reign.

Premillennialists are not agreed on the time of the rapture in relation to the great tribulation period which will be terminated by Christ's return in glory. *Pre*tribulationists hold that the rapture will occur before the beginning of the great tribulation; *mid*tribulationists place it at the middle of the tribulation period; *post*tribulationists hold that the Church will continue on earth throughout the tribulation period.

Evangelical scholarship is sharply divided on the millennial issue. All admit that the great hope of the Church is the ultimate coming of Christ which will be personal and literal. But strong differences exist as to the nature and time of the events that must precede His coming. Postmillennialism, based on an optimistic view of the future, has received severe disillusionment in the present century from the tragic development of world affairs. Within more recent times, amillennialism has been growing in scholarly favor because of the untenable character of postmillennialism and dissatisfaction with various premillennial positions. It rests on a symbolic interpretation of Revelation 20 and has no place for a Millennium in the program of the future. It does not accept at face value the many Old Testament prophecies of the coming reign of the Messiah on earth and its rejects a literal fulfillment of the prophecies of Israel's future national leadership. It cannot accept the mention of the two resurrections in Revelation 20 as literal resurrections with a time interval between them but must spiritualize the first resurrection. Premillennialism treats the account in Revelation 20:1-10 as depicting definite chronological events which form a definite link in the succession of occurrences pictured in Revelation 19:11—21:8. It allows a definite place, although not the most important place, for the Millennium in its program of the eschatological future. It recognizes the presence of symbolism but holds that behind the figurative language there are literal realities being portrayed. It holds that its understanding of Second Advent prophecies is most in harmony with the manner of the fulfillment of first advent prophecies.

It must be recognized that the basic problem behind these divergent eschatological views is how prophecy is to be interpreted, whether the language is to be allegorized and spiritualized or to be literally understood. Premillennialists hold to a literal interpretation of prophecy as far as is consistent with the presence of the figurative language in prophecy.[108]

THE STRUCTURE OF THE REVELATION

It is generally conceded that the book of Revelation was composed according to a carefully devised plan. In the words of Fraser, "It is a Book most carefully construed, curiously wrought, nicely arranged, and skillfully balanced."[109] But in the numerous proposed outlines of the book, there is no general agreement concerning its structural plan. Guthrie points out this diversity by grouping the many and varied theories concerning the structure of the book under seven different categories.[110] This variety establishes that the Revelation does not display an obvious structural outline. This diversity leads Scroggie to observe, "The architecture of this Work will vary as it is seen from different angles, and as it is interpreted in different ways."[111]

108. Paul Lee Tan, *The Interpretation of Prophecy.*
109. Fraser, p. 270.
110. Guthrie, pp. 969-74.
111. W. Graham, Scroggie, *Know Your Bible,* volume 2, *The New Testament,* pp. 369-70.

The Lord's command to John in 1:19, "Write therefore the things which thou sawest, and the things which are, and the things which shall come to pass hereafter," clearly seems to provide the key to the outline of the book as a whole. This order to John indicates that the material of his book will fall into three parts: (1) "the things which thou sawest"—the vision of the glorified Christ recorded in 1:9-20; (2) "the things which are" (cf. 1:20)—the seven churches addressed in chapters 2-3; (3) "the things which shall come to pass hereafter"—the prophetic portion of the Apocalypse, chapter 4 to the end. The fact that this third idea is repeated in 4:1 lends confirmation to this division. The three divisions, which are of unequal length, relate to the past (chap. 1), to the present (chaps. 2-3), and to the future (chaps. 4-22). That the bulk of the book is thus devoted to "things to come" is consistent with its character as a book of prophecy (1:3; 22:7, 10, 18-19). The three parts of this general outline draw attention to the authoritative source of the message as given by the risen Christ, express His concern with the present needs of the readers, and unfold the future for His persecuted Church as a whole.

In seeking to develop an analytical outline, the first three chapters present no structural difficulty, but the third main division, which comprises the major portion of the book, has been variously viewed as to its structural form. Chapters four and five, in which the sovereignty of God is central, clearly provide the setting for the unfolding of the prophetic events delineated in the remainder of the book. The apocalyptic scenes which follow in chapters 6-18 clearly look forward to the grand climax in the return of Christ in glory in chapter 19. Prominent in chapters 6-18 are three series of sevens—the seven seals, the seven trumpets, and the seven bowls.[112] All agree that these three series are part of the intentional framework of the book of Revelation. They dominate the judgments in this part of the book. The use of the ordinal numbers in each of the septenary series, as well as the recorded results under each, makes clear that the events in each series are successive. But views differ as to the intended relationship of these three series of judgments to each other. Three different views as to their chronological relationship are advanced.

The *concurrent fulfillment* view holds that the three series are

112. The contents of a fourth septenary series, the seven thunders (10:1-5), are not declared, and this series does not advance the structural development.

parallel presentations of the judgments falling on the earth and that each series terminates with the return of Christ. Hendriksen, who advocates a sevenfold cyclic arrangement of Revelation, maintains that "the cycles are no mere repetitions. Each one adds to the thought of the preceding one."[113]

The *partially concurrent fulfillment* view accepts that the three series portray distinct judgments, which while beginning successively, all terminate at the Parousia. Gundry remarks, "The fact that the contents of the seventh in each series are practically identical and seem to indicate finality—thunder, lightning, an earthquake, and various indications that the end has come—suggests that the seals, trumpets, and bowls are at least partially concurrent in their fulfillment."[114]

The third view, usually called the *consecutive fulfillment* view, holds that the seals follow in consecutive order but that the seventh seal is unfolded in the seven trumpets, and in turn the seventh trumpet is unfolded in the seven bowl judgments. The last of each series constitutes the beginning of the next series.[115] The second and third series each telescope out of the preceding series. This view is supported by the fact that the result of the breaking of the seventh seal is nowhere described, unless it is in the seven trumpets which are immediately seen (8:1-7). In the same way there is no recorded fulfillment of the "woe" connected with the seventh trumpet (8:13; 9:12; 11:14), unless its fulfillment is found in the seven bowl judgments.

Chapter 7 introduces another feature of the structure of the third major division of Revelation. Coming between the sixth and seventh seal, it constitutes an "inset" or "episode" which, while not a part of the chronological sequence, is inserted to give a clearer picture of the whole. There is a similar insert between the sixth and seventh trumpet (10:1—11:13); there also seems to be a short insert between the sixth and seventh bowl (16:13-16). There is furthermore a lengthy insertion between the seventh trumpet and the bowl judgments (12:1—14:20). Chapters 17-18 also seem to have the character of an inserted picture to provide a full portrayal of an event that has

113. William Hendriksen, *Bible Survey*, p. 452. See also *More Than Conquerors, An Interpretation of the Book of Revelation*, chap. 4.
114. Gundry, p. 374.
115. See Gary G. Cohen, *Understanding Revelation*, pp. 77-124.

already twice been mentioned (14:8; 16:19). These chapters provide a detailed description of the judgment upon Babylon because of its tremendous significance for the fulfillment of the divine program.

All the material in 6:1—18:24 brings the story to the grand climax of the book in the return of Christ to earth (19:1-21). What follows in chapters 20-22 relates to millennial (20:1-6) and postmillennial events (20:7—22:5), bringing the book of Revelation to its glorious conclusion.

AN OUTLINE OF THE REVELATION

I. The Introduction, 1:1-8

  A. The superscription, vv. 1-3
  B. The salutation and response, vv. 4-8
    1. The epistolary greeting, vv. 4-5a
    2. The dedication, vv. 5b-6
    3. The prophetic testimony, vv. 7-8

II. "The Things Which Thou Sawest," 1:9-20

  A. The setting of the vision, vv. 9-11
  B. The content of the vision, vv. 12-16
  C. The results of the vision, vv. 17-20
    1. The word of comfort, vv. 17-18
    2. The commission to write, vv. 19-20

III. "The Things Which Are," 2:1—3:22

  A. The message to the church in Ephesus, 2:1-7*
    1. The recipient, v. 1a
    2. The Speaker, v. 1b
    3. The message, vv. 2-6
    4. The invitation, v. 7a
    5. The promise, v. 7b
  B. The message to the church in Smyrna, 2:8-11
  C. The message to the church in Pergamum, 2:12-17
  D. The message to the church in Thyatira, 2:18-29
  E. The message to the church in Sardis, 3:1-6

*Each of the seven letters has the same outline, except that in the last four, the promise to the overcomer stands before the invitation to hear.

    h) Inset: The satanic preparations for Armageddon, 16:13-17

    i) The seventh bowl: final judgment in devastating earthquake and hail, 16:17-21

  5. Inset: The overthrow of Babylon, 17:1–18:24

    a) The judgment upon the great harlot, 17:1-18

      (1) The vision of the harlot, vv. 1-6

      (2) The agents of her judgment, vv. 7-15

      (3) The execution of the judgment, vv. 16-18

    b) The destruction of the great city, 18:1-24

      (1) The angelic proclamation of Babylon's fall, vv. 1-3

      (2) The voice from heaven concerning the fall, vv. 4-20

      (3) The angelic act and dirge over the fall, vv. 21-24

C. The return of Christ in glory, 19:1-21

  1. The rejoicing in heaven, vv. 1-10

    a) The rejoicing over the judgment of the harlot, vv. 1-5

    b) The rejoicing over the marriage of the Lamb, vv. 6-9

    c) The correction of John's attempted worship, v. 10

  2. The return of Christ to earth as Conqueror, vv. 11-21

    a) The coming of the King with His armies, vv. 11-16

    b) The summoning of the birds to the great supper of God, vv. 17-18

    c) The doom of the enemies on earth, vv. 19-21

D. The millennial Kingdom, 20:1-10

  1. The binding of Satan for one thousand years, vv. 1-3

  2. The millennial reign of Christ with the saints, vv. 4-6

  3. The crushing of the final Satan-led rebellion, vv. 7-10

E. The postmillennial events, 20:11–22:5

  1. The judgment of the dead at the great white throne, 20:11-14

  2. The new heaven and the new earth, 21:1-8

  3. The vision of the New Jerusalem, 21:9–22:5

    a) The description of the city, 21:9-27

    b) The delights of the city, 22:1-5

V. The conclusion, 22:6-21

A. The trustworthiness of the Revelation, vv. 6-7

B. The worthiness of God alone as object of worship, vv. 8-9

C. The concluding instructions concerning the book, vv. 10-20

1. The words of comfort and assurance, vv. 10-17
2. The warning against altering the book, vv. 18-19
3. The concluding testimony concerning the coming, v. 20
   D. The benediction, v. 21

A BOOK LIST ON THE REVELATION

Barclay, William. *The Revelation of John.* The Daily Study Bible. 2 vols. Philadelphia: Westminster, 1961.

Prints author's own translation. Volume 1, covering the first five chapters, deals extensively with the seven letters. The author's strong points are his handling of historical data and his Greek word studies.

Barnhouse, Donald Grey. *Revelation, An Expository Commentary.* Grand Rapids: Zondervan, 1971.

Prints what is called a "free translation" of Revelation. A devotional and practical commentary by an outstanding expository preacher. The material on the last two chapters was contributed by Ralph L. Keiper. The viewpoint is premillennial and pretribulational.

Beckwith, Isbon T. *The Apocalypse of John. Studies in Introduction with a Critical and Exegetical Commentary.* 1919. Reprint. Grand Rapids: Baker, 1967.

Greek text. An introduction of over four hundred pages on various introductory problems reveals impeccable scholarship. A critical commentary of nearly four hundred pages deals closely with the Greek text. Amillennial in viewpoint.

Bullinger, E. W. *The Apocalypse, or "The Day of the Lord."* 3d ed. London: Eyre & Spottiswoode, 1935.

An exhaustive treatment from an extreme futurist viewpoint. Accepting "the day of the Lord" (1:10) as the prophetic key, Bullinger insists that everything in Revelation is still future. The seven churches will be reestablished at the end of the age. Represents ultradispensational premillennialism.

Caird, G. B. *A Commentary on the Revelation of St. John the Divine.* Harper's New Testament Commentaries. New York: Harper & Row, 1966.

Prints author's own translation. Valuable for a reconstruction of the first-century setting. A scholarly commentary which takes the symbolism of Revelation to represent imminent historical rather than eschatological events.

Charles, R. H. *A Critical and Exegetical Commentary on the Revelation of St. John.* The International Critical Commentary. 2 vols. Edinburgh: T. & T. Clark, 1920.

> Greek text. The massive work of a liberal British scholar who was a master of Jewish apocalyptic literature. A mine of historical and grammatical information. Holds to preterist view.

Criswell, W. A. *Expository Sermons on Revelation.* 5 vols. Grand Rapids: Zondervon, 1961-1966. (Now in one volume.)

> A series of expository sermons covering all of Revelation by a noted conservative Baptist minister. Based on careful exegesis of the text, the sermons have a practical appeal. The viewpoint is premillennial and pretribulational.

Crow, G. R. *The Lamb and the Book. A new look at the book of the Revelation.* Bombay: Gospel Literature Service, 1964.

> A fresh work on the Revelation by an evangelical missionary in India. The author's viewpoint is premillennial and posttribulational.

Harrison, Norman B. *The End. Re-Thinking The Revelation.* Minneapolis, Minn.: The Harrison Service, 1941.

> A premillennial interpretation advocating a midtribulation rapture. Includes a colored chart of Revelation setting forth this view.

Hendriksen, William. *More Than Conquerors. An Interpretation of the Book of Revelation.* 1939. Reprint. Grand Rapids: Baker, 1967.

> An able work on Revelation by an evangelical teacher using the synchronistic or parallelistic system of interpretation. His viewpoint is amillennial.

Hoyt, Herman A. *The Revelation of the Lord Jesus Christ. An Exposition of the Book of the Revelation.* Winona Lake, Ind.: Brethren Missionary Herald, 1966.

> A concise, well-outlined interpretation from the premillennial, pretribulational viewpoint. The author holds the seven letters also give a prophetic picture of the entire Church age. Well suited to lay study groups.

Kelly, William. *Lectures on the Book of Revelation.* 1868. Reprint. London: G. Morrish, n.d.

> Expository lectures by a noted Plymouth Brethren scholar of the past century. The author uses Scripture to try to explain the symbols of the book. The viewpoint is premillennial and pretribulational.

Ladd, George Eldon. *A Commentary on the Revelation of John.* Grand Rapids: Eerdmans, 1972.

A popular commentary on Revelation that takes a premillennial and posttribulational view of eschatology. Ladd sees the Millennium and the whole book of Revelation referring chiefly to the destiny of the Church rather than to the theocratic promises to Israel. Seeks to present different viewpoints and analyze problems of interpretation.

Lenski, R. C. H. *The Interpretation of St. John's Revelation.* Columbus, Ohio: Lutheran Book Concern, 1935.

Prints author's own quite literal translation. Important for exegetical study of the text of Revelation. The work of an accomplished amillennial Lutheran scholar. Lenski adopts a topical or recapitulary method of interpretation.

Milligan, William. "The Book of Revelation." In *An Exposition of the Bible,* vol. 6. Hartford, Conn.: S. S. Scranton, 1903.

An exposition of Revelation from the idealist point of view.

Moffatt, James. "The Revelation of St. John the Divine." In *The Expositor's Greek Testament,* vol. 5. Reprint. Grand Rapids: Eerdmans, n.d.

Greek text. The work of a noted liberal British scholar who rejected the traditional authorship and followed the preterist school of interpretation.

Morris, Leon. *The Revelation of St. John. An Introduction and Commentary.* Tyndale New Testament Commentaries. Grand Rapids: Eerdmans, 1969.

A concise interpretation by a noted conservative scholar who combines the preterist and futurist views.

Newell, William R. *The Book of The Revelation.* Chicago: Moody, 1935.

A full, consistently literal interpretation of Revelation which accepts the symbolic where it is obvious. The viewpoint is premillennial and pretribulational. Has several appendixes, including "Why the church will not be in the Great Tribulation."

Pieters, Albertus. *An Exposition of the Revelation of St. John.* 1937. Reprint. Grand Rapids: Eerdmans, 1954.

The work of a conservative scholar who follows the preterist viewpoint. States his views and gives a reasoned defense.

Rist, Martin; and Hough, Lynn Harold. "The Revelation of St. John the Divine." In *The Interpreter's Bible*, vol. 12. New York: Abingdon, 1957.

> Introduction and exegesis by Rist; exposition by Hough. A liberal work which seeks to unfold the world view and apocalyptic scheme of the original author. The assumption is that upon canonization this apocalypse came to be regarded as a divinely inspired and authoritative series of predictions.

Ryrie, Charles Caldwell. *Revelation.* Everyman's Bible Commentary. Chicago: Moody, 1968.

> A concise, well-outlined study of Revelation, following the premillennial, pretribulational view. Ideal for a beginner's study of Revelation.

Scott, Walter. *Exposition of the Revelation of Jesus Christ.* London: Pickering & Inglis, n.d.

> An older, premillennial commentary by a British Plymouth-Brethren scholar that has had a strong influence on subsequent premillennial commentaries. A careful exposition, showing awareness of God's program for the future.

Seiss, J. A. *The Apocalypse. Lectures on the Book of Revelation.* 1865. Grand Rapids: Zondervan, n.d. (Originally in three volumes.)

> A series of fifty-two lectures covering all of the Revelation by a conservative Lutheran preacher-scholar who adhered to the premillennial viewpoint. Still of value as a thorough interpretation of Revelation.

Smith, J. B. *A Commentary on the Book of Revelation—A Revelation of Jesus Christ.* Ed. J. Otis Yoder. Scottdale, Pa.: Herald, 1961.

> A careful, detailed exegesis by a Mennonite scholar, known for his *Greek-English Concordance of the New Testament.* The interpretation, following a premillennial, pretribulational eschatology, is consistently literal, except where avowed symbolism demands a different procedure. A noted feature is the abundant use of statistics and comparisons.

Swete, Henry Barclay. *The Apocalypse of St. John, The Greek Text with Introduction, Notes and Indices.* 1909. Reprint. Grand Rapids: Eerdmans, 1951.

> A classic commentary on the Greek text, important for Greek exegesis. Contains an exhaustive 200-page introduction. The view-

point is eclectic, finding points of contact with the various different systems of apocalyptic interpretation. Has a full list of patristic and modern commentaries up to 1908. Invaluable for the advanced student.

Tatford, Fredk. A. *Prophecy's Last Word. An Exposition of the Revelation.* London: Pickering & Inglis, 1947.

A careful, systematic interpretation of Revelation from a premillennial, pretribulational viewpoint. While rejecting the historical view, the author sees elements of truth in that interpretation as providing partial pictures of what will be reenacted in the full future fulfillment. Seeks to unveil God's prophetic program.

Tenney, Merrill C. *Interpreting Revelation.* Grand Rapids: Eerdmans, 1958.

Not intended as a full commentary on Revelation but unique as a guide to the various methods of studying Revelation. Gives a fine presentation of various approaches but favors a premillennial stance.

Walvoord, John F. *The Revelation of Jesus Christ. A Commentary.* Chicago: Moody, 1966.

A thorough exegetical treatment from a dispensational, premillennial, pretribulational viewpoint. A leader in its class.

BIBLIOGRAPHY

NOTE: The volumes listed in the various Book Lists are not included in this bibliography except as they are cited or referred to in the body of the text.

BIBLES

The Holy Bible Containing the Old and New Testaments. American Standard. New York: Thomas Nelson, 1901.

The Holy Bible Containing the Old and New Testament. Authorized Version. London: Cambridge U.

New American Standard Bible. Chicago: Moody, 1972.

Rotherham, Joseph Bryant. *The Emphasized New Testament.* Reprint. Grand Rapids: Kregel, 1959.

Aland, Kurt; Black, Matthew; Metzger, Bruce M.; Wikgren, Allen. *The Greek New Testament.* London: United Bible Societies, 1966.

Nestle, Erwin; and Aland, Kurt. *Novum Testamentum Graece.* Stuttgart, Germany: For The American Bible Society, New York (24th Ed., n.d.).

Westcott, Brooke Foss; and Hort, Fenton John Anthony. *The New Testament in the Original Greek.* Reprint. New York: Macmillan, 1935.

NEW TESTAMENT INTRODUCTIONS

Allen, Willoughby C.; and Grensted, L. W. *Introduction to the Books of the New Testament.* 3d ed. Reprint. Edinburgh: T. & T. Clark, 1936.

Bacon, Benjamin W. *The Making of the New Testament.* London: Williams & Norgate, n.d.

Barker, Glenn W.; Lane, William L.; Michaels, J. Ramsey. *The New Testament Speaks.* New York: Harper & Row, 1969.

Bennett, W. H.; and Adeney, Walter F. *A Biblical Introduction.* 7th ed. London: Methuen, 1919.

Bleek, Friedrich, *An Introduction to the New Testament.* Translated from the German of the second edition by William Urwick. Vol. 2. Edinburgh: T. & T. Clark, 1870.

Boismard, M. E. "The Apocalypse." In A. Robert and A. Feuillet, *Introduction to the New Testament.* New York: Desclee, 1965.

Cartledge, Samuel A. *A Conservative Introduction to the New Testament.* Grand Rapids: Zondervan, 1938.

Clogg, Frank Bertram. *An Introduction to the New Testament.* 3d ed. Reprint. London: U. of London, 1949.

Dods, Marcus. *An Introduction to the New Testament.* 11th ed. London: Hodder & Stoughton, 1905.

Fowler, Henry Thatcher. *The History and Literature of the New Testament.* New York: Macmillan, 1934.

Fraser, Donald. *Synoptical Lectures on the Books of Holy Scripture, Romans—Revelation.* New York: Robert Carter, 1876.

Gloag, Paton J. *Introduction to the Catholic Epistles.* Edinburgh: T. & T. Clark, 1887.

Goodspeed, Edgar J. *An Introduction to the New Testament.* Chicago: U. of Chicago, 1937.

Gundry, Robert H. *A Survey of the New Testament.* Grand Rapids: Zondervan, 1970.

Guthrie, Donald. *New Testament Introduction.* 3d rev. ed. Downers Grove, Ill.: Inter-Varsity, 1970.

Harmon, Henry M. *Introduction to the Study of the Holy Scriptures.* New York: Phillips & Hunt, 1878.

Harrison, Everett F. *Introduction to the New Testament.* Rev. ed. Grand Rapids: Eerdmans, 1971.

Hendriksen, William. *Bible Survey. A Treasury of Bible Information.* 3d enlarged ed. Grand Rapids: Baker, 1949.

Henshaw, T. *New Testament Literature in the Light of Modern Scholarship.* 1952. Reprint. London: Allen & Unwin, 1957.

Hunter, A. M. *Introducing the New Testament.* Philadelphia: Westminster, 1946.

Jones, Maurice. *The New Testament in the Twentieth Century.* London: Macmillan, 1924.

Klijn, A. F. *An Introduction to the New Testament.* Leiden: Brill, 1967.

Kümmel, Werner Georg. *Introduction to the New Testament.* Translated by A. J. Mattill, Jr. Nashville: Abingdon, 1966.

M'Clymont, J. A. *The New Testament and Its Writers.* New York: Revell, n.d.

Miller, H. S. *General Biblical Introduction. From God to Us.* 4th ed. Houghton, N.Y.: Word-Bearer, 1947.

Moffatt, James. *An Introduction to the Literature of the New Testament.* 1918. 3d ed. Reprint. Edinburgh: T. & T. Clark, 1949.

Peake, Arthur S. *A Critical Introduction to the New Testament.* New York: Scribner's, 1919.

Robert, A.; and Feuillet, A. *Introduction to the New Testament.* New York: Desclee, 1965.

Salmon, George. *An Historical Introduction to the Study of the Books of the New Testament.* 9th ed. London: John Murray, 1904.

Scott, Ernest Findlay. *The Literature of the New Testament.* 1932. Reprint. New York: Columbia U., 1948.

Scroggie, W. Graham. *Know Your Bible. A Brief Introduction to the Scriptures.* Vol. 2. *The New Testament.* London: Pickering & Inglis, n.d.

Tenney, Merrill C. *The New Testament, An Historical and Analytic Survey.* Grand Rapids: Eerdmans, 1953.

Thiessen, Henry Clarence. *Introduction to the New Testament.* Grand Rapids: Eerdmans, 1943.

Weiss, Bernard. *A Manual Of Introduction to the New Testament.* Vol. 2. Translated from the German by A. J. K. Davidson. New York: Funk & Wagnalls, 1889.

Wikenhauser, Alfred. *New Testament Introduction.* 1958. Reprint. New York: Herder & Herder, 1963.

Williams, Charles B. *An Introduction to New Testament Literature.* Kansas City, Mo.: Western Bapt. Pub., 1929.

Zahn, Theodor. *Introduction to the New Testament.* Translated from the third German edition. 3 vols. Edinburgh: T. & T. Clark, 1909.

NEW TESTAMENT COMMENTARIES

Alexander, W. "The Third Epistle of John," *The Speaker's Commentary New Testament,* vol. 4. London: John Murray, 1881.

Alford, Henry. *The Greek Testament.* Vol. 4. London: Rivingtons, 1859; 1861.

Alleman, Herbert C., ed. *New Testament Commentary, A General Introduction to and a Commentary on the Books of the New Testament.* Rev. ed. Philadelphia: Board of Publication of the United Lutheran Church of America, 1944.

Barnes, Albert. *Notes on the New Testament, Explanatory and Practical— James, Peter, John, and Jude.* Edited by Robert Frew. Reprint. Grand Rapids: Baker, 1951.

Beckwith, Isbon T. *The Apocalypse of John. Studies in Introduction, with a Critical and Exegetical Commentary.* 1919. Reprint. Grand Rapids: Baker, 1967.

Beet, Joseph Agar, *A Commentary on St. Paul's Epistle to the Galatians.* 5th ed. London: Hodder & Stoughton, 1885.

Bennett, W. H. *The General Epistles, James, Peter, John, Jude.* The Century Bible.

Bigg, Charles. *A Critical and Exegetical Commentary on the Epistles of St. Peter and St. Jude.* International Critical Commentary. 2d ed. Reprint. Edinburgh: T. & T. Clark, 1910.

Brooke, A. E. *A Critical and Exegetical Commentary on the Johannine Epistles.* International Critical Commentary. New York: Scribner's, 1912.

Caffin, B. C. *The First Epistle General of Peter,* The Pulpit Commentary. Reprint. Grand Rapids: Eerdmans, 1950.

————. *The Second Epistle General of Peter.* The Pulpit Commentary. Reprint. Grand Rapids: Eerdmans, 1950.

Caird, G. B. *A Commentary on the Revelation of St. John the Divine.* Harper's New Testament Commentaries. New York: Harper & Row, 1966.

Callan, Charles J. *The Epistles of St. Paul with Introductions and Commentary for Priests and Students.* New York: Wagner, 1951.

Calvin, John. *Commentaries on the Catholic Epistles.* Translated and edited by the Rev. John Owen. Reprint. Grand Rapids: Eerdmans, 1948.

Carpenter, W. Boyd. *The Wisdom of James The Just.* London: Isbister, 1903.

Carr, Arthur. *The General Epistle of St. James.* In Cambridge Greek Testament. Reprint. Cambridge: U. Press, 1930.

Charles, R. H. *A Critical and Exegetical Commentary on the Revelation of St. John.* International Critical Commentary. 2 vols. Edinburgh: T. & T. Clark, 1920.

Cowles, Henry. *The Epistle To The Hebrews.* New York: Appleton, 1883.

Dodd, C. H. *The Johannine Epistles.* Moffatt New Testament Commentary. London: Hodder & Stoughton, 1946.

Eadie, John. *Commentary on the Epistle of Paul to the Galatians.* 1894. Reprint. Grand Rapids: Zondervan, n.d.

Easton, Burton Scott; and Poteat, Gordon. "The Epistle of James." In *The Interpreter's* Bible, vol. 12. New York: Abingdon, 1957.

Ebrard, John H. A. *Biblical Commentary on the Epistles of St. John.* Edinburgh: T. & T. Clark, 1860.

English, E. Schuyler. *Studies in the Epistle to the Hebrews.* Travelers Rest, S. C.: Southern Bible House, 1955.

Flack, Elmer E. "The Revelation of John." In *New Testament Commentary.* Edited by Herbert C. Alleman. Rev. ed. Philadelphia: Board of Publication of the United Lutheran Church in America, 1944.

Fronmüller, G. F. C. "The Epistle General of Jude." In Lange's *Commentary on the Holy Scriptures*. Translated from the German with additions by J. Isidor Mombert. Reprint. Grand Rapids: Zondervan, n.d.

———. "The First Epistle General of Peter." In Lange's *Commentary on the Holy Scriptures*. Translated from the German with additions by J. Isidor Mombert. Reprint. Grand Rapids: Zondervan, n.d.

———. "The Second Epistle General of Peter." In Lange's *Commentary on the Holy Scriptures*. Reprint. Grand Rapids: Zondervan, n.d.

Gibson, E. C. S. *The General Epistle of James*. The Pulpit Commentary. Reprint. Grand Rapids: Eerdmans, 1950.

Gingrich, Raymond E. *An Outline and Analysis of the First Epistle of John*. Grand Rapids: Zondervan, 1943.

Hendriksen, W. *More Than Conquerors. An Interpretation of the Book of Revelation*. 1939. Grand Rapids: Baker, 1967.

Johnstone, Robert. *Lectures Exegetical and Practical on the Epistle of James*. Reprint. Grand Rapids: Baker, 1954.

Kay, William. "Hebrews." In *The Speaker's Commentary. New Testament*, vol. 4. London: John Murray, 1881.

Kiddle, Martin. *The Revelation of St. John*. Moffatt New Testament Commentary. 1940. Reprint. New York: Harper & Row, n.d.

Knowling, R. J. *The Epistle of St. James*. Westminster Commentaries. London: Methuen, 1904.

Ladd, George Eldon. *A Commentary on the Revelation of John*. Grand Rapids: Eerdmans, 1972.

Lange, John Peter. "The Apocalypse." In Lange's *Commentary on the Holy Scriptures*. Translated from the German, with additions by E. R. Craven. Reprint. Grand Rapids: Zondervan, n.d.

Lange, J. P.; and Van Oosterzee, J. J. "The General Epistle of James." In Lange's *Commentary on the Holy Scriptures*. Translated from the German with additions by J. Isidor Mombert. Reprint. Grand Rapids: Zondervan, n.d.

Lenski, R. C. H. *The Interpretation of the Epistles of St. Peter, St. John, and St. Jude*. Columbus, Ohio: Lutheran Book Concern, 1938.

———. *The Interpretation of the Epistle to the Hebrews and of the Epistle of James*. Columbus, Ohio: Lutheran Book Concern, 1938.

———. *The Interpretation of St. John's Revelation*. Columbus, Ohio: Lutheran Book Concern, 1935.

———. *The Interpretation of St. Paul's Epistle to the Galatians, to the Ephesians, and to the Philippians*. Columbus, Ohio: Lutheran Book Concern, 1937.

Lightfoot, J. B. *Saint Paul's Epistle to the Galatians.* Reprint. London: Macmillan, 1910.

Lumby, J. Rawson. "The Epistles of St. Peter." In *An Exposition of the Bible,* vol. 6. Hartford, Conn.: Scranton, 1903.

————. "Jude." In *The Speaker's Commentary. New Testament,* vol. 4. London: John Murray, 1881.

Mayor, Joseph B. *The Epistle of St. James.* London: Macmillan, 1897.

Moffatt, James. *The General Epistles—James, Peter, and Judas.* Moffatt New Testament Commentary. Reprint. London: Hodder & Stoughton, 1947.

Moorehead, William G. *Outline Studies in the New Testament, Catholic Epistles—James, I and II Peter, I, II, III John, and Jude.* New York: Revell, 1910.

————. *Studies in the Book of Revelation.* New York: Revell, 1908.

Narborough, F. D. V. *The Epistle To The Hebrews.* In The Clarendon Bible. Reprint. Oxford: Clarendon, 1952.

Oesterley, W. E. "The General Epistle of James." In *The Expositor's Greek Testament,* vol. 4. Reprint. Grand Rapids: Eerdmans, n.d.

Pfeiffer, Charles F.; and Harrison, Everett F., eds. *The Wycliffe Bible Commentary.* Chicago: Moody, 1962.

Plummer, A. *The Epistles of S. John.* Cambridge Bible for Schools and Colleges. Reprint. Cambridge: U. Press, 1938.

————. "The General Epistles of St. James and St. Jude." In *An Exposition of the Bible,* vol. 6. Hartford, Conn.: Scranton, 1903.

————. "The Second Epistle General of Peter." In *Ellicott's Commentary on the Whole Bible,* vol. 8. Reprint. Grand Rapids: Zondervan, n.d.

Plumptre, E. H. *The General Epistle of St. James.* Cambridge Bible for Schools and Colleges. Reprint. Cambridge: U. Press, 1915.

————. *The General Epistles of St. Peter and St. Jude.* Cambridge Bible for Schools and Colleges. Cambridge: U. Press, 1893.

Purdy, Alexander C.; and Cotton, J. Harry. "The Epistle to the Hebrews." In *The Interpreter's Bible,* vol. 11. New York: Abingdon, 1955.

Ramsay, W. M. *The Letters to the Seven Churches of Asia and Their Place in the Plan of the Apocalypse.* New York: Hodder & Stoughton, n.d.

Ropes, James Hardy. *A Critical and Exegetical Commentary on the Epistle of James.* International Critical Commentary. New York: Scribner's, 1916.

Ross, Alexander. *The Epistles of James and John.* New International Commentary on the New Testament. Grand Rapids: Eerdmans, 1954.

Salmond, S. D. F. *The General Epistle of Jude,* The Pulpit Commentary. 1950. Reprint. Grand Rapids: Eerdmans.

Saphir, Adolph. *The Epistle to the Hebrews.* 2 vols. 7th Amer. ed. Reprint. New York: Loizeaux, 1942.

Scott, Robert. "The General Epistle of James." In *The Speaker's Commentary. New Testament,* vol. 4. London: John Murray, 1881.

Selwyn, Edward Gordon. *The First Epistle of St. Peter.* London: Macmillan, 1949.

Smith, David. "The Epistles of John." In *The Expositor's Greek Testament,* vol. 5. Reprint. Grand Rapids: Eerdmans, n.d.

Smith, H. Maynard. *The Epistle of S. James.* Oxford: B. H. Blackwell, 1914.

Smith, Wilbur M. "Revelation." In *The Wycliffe Bible Commentary.* Chicago: Moody, 1962.

Strachan, R. H. "The Second Epistle General of Peter." In *The Expositor's Greek Testament,* vol. 5. Reprint. Grand Rapids: Eerdmans, n.d.

Swete, Henry Barclay. *The Apocalypse of St. John.* 1906. Reprint. Grand Rapids: Eerdmans, 1951.

Tasker, R. V. G. *The General Epistle of James.* Tyndale New Testament Commentaries. Grand Rapids: Eerdmans, 1957.

Tatford, Fredk. A. *Prophecy's Last Word. An Exposition of the Revelation.* London: Pickering & Inglis, 1947.

Tenney, Merrill C. *Interpreting Revelation.* Grand Rapids: Eerdmans, 1957.

Vaughan, C. J. *The Epistle to the Hebrews.* London: Macmillan, 1890.

Walvoord, John F. *The Revelation of Jesus Christ, A Commentary.* Chicago: Moody, 1966.

Westcott, Brooke Foss. *The Epistle to the Hebrews.* 3d ed. London: Macmillan, 1909.

———. *The Epistles of St. John, The Greek Text with Notes and Essays.* Reprint. Grand Rapids: Eerdmans, 1950.

———. *The Gospel According to St. John. The Authorized Version with Introduction and Notes.* 1881. Reprint. Grand Rapids: Eerdmans, 1950.

Westwood, Tom. *The Epistles of Peter.* Glendale, Calif.: Tom Westwood, n.d.

Williams, Nathaniel Marshman. "Commentary on the Epistle of Jude." In *An American Commentary on the New Testament.* 1888. Reprint. Philadelphia: Amer. Bapt. Publn. Soc., n.d.

OTHER BOOKS

Arndt, William F.; and Gingrich, F. Wilbur. *A Greek-English Lexicon of the New Testament and Other Early Christian Literature.* Chicago: U. of Chicago, 1957.

Baxter, J. Sidlow. *Explore the Book.* Vol. 6. London: Marshall, Morgan & Scott, 1955.

Bernard, Thomas Dehany. *The Progress of Doctrine in the New Testament.* Introduction by Wilbur M. Smith. Reprint. Grand Rapids: Zondervan, n.d.

Boettner, Loraine. *The Millennium.* Grand Rapids: Baker, 1957.

Cadoux, Arthur Temple. *The Thought of St. James.* London: James Clark, 1944.

Cohen, Gary G. *Understanding Revelation. An Investigation of the Key Interpretational and Chronological Questions Which Surround the Book of Revelation.* Collingswood, N.J.: Christian Beacon, 1968.

Cullman, Oscar. *Peter, Disciple—Apostle—Martyr.* Translated from the German by Floyd V. Filson. Philadelphia: Westminster, 1953.

Dana, H. E. *Jewish Christianity.* New Orleans: Bible Inst. Mem. Press, 1937.

Deissman, Adolph. *The New Testament in the Light of Modern Research.* Garden City, N. Y.: Doubleday, Doran, 1929.

Ebright, Homer Kingsley. *The Petrine Epistles, A Critical Study of Authorship.* Cincinnati, Ohio: Methodist Book Concern, 1917.

English, E. Schuyler. *The Life and Letters of Saint Peter.* New York: Publication Office "Our Hope," 1941.

Eusebius, Pamphilus. *The Ecclesiastical History of Eusebius Pamphilus.* Translated from the Greek by the Rev. C. F. Cruse. London: George Bell, 1897.

Farrar, F. W. *The Early Days of Christianity.* Author's ed. New York: Cassell, n.d.

Feinberg, Charles Lee. *Premillennialism or Amillennialism?* Wheaton, Ill.: Van Kampen, 1954.

Gray, James M. *How to Master the English Bible.* Chicago: Moody, 1951.

Green, E. M. B. *2 Peter Reconsidered. The Tyndale New Testament Lecture, 1960.* London: Tyndale, 1961.

Grier, W. J. *The Momentous Event. A Discussion of Scripture Teaching on the Second Advent.* 1945. Reprint. London: Banner of Truth Trust, 1970.

Harrison, Everett F., ed. *Baker's Dictionary of Theology.* Grand Rapids: Baker, 1960.

Helmbold, A. *The Nag Hammadi Gnostic Texts and the Bible.* Grand Rapids: Baker, 1967.

Howson, John S. *The Character of St. Paul.* London: Strahan, 1873.

Hunter, Archibald M. *Interpreting the New Testament 1900-1950.* Philadelphia: Westminster, 1951.

Josephus, Flavius. *The Life and Works of Flavius Josephus.* Translated by William Whiston. Philadelphia: Winston, n.d.

Luther, Martin. *Works of Martin Luther, With Introductions and Notes.* Vol. 6. Philadelphia: Muhlenberg, 1932.

McCrossan, T. J. *Jesus Christ as a Higher Critic.* Seattle, Wash.: McCrossan, n.d.

Manley, G. T., ed. *The New Bible Handbook.* Chicago: Inter-Varsity, 1948.

Manson, William. *The Epistle to the Hebrews.* London: Hodder & Stoughton, 1951.

Morgan, Jill. *A Man of the Word. Life of G. Campbell Morgan.* London: Pickering & Inglis, 1951.

Moulton, James Hope. *A Grammar of New Testament Greek.* Vol. 1. *Prolegomena.* Edinburgh: T. & T. Clark, 1908.

Ramsay, William M. *The Church in the Roman Empire Before* A.D. *170.* Reprint. Grand Rapids: Baker, 1954.

Robertson, A. T. *Epochs in the Life of Simon Peter.* New York: Scribner's, 1935.

————. *A Grammar of the Greek New Testament in the Light of Historical Research.* 5th ed. New York: Richard R. Smith, n.d.

————. *The Student's Chronological New Testament, With Introductory Historical Notes and Outlines.* 9th ed. New York: Revell, n.d.

Robertson, James Alex. *The Hidden Romance of the New Testament.* London: James Clarke, n.d.

Schaff, Philip. *History of the Christian Church.* Vol. 1. 3d rev. New York: Scribner's, 1910.

Stonehouse, Ned Bernard. *The Apocalypse in the Ancient Church. A Study in the History of the New Testament Canon.* Goes, Holland: Oosterbaan & Le Cointre, 1929.

Tan, Paul Lee. *The Interpretation of Prophecy.* Winona Lake, Ind.: BMH, 1974.

Torrey, R. A. *How to Study the Bible for Greatest Profit.* New York: Revell, 1896.

Vincent, Marvin R. *Word Studies in the New Testament.* Vols. 1, 4. Reprint. Grand Rapids: Eerdmans, 1946.

Westcott, Brooke Foss. *A General Survey of the History of the Canon of the New Testament.* London: Macmillan, 1870.

Willett, Herbert L.; and Campbell, James M. *The Teachings of the Books.* New York: Revell, 1899.

ENCYCLOPEDIA AND MAGAZINE ARTICLES

Chase, F. H. "Jude, Epistle of." In Hastings *Dictionary of the Bible*, vol. 2. New York: Scribner's, 1908.

——. "Peter, Second Epistle of." In Hastings *Dictionary of the Bible*, vol. 3. New York: Scribner's, 1908.

Evans, George E. "The Sister of the Mother of Jesus." *The Review and Expositor* 44 (October 1947):475-85.

Hayes, Doremus Almy. "James, Epistle of." In *Iternational Standard Bible Encyclopaedia*, vol. 3. Grand Rapids: Eerdmans, 1939.

Helmbold, Andrew. "A Note on the Authorship of the Apocalypse." *New Testament Studies* 8 (October 1961):77-79.

Herren, A. Van Der. "Peter, Epistles of Saint." In *The Catholic Encyclopedia*, vol. 11. New York: Gilmary Soc., 1940.

Jacobs, H. E. "Brethren of the Lord." In *The International Standard Bible*, vol. 1. Grand Rapids: Eerdmans, 1939.

Kevan, Ernest Frederick. "Millennium." In *Baker's Dictionary of Theology*. Grand Rapids: Baker, 1960.

Kirsch, J. P. "Peter, Saint, Prince of the Apostles." In *The Catholic Encyclopedia*, vol. 11. New York: Gilmary Soc., 1939.

Ladd, George E. "Apocalyptic Literature." In *The Zondervan Pictorial Bible Dictionary*. Grand Rapids: Zondervan, 1963.

Law, Robert. "Elect Lady." In *The International Standard Bible Encyclopaedia*, vol. 2. Grand Rapids: Eerdmans, 1939.

——. "John, The Epistles of: The First Epistle." In *The International Standard Bible Encyclopaedia*, vol. 3. Grand Rapids: Eerdmans, 1939.

——. "John, The Epistles of: The Second and Third Epistles." In *The International Standard Bible Encyclopaedia*, vol. 3. Grand Rapids: Eerdmans, 1939.

Lockyer, Herbert. "Scripture Summaries, Apostasy in Jude." *Our Hope* 59 (May 1953; June 1953):687-94; 749-54.

Moorehead, William G. "Jude, The Epistle of." In *The International Standard Bible Encyclopaedia*, vol. 3. Grand Rapids: Eerdmans, 1939.

——. "Millennium." In *The International Standard Bible Encyclopaedia*, vol. 3. Grand Rapids: Eerdmans, 1939.

Pratt, Dwight M. "Epistle." In *The International Standard Bible Encyclopaedia*, vol. 2. Grand Rapids: Eerdmans, 1939.

Rees, T. "Hebrews, Epistle to the." In *The International Standard Bible Encyclopaedia*, vol. 2. Grand Rapids: Eerdmans, 1939.

Zahn, T. "John the Apostle." In *The New Schaff-Herzog Encyclopedia of Religious Knowledge*, vol. 6. Reprint. Grand Rapids: Baker, 1950.

INDEX

NOTE: The detailed contents of the various books as given in the outlines have not been entered in this index. See the various individual outlines.